Howard Suber's understanding of film storytelling fills the pages of this wise, liberating book. Much of it is surprisingly contrary to what "everyone knows." A remarkable work.

— Francis Ford Coppola

For years students in Howard Suber's legendary classes at UCLA begged him to write a book. Now that he has delivered it, filmmakers, scholars and anyone else with a serious interest in film can rejoice. A fascinating and thought-provoking work.

— Alexander Payne, Director/Screenwriter, *Sideways, About Schmidt*

What Aristotle did for drama, Howard Suber has now done for film. This is a profound and succinct book that is miraculously fun to read.

— David Koepp, Screenwriter, *War of the Worlds* (2005), *Spider-Man, Mission Impossible, Jurassic Park.*

William Goldman, who said "nobody knows anything" about Hollywood films, probably never took a class from Howard Suber. Put this book on the shelf between Aristotle's "Poetics" and your O.E.D.; Professor Suber knows more about what's important about film storytelling than anyone I've ever encountered, and he presents it here in an incredibly clear, useful, and provocative way.

— Dan Pyne, Screenwriter, *The Manchurian Candidate* (2004), *The Sum of All Fears, Any Given Sunday.*

The Power of Film is destined to become a classic. People will return to it again and again because it is useful -- not just for those learning their craft, but for seasoned veterans who face specific problems in developing stories and characters. Suber's ability to distill his wisdom, insight, and experience with such succinctness and wit provides an added bonus -- this book is a joy to read.

— Gil Cates, Director/Producer; former President, Directors Guild of America; Producer, Academy Awards

Suber understands the alchemy of movies. *The Power of Film* captures his unique ability to demystify the process of filmmaking, beginning with the epiphany of the artist to the eureka of the audience. It's not a "how to" book but a "how come" movies get made.

— Peter Guber, former CEO, Sony Studios; CEO, Mandalay Pictures; Producer/Executive Producer, *Midnight Express, Missing, The Color Purple, Batman, Rainman*

Each of the nearly 300 entries in this particular aspect of the film making art delightful to read. This is a wonderful b ested in the art of film.

— Fred Roos, Producer, *The Godfather: Part II, The Godfather: Part III, Apocalypse Now, The Conversation, The Black Stallion*

Suber knows the industry, the creative process, and the audience. This book comprehensively analyzes the elements of film storytelling, and is especially useful for understanding the psychological processes at work in popular films.

— Joe Roth, founder, Revolution Studios; former Chairman, Twentieth Century-Fox and Walt Disney Studios

In my thirty-five years in the motion picture industry I have met many people who know a great deal about the business. Others are steeped in the knowledge of film history, or the principles of storytelling. Rarely have I known someone who has the in-depth knowledge of both the creative and business workings of this tight-knit community *and* has such an in-depth knowledge of film history and film storytelling. Suber is that rare one, and this a rare and immensely valuable book.

— Tom Sherak, Partner, Revolution Studios; former Chairman, Twentieth Century Fox Domestic Film Group

When I was a student at UCLA, I wanted to know as much about film as Howard Suber did. When I got my first job in the industry, I still didn't know as much about film as Howard did. Now that I've been working in the film business for over twenty years, I have reached the conclusion that I will never know as much about film as Howard Suber and should abandon all hope that I ever will. He is everything you wish for in a teacher and author. *The Power of Film* confirms his status as one of our most profound film chroniclers.

— Terry Press Marx, Marketing Executive, Dreamworks SKG

Just because you can spell, doesn't mean you can write. Be thankful you have Howard Suber's book from which to learn the principles of storytelling.

— Stefani Relles, Vice President, Fox Broadcasting Company

When I first received Howard Suber's book, I was in the middle of producing a movie but I thought I could speed-read the entries at random between takes. After reading the first one, I e-mailed it to a director I know who was struggling with a similar aspect of the creative process. After reading the second one, I scribbled a note to myself that I should rethink part of a screenplay I'm developing. After reading the third one, I walked across the set and showed it to the cinematographer to settle an argument we'd been having about Russian cinema. This isn't good. I don't have time for this book. It's too interesting. I may have to give up producing.

— Lindsay Doran, former President of United Artists; Producer of *Dead Again, Sense and Sensibility, Nanny McPhee,* and *Stranger Than Fiction*

Studying with the brilliant Howard Suber radically liberated the way I think about movies and gave me crucial tools for understanding how/why films work (or don't). How wonderful that his profound insights into patterns of storytelling, human psychology and the history of cinema are finally accessible to all! His contagious spirit of inquiry and elegant conclusions will provoke and inspire film artists, executives and cinephiles for generations to come.

— Caroline Libresco, Senior Programmer, Sundance Film Festival; Independent Producer

Nothing left to say about film? *Au contraire.* Here's Howard Suber, exploding with originality. ...We don't know of another book like it. Demand for it will be permanent.

— Arden Heide, Samuel French Theatre & Film Bookstores

The notes I took in Suber's classes years ago have grown dog-eared over the years as I've referred to them again and again in preparing to direct both independent and mainstream films. The distillation of his wisdom into concise and entertaining essays makes *The Power of Film* a book that will enlighten –and liberate – filmmaker/storytellers around the world. I will be keeping the volume on my desk where I know I'll be reaching for it daily.

— Charles Herman-Wurmfeld, Director, *Kissing Jessica Stein, Legally Blonde 2*

I spent twenty years as a writer/producer in Hollywood, and yet Howard Suber was able to teach me more than a thing or two when I came back to sit in his class at UCLA. It would cost you a fortune to learn what's in this book the "hard" way, by trial and error. Sit back and enjoy learning it the pleasurable way. Professor Suber has for many years been a mentor to countless people who want to understand great films – especially *why*, from the psychological standpoint, they are great.

— Judy Burns, Television Writer/Producer, *Star Trek*

Evoking Roland Barthes' playful *A Lover's Discourse*, Howard Suber's *The Power of Film* is a rousingly profound and loving set of meditations on the movies. Indeed, it's hard to stop reading: the entries are wise, witty, practical, illuminating, and often very, very funny! Whether one makes movies, studies them, or just loves to see them, this is a book for film lovers everywhere.

— Vivian Sobchack, former President, Society for Cinema Studies; *author of Carnal Thoughts: Embodiment and Moving Image Culture, The Address of the Eye: A Phenomenology of Film Experience*, and *Screening Space: The American Science Fiction Film*

Clearly, over forty years of inspired teaching have taught Professor Suber that accessible, articulate prose and examples mean more than pedanticism and verbosity. This crowning work is wonderful!

— Frank Manchel, Author of *Film Study: An Analytical Bibliography*; Professor Emeritus, University of Vermont

If UCLA is the Camelot of screenwriting schools — which it is — Professor Howard Suber is its Merlin. For over four decades, students have entered his classroom to see the secrets of screen magic revealed — not only how movies work, but why they affect us so deeply, and how we can apply those secrets to our own concoctions. Here it is at last, a witty A-to-Z of the raw ingredients out of which the magic of film is spun. From now on Prof. Suber's book will sit on the screenwriter's desk, next to the dictionary and the thesaurus.

— Robin Russin, professor of screenwriting, University of California, Riverside; co-author of *Screenplay: Writing the Picture*

As a psychotherapist who has specialized in dealing with artists, I look for works I can recommend that will liberate their creativity, not constrict it. This book does exactly that. Suber has obviously thought long and deeply, and everywhere demonstrates a clear understanding of the creative and commercial processes involved in popular movies. He says his writings "deal not so much with style and technique as with the psychology of storytelling, which ultimately is the psychology of human beings." He is absolutely right. Like the films he discusses, this is a memorable work.

— Roberta Degnore, Psychotherapist; Independent Director/Writer

I'm a screenwriter who used to teach poetry and philosophy. Howard Suber has taught generations of screenwriters, and he's *both* a poet and philosopher.

— Adam Kulakow, Screenwriter

Nowhere else can one find a concise compilation of the crucial elements that make up the emotional content of films. What makes a movie memorable? What themes recur in popular films over and over again? Suber has the answers. In an easy to read style, Suber de-bunks the mystery of popular film and hands the goods to us on a silver platter.

— Diane Ambruso, Screenwriting Professor, California State University, Fullerton, former Program Acquisition Executive, DirectTV

Suber has influenced generations of film students and the film industry itself. This book is not merely the summation of a lifetime's work — it is a guarantee that his work will live beyond him.

— Steve Montal, Founding Associate Dean, North Carolina School of Filmmaking

No matter where you're from in the world, no matter how much experience you've had as a filmmaker, storyteller, or member of the audience, read *The Power of Film* and reconsider. Howard Suber's book is more than a provocative guide to filmmaking, more than an analysis of film audiences, more than the ultimate reference for creative persons. It's really about the forces that drive our craving for stories and our lives. Suber is concerned with memorable films. Well, this is a truly memorable book.

— Cyril Tysz, French Writer-Producer

I packed my New Delhi life into two suitcases and flew half way across the world to study with Howard Suber. We all have many teachers in life, but gurus are rare. I am one of a large number of people who have found this man to truly fit that role.

— Akshat Verma, Screenwriter

Instead of another "how to" book on film that offers up tried but not necessarily true rules, *The Power of Film* provides an immense treasure trove of sparkling creative ideas about the nature of film. With the humor and natural ease of a sage, Howard Suber explains the psychological and emotional mechanics of film in simple terms – and the alphabetical structure makes it wonderfully accessible. Suber bases his conclusions on a wide range of American popular films that have been proven over time to have worldwide appeal, but I know from experience that his ideas and insights apply, not just to American films, but to those of the rest of the world as well. This is a profound work!

— Frank Suffert, German Director/Screenwriter

Ever since I took his screenwriting seminar for FIND (Film Independent, formerly Independent Feature Project, West), Howard Suber's ideas have guided my career in Latin America and the USA. As an independent filmmaker, I look for books that are not simply focused on getting rich and famous in Hollywood, but are concerned more with creativity and using film to say something meaningful about our lives. The *Power of Film* is that book.

— Patricia Cardoso, Director/Screenwriter, *Real Women Have Curves, The Water Carrier*

I have learned more about film, and I think about life, from Howard Suber than from anyone else. The wisdom in this book is all about the power, beauty and compassion of film storytelling that lasts.

— Dirk Dotzert, Film Consultant, Berlin, Germany

As a Chinese film producer, I know that there is a real need for a book like this, which will be well-received in China and have an important influence on the development of its film industry. Although Professor Suber uses America's greatest films as the basis for his conclusions, the principles he derives from them have universal application.

— Yennie Hao, Chinese Producer

I am the farthest thing from a Hollywood filmmaker on the planet, and my films might even be said to be in opposition to what Hollywood stands for. But I find so many of Suber's insights totally applicable to third world and independent films. This work is amazing for its breadth and depth.

— Jorge Preloran, Argentine filmmaker

This book is a collection of absolute gems from Howard Suber's legendary film courses at UCLA. Dip in anywhere and find something profound or provocative (or both at the same time). The insights Suber offers are fresh and original and will change forever how you look at movies. This is a must-have book for anyone who cares passionately about stories and storytelling in cinema.

— Laurie Hutzler, Screenplay Consultant; Screenwriting instructor, UCLA Professional Screenwriting Program.

We all know the films we love, but can anyone ever explain *why* we respond to them the way we do? Howard Suber can. Memorable films have made Hollywood a global industry that both defines and is defined by American culture. Read this book from cover to cover, for *The Power of Film* is nothing less than an analysis of the underpinnings of American values — and much of the world..

— Yoshi Nishio, Producer & International Media Financier

I was an experienced fifty-year-old writer when I first encountered Howard Suber, and thought I already knew what I needed to know. His ideas changed the way I thought about stories because he helped me see that the principles used to construct memorable films are the same principles we use — if we're wise — to create meaningful lives. What a gift that was!

— Murray Suid, screenwriter/producer

Not since Aristotle's *Poetics* has anyone made such a comprehensive analysis of storytelling. A must-have work for anyone anywhere who cares about film.

— Isobel Gardner, Swedish Producer/Screenwriter

A cornucopia of Suber's film wisdom over his long and productive career, one that any screenwriter, filmmaker, or movie-goer will treasure for decades to come. This book distills in clear, precise language what makes great films great, and simultaneously offers fresh insights to aspiring and experienced filmmakers.

— Cecilia Fannon, Screenwriter/Playwright

Howard Suber is the bright star that guides us through the dark nights of the cinema.

— Chuck Bigelow, MacArthur Fellow; former professor, Stanford University; Screenwriter

Howard Suber defines why popular American films work with amazing clarity, thankful simplicity and memorable wit. This is a brilliant must-read for anyone and everyone who takes pleasure in watching, analyzing, or making memorable feature films.

— Hammad H. Zaidi, Producer

A highly readable lexicon covering what every movie-lover needs to know.

— Jason Squire, Professor, University of Southern California Professional Writing Program; editor, *The Movie Business Book*.

Like a great many of Howard Suber's former students, I've saved every note I ever took in his classes, and there isn't a smeary page I haven't gone back over many, many times. Now, all that wit and wisdom is distilled into one handy A to Z guide, a Rosetta stone than can be used to unlock the secrets of memorable film storytelling. *The Power of Film* is not remotely about screenplay formulas — from the moment Howard challenges the idea of "acts," you know you're off the reservation. But where you are is far more exciting. You're in the world of the "essential," the fundamental principles that so many popular films share — and if you get this part of the story right, everything else falls into place. This book is filled with truly memorable writing from one of the world's most memorable film teachers.

— Rita Augustine, Screenwriter

The Power of Film is the most insightful book I've read since the *Kama Sutra*. Filmmakers can apply Suber's ideas to their own work and parrot them in meetings and pretend they thought of them themselves. Ordinary people who love movies will have to settle for wowing their friends with their brilliance.

— Eric Barker, Screenwriter

Suber pulls back the curtain and shows the art, commerce, philosophy, and culture behind cinematic storytelling. This groundbreaking work goes well above and beyond Hollywood films — every word in this book rings true universally for the independents and ethnic driven films. In my own works dealing with Asian and Asian American themes, I've applied Suber's principles religiously. I consider it the bible of modern screenwriting and a mandatory text for anyone who creates or just loves film.

— Weiko Lin, Assistant Professor, Screenwriting and Playwriting, University of California, Riverside

If all films were destroyed by a war of the worlds and only one book survived to recall the glory that was once Popular American Cinema, I would hope it would be *The Power of Film*.

— Kris Young, Screenwriter

Howard Suber's insights into film have guided me to find cohesive narrative stories from the most chaotic bodies of disorganized, raw footage imaginable! Moreover, I have found that the principles he discusses apply to all forms of filmmaking: documentaries, music videos, commercials, art films, shorts, and writing in general. Suber never says the work is easy, or that you can follow some formula, but what he offers has helped me immensely. This is required reading for all storytellers!

— Doug Pray, Director, *Hype, Scratch, Infamy*

Suber's study of storytelling applies not only to live action but to animation. It is profoundly insightful, which is why I apply his ideas on a daily basis to my own work in animation.

— Margaret Dean, Producer, Warner Bros. Animation

Try this experiment: read Howard Suber's book, then go back and watch your all-time favorite movie — the one you've seen twenty times and know by heart. You'll be absolutely astonished at how much you notice for the very first time. *The Power of Film* will change the way you look at movies. It may even change the way you look at life.

— John Wray, Screenwriter/Animator

THE POWER
OF FILM

HOWARD SUBER

MICHAEL WIESE PRODUCTIONS

Published by Michael Wiese Productions

11288 Ventura Boulevard

Suite #621

Studio City, CA 91604

(818) 379-8799, (818) 986-3408 (FAX).

mw@mwp.com

www.mwp.com

Front cover by agdesign.com

Interior design by William Morosi

Copyedited by Paul Norlen

Printed by McNaughton & Gunn

Manufactured in the United States of America

Library of Congress Cataloging-in-Publication Data

Suber, Howard, 1937-
  The power of film / Howard Suber.
    p. cm.
  Includes index.
  ISBN 1-932907-17-3
  1. Motion pictures. I. Title.
  PN1994.S86 2006
  791.43--dc22

                        2006019683

Contents

FOREWORD

HOWARD SUBER WOULD, in all certainty, warn you against
accepting at face value any of the plaudits and accolades that
accompany forewords to books. And it isn't false modesty
or curmudgeonly cynicism that would drive this response
(although he is uncommonly self-deprecating for a man of
his accomplishments). Instead, he has always exhibited an
extremely persistent aversion to the empty cacophony of hype,
of academic self-congratulatory grandiosity, and of mean-
ingless film industry bullshit. So it is with a strong degree of
trepidation that I attempt to avoid these pitfalls and seek to
reflect and comment on this book and its author.

Howard Suber is not necessarily a name you would know
as an author or critic (although I think that will change once
this book is published), nor is he part of some film industry elite. He is, however, a man with many admirers inside
that industry, and countless former students lavish praise on
him — many of whom are among the biggest names in film
and television.

Suber has spent most of his life tearing down the walls
that define the traditional university and creating something
else. Let me briefly list for you just some of Suber's accomplishments: He is responsible for starting the UCLA Critical
Studies Program, for founding the UCLA Film Archive, and
for developing and forging the UCLA Film and Television
Producers Program. He drastically reformed the Society
for Cinema Studies, the most important association of film
teachers, theorists, and historians in the nation, and he led
the campaign to establish the School of Theater, Film and

Television at UCLA. He was largely responsible for recruiting much of that department's estimable roster of talent, including its present Dean and Chairperson. In short, he transformed the UCLA Film School.

Companies in the film and television industry have frequently hired Suber as a consultant and expert witness on issues involving authorship, creative control, the creative process, and copyright. Other corporations have asked him to advise them on strategic business plans and to explain to their employees the structure of the film business. The diversity of these various academic and professional activities has given him a perspective that brings together the artistic and business aspects of film storytelling in an unparalleled way.

But these are not his most significant accomplishments. His most enduring legacy is his impact on students.

Howard Suber is one of the foremost teachers of film in the world. He has taught sixty-five different courses in every arena of the UCLA film program (except animation), including screenwriting, direction, production, film history, theory, and criticism. He is clearly a man of incredibly restless, eclectic intellect and creative energy.

Which leads me from the man to the work.

The book you are holding is neither a standard work of criticism nor some foolish arbitrary set of rules for the nascent screenwriter or writer/director. It is, instead, a remarkably rich compilation of concepts, ideas, and observations accrued from years of teaching. This volume will give you at least an idea of why Howard Suber is so admired and valued, not only in the academic world, but by some of the most important creative people in the film industry.

To summarily encapsulate *The Power of Film* is difficult, for it has a profound scope and many dimensions, and operates on multiple levels of comprehension that makes any reductive summary woefully inadequate.

That said, the task — the voyage through popular film culture — that Suber has set out for himself is no less than a basic understanding of why film "works." "It works" is a phrase that is often used by buyers, distributors, and others in the film industry to describe the effect of a film on an audience, differentiating the film that succeeds versus one that doesn't. Suber tells us *why* certain elements "work" in films and why others do not.

Suber's examples are all from "memorable popular films." As he explains, these are two separate qualities: the films must have been extremely popular in their own day, and they must also have *remained* in our cultural memory. Given Hollywood's enormous popularity over the past seventy-five years, it is not surprising that the films he cites are mainstream American classics. But the vast majority of Suber's insights apply equally well to independent films and to filmmaking around the world that aspires to appeal to an international audience.

This book does not try to categorize audiences or to provide simplistic "rules" for screenwriting and filmmaking. (In fact, true to his always skeptical spirit, Suber debunks a good portion of the so-called rules.) Instead, Suber genuinely helps us understand "the power of film" — why it has been the predominant art form for more than a century, and why it continues to have such power over the lives we all lead.

One of the joys of reading this book is Suber's ability to state things with breathtaking simplicity and elegance. This book is provocative and insightful, and whether or not you agree with a particular observation or point that Suber has made, you will find yourself time after time being transported to a higher level of sophistication than most people ever bring to film.

By pointing out contradictions, popular misunderstandings and misapprehensions, and by making the kind of distinctions that create insight, Suber merges the analysis of film culture with a very broad base of knowledge of other areas of modern life, leading us to truths and even, at times, to revelations that transcend film itself.

Suber's text moves freely among its nearly three hundred entries, connecting, for example, a discussion of Character to Disaster films, Aristotle and Happiness, Film Noir and Structure, the "Willing Suspension of Disbelief" and a discourse on Love.

One cannot, and probably should not even try, to read this book as a whole from cover to cover in one sitting. It is far too encompassing, far too complex — and yet condensed — for anyone to attempt to absorb it all quickly. It must be savored, slowly, and repeatedly.

Suber's writing has such a fluidity of style and incessant thoughtfulness that the best way to take it all in is like a hiker walking through a fertile and varied forest, where the pleasure lies in discovery, not merely in reaching a destination.

All of us who have had him as a teacher have been given a gift. For those who have not, this work richly demonstrates why Howard Suber has always been such a pleasure to spend serious time with, and why for forty years he has been so highly esteemed as a molder of lives.

Geoffrey Gilmore
Director, Sundance Film Festival

ACKNOWLEDGMENTS

IN KEEPING WITH the rest of this book, I will try to make this as concise as I can, and will therefore identify the four people whose efforts have been most helpful in one specific area, getting this book finished:

- Cecilia Fannon, a successful playwright and editor who came into my life as a screenwriting student and, after looking at five hundred pages of handouts during a course, offered to help edit my writings. Perceptive, rigorous, inventive, and always funny and engaging, she made the process of distilling my work into this book an exciting adventure.

- Charles Bigelow, former Stanford professor and MacArthur Foundation prize fellow, who also came into my life as a screenwriting student, and later spent an enormous amount of time and energy writing extremely helpful notes more than half as long as my own manuscript.

- Murray Suid, who also came into my life as a screenwriting student after a successful career as a writer and editor, who helped edit an earlier attempt to distill my ideas into book form.

- Stuart Brown, M.D., the psychiatrist who was the first person to document on film the ideas of Joseph Campbell and then honored me with the belief, expressed through many years of discussion and encouragement, that my ideas should be permanently recorded.

I would also like to thank Ken Lee, William Morosi, and Paul Norlen, each of whom went far beyond the call of duty in the editing, composition, and layout of this book. Finally, I want to acknowledge the person whose caring, understanding, and support make him the kind of publisher every writer hopes to find: Michael Wiese.

INTRODUCTION

FOR MORE THAN forty years, I have had the good fortune of teaching a fascinating succession of gifted writers, directors, and producers in UCLA Film School who are now expressing their creativity around the world. I want to begin by thanking all the committed and talented people who listened to me pontificate, challenged me when I needed it, and inspired me to keep on working in what has always been a collaborative effort to understand the nature of popular film.

I have taught sixty-five different courses covering a great variety of subjects in film and television, and in these courses I often distributed more than five hundred pages of notes in a single term. When I crossed paths with former students, they would frequently ask why I've never organized and published these handouts in book form. After hearing the question for decades, I finally decided to do something about it.

I have tried to make each entry in this book as succinct as I possibly can. Many of these entries are a summation of an entire course that I have taught, or of a series of lectures on the topic that I've tried to distill to its essence. I fear that some of the entries may feel like the punch lines of jokes that I've forgotten to give you the setup for, but that danger seems to me to be outweighed by the desirability of keeping these entries as succinct as I can make them.

Some who have read the manuscript for this book have commented that it can easily be read from start to finish. While that is gratifying, the point of the alphabetical arrangement is to allow you to skip around, as your needs, interests, or moods may lead you.

THE FILMS THIS BOOK IS ABOUT

POPULAR FILMS ARE a special kind of drama. While much that is in them can be traced back to the ancient dramas of Aeschylus, Sophocles, and Euripides, whose works were performed in a kind of popular theater for Athenians, only some of what was true for dramatists and their audiences then continues to be true twenty-five centuries later.

Popular films have their own principles, patterns, and structures. These deal not so much with style and technique as with the psychology of storytelling, which ultimately is the psychology of contemporary human beings.

The observations and principles contained in this book do not apply to *all* films. I can no more generalize about "film" than someone else could generalize about "books," "paintings," or "people." I have been a student of world film all my life, but because I teach in an American university adjacent to that mythical place called Hollywood and most of my students are Americans who want to make American films, my examples are confined to American films of the sound era. This is not because I believe them to be the only important films nor because I consider them the "best." Rather, I confine myself to American films because I can be reasonably sure most people listening to or reading what I have to say will be familiar with a good proportion of the examples I use.

Nor am I talking about all "American films" or "Hollywood films." There have been over 80,000 American feature films, and no statement can apply to all of them. My observations and conclusions are focused on the body of films I call "memorable popular films." There are two different categories here, and both of them must be present:

1) *They were popular in their own day*. The vast majority of the films I base my conclusions on were in the top ten films at the box office in their year of release, often in the first or second position.

2) *They have remained popular for at least a decade*. Many films do very well at the box office when they are released, but nobody ever wants to see them again. I think it is a modest requirement to insist that before we refer to a film as "memorable," it must have remained popular for at least a decade.

In ordinary language, when we say something is "memorable," it usually means no more than "I liked it." But what I choose to remember may not be what you choose to remember. In this book, "memorable" is not my personal judgment of value or what I think *ought* to be remembered — it is a statement of the fact that large numbers of people *do* remember these films.

If someone can say, "Frankly, my dear, I don't give a damn," "We'll always have Paris," or "I'll make him an offer he can't refuse" and large numbers of people years after the films first came out can still recognize that these lines come from *Gone with the Wind, Casablanca,* and *The Godfather*, it is clear these films are, by definition, memorable. My life's work has been devoted to trying to understand *why* certain films are memorable and popular and others are not.

A small group of films have been included over and over again in lists such as those selected by the Library of Congress' National Film Registry committee (of which I used to be a member), the American Film Institute, the Internet Movie Database, and the many other organizations that compile data on popular films. Many of these films are discussed in film history books, are re-released in theaters, remain consistent sellers on DVD and video, and air frequently on television.

"Popular," then, means here that the film appealed to large numbers of people in the United States and elsewhere, both at its time of release and in later years.

When, as I often do in this book, I use the term "memorable popular films," I am referring to films such as these:

The African Queen
All About Eve
Amadeus
American Graffiti
Annie Hall
The Apartment
Apocalypse Now
The Best Years of Our Lives
Bonnie and Clyde
The Bridge on the River Kwai
Butch Cassidy and the Sundance Kid
Casablanca
Chinatown
Citizen Kane
The Deer Hunter
*Dr. Strangelove Or: How I Learned to Stop Worrying and
  Love the Bomb*
Doctor Zhivago
Double Indemnity
E.T., The Extra-Terrestrial
Frankenstein
The French Connection
From Here to Eternity
The Godfather
The Godfather: Part II
Gone with the Wind

The Graduate
The Grapes of Wrath
High Noon
It's a Wonderful Life
Jaws
King Kong
Lawrence of Arabia
M*A*S*H*
The Maltese Falcon
The Manchurian Candidate
Midnight Cowboy
Mr. Smith Goes to Washington
Mutiny on the Bounty
North by Northwest
On the Waterfront
One Flew Over the Cuckoo's Nest
Platoon
Psycho
Raging Bull
Raiders of the Lost Ark
Rebel Without a Cause
Rocky
Schindler's List
The Searchers
Shane
The Silence of the Lambs
Singin' in the Rain
Snow White and the Seven Dwarfs
Some Like It Hot
The Sound of Music
Star Wars
A Streetcar Named Desire

Sunset Boulevard
Taxi Driver
To Kill a Mockingbird
Tootsie
The Treasure of the Sierra Madre
2001: A Space Odyssey
Unforgiven
Vertigo
West Side Story
The Wild Bunch
The Wizard of Oz

I have also included some references to more recent films that have not yet been proven to stand the test of time but that I believe stand a good chance of doing so in the years ahead.

The memorable popular films referred to in this book are not meant to be sacred objects worthy of veneration. They are merely *reference points* that, in most cases, are familiar to people seriously interested in popular film. Like classics in all the arts, the past popularity of these films does not provide us with a formula for creating successful films in the future. The fact that they were popular in their own day and continue to remain memorable may, however, help us understand the *principles* that have been effective in the past.

The term "popular" as used in this book refers to audiences, but this does not necessarily include *all* potential audiences. As with every other popular medium, the norm for films is defined by the dominant audience and its culture. In the United States and Europe, which are economically the most important markets for film, young, Caucasian, Judeo-Christian males of European extraction between the ages of fourteen and thirty have historically dominated this audience.

When people talk or write about "the audience," they are generally referring to this demographic group. But what is a cultural norm need not be the only yardstick of what is "normal." Women, non-Europeans, non-Caucasians, non-Judeo-Christians, gays, lesbians, and other groups that have sometimes not been considered the primary audience for motion pictures may — or may not — have different values.

Popular films operate in much the same way as democratic politics. Although cynics claim that both politics and popular entertainment work by appealing to the lowest common denominator, this is a superficial assumption. In both politics and popular culture, there are many different constituent groups, and the key to success lies not in finding something that everyone finds appealing but in finding different elements that appeal to these different constituencies. Memorable popular films are frequently complex and paradoxical. It may be one of the reasons they *are* memorable and popular.

Part of the complexity of films is that they combine elements of nearly every art form that preceded them. Some people focus on what we *see* in films, and spend their time discussing camera movement, framing, angles, lighting, editing, special effects, etc. Others focus on what we *hear* and focus on plot, character, and dialogue.

With some films, you could simply listen to the soundtrack and take in most of what is creatively important in the work. With others, you could turn off the soundtrack and just watch the images, and you would take in most of what is creatively important in the work. In a small percentage of films, sight and sound are inseparable and fuse into one expressive whole. Most of the films that I discuss in this book are in this category.

But, because my focus here is on storytelling, it should be understood that a film's "story" goes well beyond what can be expressed in words. If I do not discuss the visual elements of film in this book, it is not because I consider them unimportant or of lesser importance. In my classes, I discuss the visual elements of film constantly, but my students and I have the films themselves on hand to look at, and we have all just seen them shortly before the discussion. Attempting to incorporate the visual elements of film into this book would require a work that is quite different from what you have in your hand.

Movies entertain us, and often they are nothing more than grab bags of gimmicks, gags, and gab. But those that continue to appeal to audiences over time and to lodge in our individual and collective memories do so because they reveal patterns of how we live our lives. Our hopes and fears, our aspirations and our failures, our longings and our frustrations, our loves and our hates are all embodied in the memorable popular films.

To study such movies is therefore to study ourselves, not as we are, but as we wish we could be. Memorable popular movies do not show us just the world, they show us a *just world* — one in which the people we identify with not only stand for the things we would like to stand for, they *stand up* for what we would like to believe are the most important values of individuals and societies.

Perhaps that is *why* they are memorable as well as popular.

A

*There is no such thing as an
antihero. There are only characters
who act heroically and those who do not.*

ACCIDENTS

IMAGINE YOU'RE WATCHING an early cut of *Annie Hall*, the story of two lovers who have quarreled and parted. Imagine that, as the film nears its conclusion, Annie and Alvy talk on a street corner and then Annie turns and crosses toward the other side. When she's halfway across, a passing truck strikes her dead.

Would such a version of *Annie Hall* have helped it receive its Academy Award? Would it have helped it get on almost every list of the great American films? Or would audiences have demanded their money back?

Woody Allen could have appeared in every theater in the United States where the film played to explain that ending *Annie Hall* with an accident was a realistic conclusion to the story because, after all, 55,000 Americans die in traffic accidents every year and a good proportion of them were undoubtedly lovers. But, as the audience hanged him from the nearest rafter, they would have responded, "Yeah, but I didn't pay good money for *that!*"

In the film as it was actually made, Annie successfully crosses the street, has a conversation with Alvy that we don't hear, and then leaves him forever while he prattles on about needing some eggs. That's an acceptable ending because most of the world's memorable love stories end with the separation of the lovers.

If the story had ended with an accident, we would have felt cheated, like buying a jigsaw puzzle and discovering one of the key pieces was missing just as we thought we were completing it.

The important events in drama are not accidents of nature, disease, or automobiles — things that occur because of some outside force that we call Fate. Drama is about individual human decisions and actions, and the consequences of both. Characters must be *responsible* for what happens to them.

In modern drama, as a general rule, nothing is accidental.

(See also: INTENTIONALITY; DEUS EX MACHINA; DESTINY)

ACTING

THE FRENCH PERFORMER Sarah Bernhardt was called "the greatest actress in the world" in the early years of the twentieth century when films were becoming a mass art form. Enterprising producers sought to capitalize on her worldwide fame and they convinced her to repeat some of her greatest roles in film versions of *Hamlet, Tosca, Camille,* and *Queen Elizabeth.* Adolph Zukor bought the American rights to these films and formed a company whose announced goal was to present "famous plays with famous players."

While Zukor survived into his nineties, heading the company that became Paramount Pictures Corporation, most of the early films of Bernhardt and other famous actors and actresses of the day did not. That's because one of the first lessons early filmmakers had to learn was that great theater acting is not great film acting.

When the Bolshevik Revolution gave Lenin dictatorial power over the newly formed Soviet Union, his minister of education declared that film was the most important of all the arts. The world's first school devoted to teaching film was established in Moscow to further this uniquely powerful new medium, and one of its first professors was the noted director, Lev Kuleshov, who conducted an experiment that is cited to this day in film classes.

There are different versions of the details, but the gist of the story is this: Kuleshov used footage of Ivan Mozhukhin, a popular stage actor of the day. Unlike Sarah Bernhardt, who was allowed to do on film what she did on stage, Mozhukhin did the thing that actors find hardest: express *no* emotion. Kuleshov repeated the same shot of Mozhukhin and juxtaposed to it bits of stock footage, which some versions of the story say consisted of a steaming bowl of soup, a young child coming toward the camera, and an old woman in a coffin. He cut together Empty Ivan and the bowl of soup, Empty Ivan and the young child, Empty Ivan and the old woman in the coffin.

Audiences marveled at Mozhukhin's superb acting ability — how he expressed extreme hunger as he approached his bowl of soup, tender fatherly emotions as *his* child came toward him and overpowering grief at the death of *his* mother.

Thus was revealed the secret of great film acting: it is not action, but *reaction* that counts. The emotional response of the audience comes not just from what is projected *from* the screen but also from what the audience projects *onto* it.

The implications of the Kuleshov experiments lie at the foundation of popular American film to this day. We are likely to see this most clearly when the Academy Awards for Best Actor are given. The archetype of the American male screen hero is The Strong Silent Type. Year after year, when they show clips from films that garnered nominations for qualified actors, what dominates are reaction shots. If we study publicity stills of popular male actors over the years and ask, "What are they expressing?," the answer is usually: *nothing*.

The audience projects *onto* the image on the screen the relationship between thought and emotion. It is therefore an active collaborator in the process of constructing the story.

The trick, of course, is to get the audience to project onto the screen what you *intend* them to. That is as much the writer's job as it is the actor's — if we can't imagine in our heads how a character might look when we read the script, it is probably not our imagination that is at fault, but rather the writer's.

WHEN THE CAMERA starts rolling, American directors
do not yell, "Dialogue!" — they yell, "Action!"

ACTION

In real life, our "character" is often considered
to be some inherent quality within us. In film, however, character is the result of what someone *does*.

Action is often disdained by intellectuals and
critics, perhaps because Aristotle placed "spectacle"
at the bottom of his list of the elements of drama,
and dismissed it by saying, "The production of
spectacular effects depends more on the art of the
stage machinist than on that of the poet."

In the history of theater, which operates in real
time and within very limited space, it has always
been difficult to stage expansive and fast-paced
action sequences. That staple of action films, the
chase, works well when an actor can run, ride a
horse, car, airplane or rocket ship across considerable distances. Editing, which has no analogous
technique on the stage, can condense and manipulate time to produce thrills, suspense, fear, and the
kind of emotional rush found in roller coaster rides.
But the necessity in the theater of staging a chase in
real time and limited space prevents it from being as
effective as it could be in film.

The Birth of a Nation, one of the cornerstones
of American feature film history, has become dated
in many ways, but the chase scene at the end of the
film holds up quite well. Other classic films, such
as *Stagecoach, The French Connection, Bullitt, The
Terminator,* and *The Fugitive,* are memorable in large
part because of their chase scenes.

ACTION

Action scenes revolve around the fulcrum of
power. The relationships are simple and clear, and
yet they can reverse themselves in the blink of an
eye — the pursuer can become the pursued, as so
often happens in cartoons.

In the theater, conflict is almost invariably
between human beings. In film, however, the
conflict can also be between human beings and
firestorms, tornadoes, floods, volcanic eruptions,
earthquakes, meteors, and many other non-human
sources of power.

The chase is one of the basic building blocks of
drama, but it does not necessarily have to involve
physical movement. Detective films involve the pursuit of the killer; in conventional love stories, the
boy pursues the girl.

Some filmmakers, producers, and executives act
as though there is a dichotomy between action and
character, that you can have one or the other but not
both. This is why, when stories are referred to as "a
character piece," eyes sometimes glaze over — many
people in the industry take this to mean it's devoid
of action and, therefore, dull.

Because character development and action
sequences are so often seen as antithetical, many
modern action films give us an action sequence,
then stop for a little "character development," then
rush to another action scene. There is no reason,
however, why characterization cannot proceed
through the chase. The long scene in *The French
Connection* in which Popeye Doyle chases a killer in
an elevated train while he is driving a careening car

8   THE POWER OF FILM ⌣ HOWARD SUBER

below does more to develop his character than any other scene in the film. *The Terminator*, *Alien*, *The Matrix* and many other recent films revolve around one long chase. One reason they work so well with audiences is that, rather than alternating between action and character development, the two proceed simultaneously.

The prejudice against action films that some intellectuals, critics, and writers demonstrate may stem from a prioritization of words over images. How does one *write* an action sequence — "The villain chases the hero across the galaxy for the next twenty minutes"?

Action is generally visual, which explains why action films are the most successful exports of the American film industry — difficulty with the English language does not hamper non-Americans from appreciating such films. The fact that that there is less dialogue in action sequences does not, however, mean that the writer has nothing to contribute to action scenes; it just means the writer's contribution will lie more in scene description than in dialogue. That, too, is an essential art of the screenwriter.

ACTS

THERE ARE THOSE who claim that a film must have a three-act structure, and they often claim that Aristotle gave this "rule" to us. In fact, there were *no* acts as we define the term today in Greek drama, and Aristotle did not talk about acts at all because the plays he analyzed were all presented in a single continuous performance.

Nor, for that matter, is the five-act structure that many people associate with Shakespeare something he was hung up on. While he did use a five-act structure occasionally, it wasn't until nearly a hundred years after his death that a publisher imposed a consistent five-act structure on his plays.

In the theater, the audience is aware of acts because the curtain comes down, the house lights come up, and they get a chance to go to the bathroom. In film, the curtains don't come down, the houselights don't come up, and anyone who goes to the bathroom has to miss whatever keeps running on the screen.

Thinking in terms of acts is similar to erecting a scaffold to build a building: it may be a useful tool for the craftsmen during the construction phase, but it obscures the view of the work itself, and the people who gaze on the finished project will not know or care what kind of scaffold was used.

If the Greeks and Shakespeare had no need to worry about acts, maybe we have no need to, either. But because so many people in our time *do* worry about acts, entries follow for three possible ways of thinking about them (see: PARADOX).

(See also: ARISTOLATRY; ACTS, FIRST; ACTS, SECOND; ACTS, THIRD)

Beginnings and endings are the most interesting and most dynamic parts of any experience. Birth and death. Weddings and divorces. The beginning of a film and its ending.

The function of first acts has changed over time. In nineteenth-century European and American theater, "well-made plays" customarily began quite leisurely, with exposition that told us something about the characters, the setting, and events that had occurred prior to the raising of the curtain (see: Exposition). American films followed this theatrical tradition until the 1960s.

Then, perhaps through the influence of television, American films increasingly dispensed with leisurely beginnings and instead started with a scene intended to hook the audience (see: Hooks). While a hook is structurally necessary in television, where the viewer is ever ready to change to another channel, the audience in a movie theater has already paid its money and is not likely to wander out. Even though an early hook was not really needed, it became the standard way of beginning American films, and thus leisurely exposition was no longer allowed in most first acts.

In *Jaws*, the first scene quickly plunges us into the quick and sudden consumption of a nubile young woman by the film's title character. In *The Wild Bunch*, the first scene culminates in bloody crossfire during a bank robbery that kills many innocent men, women, and children. In *Bonnie and Clyde*, sex and violence are almost immediately linked together.

Acts, First

There is, however, a problem in beginning a movie with such major dramatic scenes. It is axiomatic that drama is structured around rising action; that, as we move through the real time of the film, the tension increases, emotions rise, and the pace often quickens until we reach the climax. If the first scene is intensely dramatic, it sets up the expectation that the film will reach even higher levels, which can be a problem when it doesn't.

In a great many films, most of the characterization occurs in the first act, the second act is usually devoted to action, and if there is any further characterization, it often doesn't occur until the third act. If, however, the first act is devoted to action, it is too late to begin dealing with characterization in the second or third act.

(See also: ACTS; ACTS, SECOND; ACTS, THIRD; ARISTOLATRY; HOOKS; COMPLETION AND RETURN)

THE REVOLUTIONARY FRENCH director, Jean-Luc Godard, attracted considerable attention when he said that of course films have a beginning, middle, and end — "But not necessarily in that order."

It's a funny but illogical witticism. Screenwriters, studio executives, and producers who think in terms of a three-act structure often note that the hardest act to get right is the second. With regard to any specific movie, everyone will agree on where the first act begins and where the third act ends, but there is often no agreement about where the second act begins and ends — even among the people who make the film.

A second act is not something you know when you see it. In part, this is because it's not clear what the *function* of the second act is.

The insistence that there must be three acts may, in itself, create the "Second Act Problem." When cuts are made in a film, they often come from the second act. This is because the second act is often where the film starts to meander, loses sight of where it's going and gets boring — just as often happens in life, when many people experience a "midlife crisis." The several robberies and chases in the second act of *Butch Cassidy and the Sundance Kid*, the "marriage" of Martin Pawley in *The Searchers*, and the journey upriver in *Apocalypse Now* all lack the sense of urgency, necessity and purpose that scenes in the first and third acts have.

The solution to the "Second Act Problem" is often found in the third act. That is, when the filmmakers figure where the story is going, it becomes

ACTS, SECOND

easier to assure that the second act makes progress towards that destination, rather than meandering aimlessly.

(See also: ACTS; CRISIS POINT, ONE-HOUR; ACTS, FIRST; ACTS, THIRD)

THE THIRD ACT is where the action either raises
to its highest emotional state, or the conflict that
was set up earlier is resolved. Often, the highest
state takes the form of a bloodbath, as we see in
Bonnie and Clyde, The Godfather series, *High Noon,
The Searchers, Butch Cassidy and the Sundance Kid,
The Wild Bunch, Unforgiven,* the *Alien* series, *The
Terminator* series, *The Bridge on the River Kwai,
Apocalypse Now, Taxi Driver, Dr. Strangelove,* and
The Manchurian Candidate.

Some people might find it astonishing how many
memorable popular films end in violence and death,
but the history of drama is filled with them. The
Greeks had them, Shakespeare had them, and it is difficult to find any period that is not filled with them.

If death is the ultimate separation, the next
worst is the separation of people who love one
another: Rick and Ilsa separate in *Casablanca,* Elliot
and E.T. separate in *E.T., The Extra-Terrestrial,*
Tom Joad and his mother separate at the end
of *The Grapes of Wrath,* Sam Spade and Brigid
O'Shaughnessy separate in *The Maltese Falcon.*

The story that resolves itself in unification is
most often a comedy, as *It Happened One Night,
Some Like It Hot,* and *Tootsie* demonstrate.

(See also: BEGINNINGS AND ENDINGS; ACTS; ACTS,
FIRST; ACTS, SECOND; ENDINGS, HAPPY)

ACTS, THIRD

ADAPTATIONS

As *Gone with the Wind, The Grapes of Wrath,* and *The Godfather* demonstrate, many of the most memorable films have been adaptations from novels. If the book was very popular, however, the filmmaker has severe limitations on how much can be changed. As David O. Selznick pointed out with regard to adapting *Gone with the Wind* into a movie, audiences understand that a film cannot include everything that was in the original book, and they will forgive the filmmakers for deleting scenes and characters — but they will never forgive them for creating new scenes and new characters.

Other forms of film that might be considered adaptations are biographical films and those dealing with specific historic events. *Lawrence of Arabia* and *Gandhi* are based upon pre-existing materials and the storytellers' major contributions often come from identifying the most essential elements of the story and structuring them in the most powerful manner possible. This is not necessarily less creative than inventing new characters and scenes; it is merely a different kind of creativity.

PROTAGONISTS CAN BE as young as Elliott in *E. T.*
and Dorothy in *The Wizard of Oz*, or they can
be as old as Charlie Allnut and Rose Sayer in *The
African Queen*. But if asked to name the memorable
heroes in films, people would probably not name
these characters first. This is because many of us are
ageists when it comes to heroes — we often think of
heroes as people who are beyond childhood but not
yet into middle age.

AGE

There has always been a gap between generations. When were the young not convinced deep
inside that they were morally superior to the old?
And when were the old not convinced deep inside
that their generation was morally superior to the
young? When were both not wrong?

When ages are mixed in film — when generations collaborate rather than being antagonistic
— the results can be quite memorable, as the
combination of Ben Obi-Wan Kenobi and Luke
Skywalker in *Star Wars* and Vito Corleone and
Michael Corleone in *The Godfather* demonstrate.
The gift that age gives to youth is wisdom and
experience, as Obi-Wan and Vito illustrate; what
youth gives to age is energy and hope, as Luke and
Michael demonstrate.

Near the end of *Lawrence of Arabia*, Prince
Feisal says in his last scene with Lawrence:

> Young men make wars, and the virtues of war are
> the virtues of young men: courage and hope for the
> future. Then old men make the peace, and the vices of
> peace are the vices of old men: mistrust and caution.

Bringing together people of different ages can result in powerful characters and scenes. There is also poignancy in such juxtapositions, perhaps because they are so seldom seen.

Two THINGS ARE necessary for the creation of interesting characters: the invention of interesting enemies and the invention of interesting allies.

As is so often true in life, the hero doesn't choose his allies — they simply appear. Harry Callahan in *Dirty Harry* is assigned a new partner; Chris Taylor in *Platoon* is assigned to work under Bob Barnes and Elias Grodin.

But the hero *chooses* his enemies. Much of the time, the villain would be perfectly happy to have the hero as an ally — it is the *hero* who makes himself an enemy by opposing what the villain does.

Often, someone who initially appears to be an ally turns out to be false, as often happens in detective, police, western, and war films in which one social unit faces another.

When the story involves a male and female, the relationship frequently begins with the two parties being antagonistic to one another and is followed by their becoming allies. In *North by Northwest*, Roger Thornhill and Eve Kendall are antagonists who become lovers, but it is not certain until quite late in the film whether she will end up betraying him again.

Interesting characters are often not all that interesting in themselves — think of Butch Cassidy and the Sundance Kid — they are interesting in large part because of their *relationships* with their allies and their enemies.

(See also: CHARACTER RELATIONSHIPS; VILLAINS; LOYALTY; BETRAYAL)

ANIMATION

THE STUDIO THAT has turned out the highest proportion of memorable popular films is the Walt Disney
Company. Some attribute this to Disney's domination in the area of animation, but animated films do
not necessarily attract huge or reliable audiences.
What Disney at its best mastered and sustained was
the art of telling stories that appeal to multiple constituencies. In this, they have been a model of the
process underlying all filmmaking that must appeal
to large numbers of people.

Contrary to popular belief, animated films are
not made for children; they are made for *parents* and
their children. Parents must be persuaded to take
their children to the theater or bring the films into
the house, and this means they usually must watch
the films with their children. If both adults and
children are not to be bored, there must be levels of
story, dialogue, and action that appeal to each on
their own level. Success in the field of animation
depends, therefore, not merely on the techniques of
animation, but also in the ability to tell stories that
appeal simultaneously to different constituencies.

(See also: CUTE)

CHEWBACCA AND THE Ewoks in the *Star Wars* series,
The Cowardly Lion and Toto in *The Wizard of Oz*,
the wolves and horse in *Dances with Wolves*, Flipper,
Lassie, Benji and the countless friendly animals or
other life forms who come to the aid of humans in
stories might be called "anipals."

The distinguishing feature of anipals is that
they are almost invariably cute and, with a few
exceptions such as Chewbacca, small. Their function is to be the pal of the protagonist, guiding him
in moments of danger, comforting him when he is
feeling lonely, and providing laughs both for the
main character and the audience — which is why
cuteness is an imperative (see: CUTE).

The chimeras of ancient myth were, like anipals, part animal and part human, but they were not
generally "cute" and they were as often antagonists
as allies. Anipals are just that — *pals*.

Traditional storytelling for thousands of years
anthropomorphized animals, imputing human characteristics to them. In modern times, the process of
anthropomorphization has often been applied to
machines, as Robby the Robot in *Forbidden Planet*
and R2-D2 and C-3P0 in *Star Wars* demonstrate.

(See also: CHIMERAS; MONSTERS)

ANIPALS

ANTAGONISTS

LIKE MOST OF the other key terms used in discussions of drama, "antagonist" comes from a Greek word. An "agon" is simply a contest or game.

All villains are antagonists, but not all antagonists are villains. When someone climbs a mountain, blazes a trail through a forest, uncovers a secret of nature, explores outer space or the oceans below, we may say the protagonist "battles" with nature, but it is not the same as a protagonist's battle with a villain.

Heroes and villains possess consciousness, will, and intention. Nature has none of these. Nature is not concerned with good or evil, but man is. Villains are immoral; nature is amoral. Villains intend harm to others; nature has no intention at all — it merely *is*. That doesn't prevent nature from being an antagonist, and when it is, the audience will always be on the side of the humans. Even the most dedicated ecologist would find it difficult to construct a satisfying dramatic story in which a flood, fire, hurricane, or earthquake "wins." That is something that only happens in real life.

The absence of good and evil in conflicts with nature poses a dramatic problem, because without this moral component, interest in the story becomes more difficult to sustain. This is why disaster films — which by definition deal with some conflict with nature — almost always have a second conflict, which involves other humans.

It is possible to construct a story in which there is simply an *agon* in the original Greek sense of a contest or game. The competition between two athletic teams or businesses could, for example, involve

likeable people on both sides who do not have an
evil bone in their bodies. Films *could* present such
stories — but who would watch them?

When we look at lists of memorable popular
films, it is clear that we choose to remember those
stories that are morality plays, in which the protagonist is on the side of good and the antagonist is on
the side of evil.

ANTIHEROES

A MAN IS driving to work one day and sees a house on fire. He rushes in and rescues an elderly woman confined to a wheelchair. Is he a hero? The nightly newscasts will describe him that way, as will his friends and former grade school teachers, who will say they always knew he had it in him. But the man (let's call him Mr. Samaritan) will probably say he was just "an ordinary guy doing what any decent person in that situation would do." Many others, while praising his courage and selflessness, would agree.

What does Mr. Samaritan do after people stop talking about his good deed? Does he go looking for more burning houses? Probably not. An "ordinary guy" does not go *looking* for the chance to be a hero.

But consider Superman, Batman, Spider-Man, and other "superheroes." Such characters are "super" in part because they are not "ordinary guys" — they are *professional* heroes. If someone said to Mr. Samaritan, "What do you do?" he would probably respond with a description of his day job. If, on the other hand, someone says to a superhero, "What do you do?" his response would have to be, "I rescue people."

Everyone, regardless of age, can identify with a man who plunges into a burning house. However, it takes a young mind, probably no more than fourteen years of age (psychologically, if not necessarily chronologically) to identify himself with a superhero.

Now, what would you say if the man driving down the street saw the fire, heard the screams coming from within the house, but looked at his watch, muttered something to himself about being late for an appointment and sped away? If the person who rushes into the fire is a hero, what would you call someone who chooses not to?

While the opposite of a hero is a villain, the decision not to rush into a burning building does not in itself make someone a villain. What, then, is such a person? Some people say he is an "antihero."

Critics love to talk about antiheroes and it is often claimed that antiheroes suit the temper of our times. But "anti" means "against" and the antihero is not someone who is *against* the hero — that, to repeat, is the villain. Nor are antiheroes people who are against being heroic. Travis Bickle in *Taxi Driver* and R. P. McMurphy in *One Flew Over the Cuckoo's Nest* may be scruffy, crude, cynical, hostile, and apparently unwilling to stick their neck out for others. Yet Travis Bickle kills pimps and drug dealers to save the teenage prostitute, Iris, and McMurphy tries to avenge Billy's death after Nurse Ratched drives the boy to suicide.

Bickle and McMurphy are like a great many other memorable dramatic heroes — they do not want to be involved. But they are not antiheroes; they are merely people who are not *yet* heroes. Before the story is over, they will perform some heroic act that is quite *un*characteristic of them. And then, like the guy who saves the old woman from the fire, they will go back to their day job.

There is no such thing as an antihero. There are only characters who act heroically and those who do not. It is difficult to find a memorable popular film whose central character is in the latter category.

ARISTOLATRY

ARISTOTLE WAS A very smart man who lived nearly twenty-five hundred years ago. Many have treated his brief lectures on drama as Holy Writ. Scholars tell us that he didn't actually write the *Poetics;* his students took notes during his lectures and it is these approximately forty pages that posterity has been left to puzzle through. Whether Aristotle's students fully comprehended what their teacher was saying has long been unclear. Several of his key phrases and ideas have been subjected to so many different interpretations over the years that it is unclear whether he was as ambiguous as the text we have received appears, or whether his students were just lousy note takers.

Too often, people practicing Aristolatry, which is the invocation of his name to support something he never actually said, have used Aristotle's brief lectures on tragedy to put drama into a straitjacket.

Take Aristotle's observation that drama has a beginning, middle, and end. Aristotle said this in passing, but this is such a self-evident statement that one has to wonder why he bothered to make the point or his students thought it worthy of preserving for posterity. World War II, this sentence, and your last bowel movement all have a beginning, middle, and end. *Everything* that takes place in time or space has a beginning, middle, and end.

As noted in the entry, Acts, not a single one of the plays Aristotle was familiar with had acts in the modern sense. Aristotle said absolutely nothing about an act structure — a significant omission, since Aristotle loved to number things.

The three-act structure that so many people ascribe to Aristotle was, in fact, invented more than two thousand years later when Ibsen and other nineteenth-century dramatists found that their audiences — unlike the drama groupies of Periclean Athens — were unable to sit still for the entire duration of a full-length play.

Nor did Aristotle prescribe a rigid adherence to the "Three Unities" of time, place, and action. That formula was invented three hundred years ago when the French playwrights Molière, Racine, and Corneille were the rage. Like the three-act structure today, its incorrect attribution to Aristotle was used by people who felt that art needed laws rather than license.

Making up "laws" about drama and then ascribing them to Aristotle is an ancient game. The point here is not to knock Aristotle, but rather his interpreters. As with the words of many other smart and insightful teachers (the carpenter from Nazareth comes to mind), those who claim to be Aristotle's disciples and speak on his behalf are all too often obsessed with inventing "rules" that choke the life out of human experience and diversity.

(See also: ACTS, FIRST; ACTS, SECOND; ACTS, THIRD)

ARMOR

WE ARE BORN naked and defenseless, but the first thing we develop in dealing with the world is armor. (The second is tools, which has its own entry.) Armor protects us. It can consist of physical strength, education, class, attitude, looks, or anything else we wrap around us to protect ourselves from danger and injury.

Early in *Gandhi*, the title character rides in the first-class compartment of a train in racist British-controlled South Africa. An officious white guy walks by Gandhi's compartment, does a double-take, and summons the porter, demanding he be evicted. Gandhi responds that he has a first-class ticket. When he is told that it doesn't matter, Gandhi protests and the Englishman responds to his protest by calling him a "cheeky wog," demanding to know why a such a person thinks he is entitled to sit in the first-class section reserved for Europeans. Gandhi buttons his proper British suit, rises to his full diminutive stature and responds, "I am a barrister admitted to the Court of Saint James."

In the next shot, Gandhi stands beside the train track in the middle of nowhere, his luggage beside him as the train recedes into the trackless horizon. The person who will become a mahatma ("great soul") has learned that his proper British suit, his financial means to purchase a first-class ticket, his fancy education and admission to the bar in London are not enough to protect him. As is always the case, there is no armor sufficient to protect one from racism and prejudice.

This is a familiar scene in drama because it causes a moral crisis, which drama constantly seeks. What will the hero *do* when he discovers his armor doesn't protect him, that he can be violated — now and in the future? There is only one satisfactory answer: he can pick himself up, dust himself off, and start all over again.

Gandhi stops wearing British armor and dons khadi, the cheap cotton cloth of India's poor, which he will wear henceforth. Later, this becomes a kind of armor, and in the end, it, too, will be insufficient to protect him when he is assassinated by one of his own people, whom he has devoted his life to freeing.

Armor is exterior. That is why, in many memorable stories, it is ultimately useless. What matters is what is *inside* the hero, not outside.

(See also: WEAPONS; TOOLS)

ART VS. CRAFT

Is MAKING A film an art or a craft? The artist often doesn't know what he is creating until it's finished. The craftsman, on the other hand, usually *does* know — otherwise, he wouldn't begin work. The artist is thus the more daring of the two because he has to plunge into ambiguity, uncertainty, and darkness. It is, in fact, the quality of daring that distinguishes all artists, whatever their medium. This does not mean the artist need not be a skilled craftsman — most of them are — it means that art goes *beyond* craft.

ONE OF THE most important elements of filmmaking is attitude.

The English writer Horace Walpole once said, "Life is a comedy to those who think; a tragedy to those who feel." The difference between the two is a matter of attitude. In aviation, "attitude" describes your relationship to the ground; in psychology, it describes how you're grounded — how you locate yourself in relation to others, and to life itself.

Stars are actors with attitude. Charlie Chaplin and Marilyn Monroe wanted desperately to please, while Gary Cooper and John Wayne couldn't have cared less whether you liked them. Woody Allen's pessimistic attitude defines him, just as Tom Hanks' optimism defines him. Every actor's attitude is, along with their looks, the main thing they have to sell.

Character *begins* with attitude, but it cannot end there. While one of the defining attributes of heroes is their defiance, anyone who has dealt with teenagers can testify that when defiance is merely an attitude, it can be annoying.

An attitude is embedded in every film — we sometimes call it "mood." (See that entry.) In the early 1960s, Columbia Pictures bought two serious novels dealing with a technological glitch that sets off an unintended nuclear war. Sidney Lumet, the director of the first project, *Fail-Safe*, produced a bleak and depressing film that left the audience numb with despair. Stanley Kubrick worked for several months on the second novel Columbia had purchased, *Red Alert,* which contained remarkably similar scenes, situations, and characters. (Columbia bought both precisely *because* they were so similar and they feared a lawsuit.) Finally, Kubrick concluded that people engaged in the kind of mutually assured destruction depicted in the book had to be crazy, and it was therefore impossible to treat them seriously. With that change of attitude, Kubrick turned the dark, despairing *Red Alert* into a comedy he called, *Dr. Strangelove Or: How I Stopped Worrying and Learned to Love the Bomb.*

Attitude is also crucial within the audience itself. While it is often said that a character must change, there are films — *Citizen Kane* being one — in which the fundamental nature of the character does not change. Kane's inability to change, in fact, is what makes his story a tragedy. When the audience recognizes this fact, it changes its attitude toward him — which is all that is required for an emotionally satisfying story.

32   THE POWER OF FILM   ⌒   HOWARD SUBER

ATTRIBUTES ARE THOSE elements of character that people have little or no control over because they have been received as part of genetic inheritance or socialization. People can't change their height, hair, pigmentation, the shape of their eyes, or other parts of their anatomy — at least not until recently. Nor can they change their unconscious behavior patterns — at least not without extensive therapy. The way we walk, talk, eat, and go about the ordinary routines of life — not to mention the extraordinary ones that are the stuff of drama — are attributes we seldom consciously developed.

Aptitudes, similarly, are largely beyond conscious intention or control, and thus part of our "fate." Someone may have an aptitude for French, differential calculus, the flute, basketball, writing, or baking bread, but while one has to work to become proficient in them, the aptitude that enables someone to do them well is often beyond conscious will or control.

Memorable characters are those that go *beyond* their attributes and aptitudes — they are defined, not by what they *are*, but by what they *do*.

(See also: CHARACTERIZATION; CHARACTER, POWER; CHARACTER STUDIES; CHARACTERS, STOCK; CHARACTERS: WHAT ARE THEY? WHO ARE THEY?)

ATTRIBUTES AND APTITUDES

Audiences

THE CLAIM THAT the key to popularity lies in appealing to the lowest common denominator reveals a profound misunderstanding of how audiences for movies function. Popular films achieve success the way democratic politicians do: by appealing to multiple *constituencies*; that is, different segments of the total population. What appeals to men may not appeal to women; what appeals to the young may not appeal to the old. Because the audience is not an undifferentiated "mass," movies, like political platforms, religions, and other endeavors that aspire to attract large numbers of people, must contain different *elements* that attract different kinds of people.

B

*The most important
word in storytelling is "but."*

BACKSTORIES

GEORGE LUCAS BEGAN the first *Star Wars* "A long time ago, in a galaxy far, far, away." After three films, he ran out of material that would enable the story to go forward, so he used a gimmick that creators of popular stories have often reverted to: he went *backwards* in the sequence of storytelling. Although some in the press created the term "pre-quel" for his three successive sequels, what Lucas did was make three more episodes dealing with the "backstory" of the original *Star Wars*.

Deciding how much of the backstory to include is a difficult creative decision. Where do you begin the story of famous people such as Jesus, Lincoln, and Gandhi? It depends on what you think the film is about.

In the story of *Oedipus Rex*, the audience learns that, as a young man, Oedipus killed a stranger on a road, and it turns out that man was Oedipus' father, and that he had unknowingly fulfilled a prophecy made before he was born, which in turn explains why there is now a plague upon the land of Thebes. Mel Gibson's *The Passion of the Christ* is about the crucifixion, and everything before it is backstory.

Backstories are often hinted at, rather than fully developed. In *Casablanca*, there are two back-stories — the first concerning Rick and Ilsa's love affair in Paris, and the second one dealing with Rick before he met Ilsa, when he fought in the Spanish Civil War, ran guns to the Ethiopians when Italy attacked it, and perhaps killed a man back in the United States. Rhett Butler in *Gone with the Wind* ran the Union blockade of Southern ports and ended up with a considerable amount of Yankee silver, Sam Spade in *The Maltese Falcon* had an affair with his partner's wife, Tom Joad in *The Grapes of Wrath* killed a man and was sent to prison, Michael Corleone in *The Godfather* defied his father's wishes and became a decorated war hero, Benjamin Braddock in *The Graduate* was a star student and athlete, and William Munny in *Unforgiven* did terrible things in his past. But all of these things *remain* in the past, backstories that are hinted at or dimly seen but not dramatized.

Drama is built upon cause and effect. When backstories *cause* events in the present, they can be powerful elements in the story. But when they are simply events that happened earlier, and the audience doesn't really need to know about them in order to understand the present, backstories can be a waste of time.

(See also: EXPOSITION; FLASHBACKS; MOTIVATION)

BEGINNINGS AND ENDINGS

WE SEE A locked gate with a "No Trespassing" sign on it, and then slowly move towards a castle on a mountaintop, and then go through the window from which light shines. A dying man lies on a bed and his lips fill the screen in a very tight closeup. He whispers, "Rosebud!" and dies. At the end of the film, we see a roaring fire in a furnace and, as in the beginning of the film, move into it until, in the middle of the flames, we see a sled with the name "Rosebud," and we know *Citizen Kane* is over.

The two most important elements of any story are the beginning and the ending. That's why, in the story of our lives, our mothers often recorded our first words, and why, if we accomplish something of note, journalists will record our final words.

A film with a brilliant first scene and last scene are halfway to greatness. All the rest is padding.

(See also: ACTS; ACTS, FIRST; ACTS, SECOND; ACTS, THIRD; COMPLETION AND RETURN)

THE HISTORY OF our species, as well as the history of fiction, is filled with stories of betrayal. The foundation and continuation of all social relationships depends on loyalty, and betrayal leads to their destruction. Betrayal, therefore, is a powerful action on both the personal and social level — which is why it appears so often in memorable stories.

BETRAYAL

The person who betrays someone else or an institution often claims he did it for a principle. But a person who betrays others for a principle sometimes *has* no principles, because the destruction of the human community leaves every other potential principle at risk.

The worst wars are civil wars, which are by definition conflicts between people who have almost everything else in common. People *assume* that others are loyal, which is why they feel so deeply betrayed when they discover they are not. This is why civil wars such as those fought in America, France, Russia, China, and Vietnam generated so much passion and had such long-term - consequences.

When loyalty and betrayal are major elements, much of the first half of the story will be spent on the development of loyalty and trust that *enables* characters to become a community, as we see in such different films as *Lawrence of Arabia*, *Star Wars,* and *The Dirty Dozen.*

Betrayal usually occurs late in memorable stories, and often creates one of most important scenes in the story. Judas kisses Christ. Tessio proposes that Michael meet Barzini in *The Godfather*. Michael realizes in *The Godfather: Part II* that his brother Fredo has betrayed him in Havana and, in a mirror of the Christ story, bestows a kiss on him.

Betrayal is fertile ground for drama. Where would gangster, science fiction, and horror films be without it?

(See also: LOYALTY)

In real life many successful, powerful, or merely famous people got where they were because they happened to be in the right place at the right time. But, as one of the most famous lines in *Lawrence of Arabia* declares, "Truly for some men nothing is written unless they write it."

The underlying premise of nearly all biographical films is that people who deserve to have films made about them have controlled the story of their own lives, that they were *responsible* for what happened to them (see: Individualism).

Drama is built on cause and effect; that is, what happens in one scene determines what happens in later scenes. Life, however, is one thing after another. Work, love, family developments, politics, economics, wars, depressions, accidents, and events that one has no responsibility for consume the lives of most people.

When filmmakers decide to make a biography about a real person, they invariably discover that their subject's life was episodic rather than dramatic (see: Structure, Episodic). Their first and primary task, then, is to change the episodic structure of real life into the dramatic.

The prologue to *Lawrence of Arabia* begins, as biographies so often do, with his death. When the flashback into the story of how he lived begins, it does so with Lawrence in Egypt and it ends with him leaving Damascus. While the film runs for three hours, it actually covers only a few years of Lawrence's life. *Patton* famously begins with its title character in front of a huge American flag

BIOGRAPHIES

commanding his troops, but how he got to his position of authority is not shown. *Gandhi* begins and ends with the Mahatma's death, but once the inevitable flashback begins, we meet him as a grown man practicing law. What happened to him before then is not shown, nor are long periods of his life later on.

If a real person is important enough to make a film about, the audience already knows how the story ends; the major problem, therefore, is deciding where to *begin*. It will be creative decisions — rather than biographical facts — that determine how much to show of the great amorphous middle that is a feature of everyone's life.

Almost invariably in shaping a film, real-life events will be structured in a way that confirms the audience's need to believe that the subject of the film fulfilled his Destiny and was not merely subject to Fate (see: DESTINY). If the biography is about a composer, singer, or bandleader, for example, much of the film will consist of their search for their unique "sound"; if a writer, they will be searching for their unique "voice"; if an artist, it will be their unique "vision"; if a religious, political or social figure, it will be their search for their unique "mission."

Most of us struggle just to get through the day; we *react* to events, but seldom see a goal clearly and move directly toward it. When people are farsighted enough to do so, they often become the subjects of movies.

In his seminal book, *The Creative Process*, Arthur Koestler coined the term "bisociation" and argued persuasively that it is what accounts for creativity, scientific discovery, and humor. Bisociation consists of bringing together elements that previously had not been brought together — and were often thought not to *belong* together — so that they produce something new, useful and/or humorous.

BISOCIATION

Bisociation is not the same as the Marxian dialectic of opposites, nor are there necessarily contradictions between the things that are brought together — they just haven't been brought together before.

Early in *Alien,* the crew is eating together and chatting amiably when suddenly a monstrous fetus erupts through the chest cavity of one of the crewmen, providing a very dramatic introduction for the film's title character. Early in *The Terminator,* thunder and lightening crackle and pop across the Southern California sky, and a totally nude Adonis is "born" on the pavement. In *2001,* a spaceship with the markings of a well-known airline docks at a huge revolving space station while the nineteenth-century "Blue Danube Waltz" by Johann Strauss plays on the sound track, capturing its grace and beauty, however anachronistically.

Bisociation consists of the juxtaposition of the unexpected, the unlikely, and often the "unnatural," which is why it is so often found in the most memorable science fiction and horror films, where two cultures (earthlings and "others") or two states of existence (natural and "supernatural") are brought together.

In comedies, which are scarcely possible without bisociation, people who have little in common, who don't appear to "belong together," develop into romantic couples, as we see in films such as *Some Like It Hot, Annie Hall, The Graduate,* and *Tootsie.*

The Exorcist is not just another horror film; it merges the story of a family with elements of the horribly supernatural. Similarly, *The Godfather* is not just another gangster film; it merges the story of a family with some of the most violent and brutal scenes in film.

When no one has ever thought of bringing two elements together or, better yet, when the common wisdom says that you must *not* mix two different elements together, the creative potential of bisociation may produce a work that is fresh, original, and memorable.

(See also: PARADOX; OPPOSITES; INCONGRUITY; DUALITY; IRONY; CHIMERAS; FISH OUT OF WATER; ORIGINALITY; TEAMS AND COUPLES; DEFIANCE)

BLESSINGS

THE GREATEST GIFT one human being can give another is a recognition of his or her own potential. And the greatest curse is to cause that person to lose faith in his or her own potential.

This is why parents, mentors, teachers, and other authority figures have such power over us. We trust their ability to judge what we are capable of. When they believe we can do something, we believe we can; when they doubt it, so do we.

The function of Obi-Wan Kenobi and a host of other mentors, teachers, trainers, and authority figures is not to exert their power *over* other characters — it is to help them realize that they have it.

(See also: CURSES; MENTORS; POWER)

BLOCKING

IN OLD CARTOONS, the central character is often run over by a steamroller, falls to the bottom of the Grand Canyon, or is blasted point-blank in the face with a shotgun. In the very next scene, he goes blithely on his way, oblivious to the pain and death inherent in the preceding scene.

If you are at the supermarket and see someone slip on a banana peel, you might rush up to see if that person is okay; but when you see someone slip on a banana peel in a motion picture, the proper reaction is laughter.

While tragedy is based on a cause-and-effect relationship between actions, comedy is usually based on cause *without* effect, as these examples demonstrate. We see the cause, but the consequence — usually pain — is blocked.

In a war film, a minor character pulls out a picture of his girlfriend or his wife and kids. The audience is invited to feel empathy for him and as often as not he will die poignantly a few scenes later. But we are seldom shown the pictures of the wife and kids of the *enemy*. The "other" side in war films is usually a faceless, anonymous horde. Enemies die in long shots, whereas good guys die in closeup. In the first, the filmmaker is trying to block identification with the characters; in the second, he is trying to enhance it.

Filmmakers are well aware that their job is to elicit feelings from their audience; what is equally important is to the ability to block them.

(See also: MISDIRECTION)

The claim that something is boring often tells us as much about the bored as it does about the bore. What is boredom? Not repetitiveness — much of the world's most enduring art is built on the principle of repetition. Something is boring because it's predictable.

The cure for boredom is unpredictability. This is why the most engaging stories are often filled with misdirection; that is, we expect the story to go in one direction, but it goes in another.

This is more complicated than it might appear, for it requires the filmmaker to be able to predict what the audience will expect, and then to go in some other direction that will still manage to please them.

(See also: MISDIRECTION; BUT)

BORING

BUT

THE MOST IMPORTANT word in storytelling is "but." Inexperienced storytellers tell us that first one thing happened, and then another thing happened, but they don't connect the events in an entertaining and dramatic way. Experienced storytellers constantly say, "The good news is …" *but* "The bad news is…"

It is the reversals and contradictions, the paradoxes and incongruities, that make a story interesting.

(See also: PARADOX; DECEPTION, FLOW)

C

*Like religion, people go to movies, not to
see the world as it really is but to see a world
that compensates for the one they know.*

CALL TO ADVENTURE

JOSEPH CAMPBELL'S *The Hero with a Thousand Faces* and his later television series led some people to treat Campbell's observations of ancient Hindu, Buddhist, and Greek mythologies as if they were a sure-fire formula for creating popular films. Among the most famous elements of Campbell's writings was the hero's "Call to Adventure."

What escaped many of Campbell's followers was that while "the call to adventure" was certainly present in the *Star Wars* series, in part because George Lucas studied *The Hero with a Thousand Faces* before writing the screenplay, such a "call" is most often heard by adolescent males who have nothing better to do with their time.

Jimmy Dean's character is certainly looking for adventure in *Rebel Without a Cause*, as are the kids in the hot rods in *American Graffiti*. Bonnie and Clyde also like hot rods and the call to adventure, but look what it gets them. Benjamin Braddock isn't looking for much of anything in the beginning of *The Graduate*, but when a roll in the hay is offered by an older woman, he succumbs, only to discover it wasn't much of an adventure after all. And George Bailey, early in *It's a Wonderful Life*, tells his pop, "I just feel like if I didn't get away, I'd bust," but it may be possible that one of the reasons the film is so memorable to so many people is that it ultimately makes the point that *not* heeding the "call to adventure" is what makes someone a *mensch*.

In real life and even in film, most people past adolescence are too busy trying to make it through the day to hear — or take — any "call." The older the person, the more likely it is that he or she simply wants to be left alone. That would describe the state of most post-adolescent protagonists in the world's memorable films, for whom "I stick my neck out for nobody" — the principle enunciated by Rick Blaine in *Casablanca* — is an appropriate motto. William Munny in *Unforgiven* is just trying to raise his kids and figure out how to cure his sick pigs. Michael Corleone just wants to marry the WASP nebbish he brings to his sister's wedding and it is clear he wants go into something *less* adventurous than the family business (in Mario Puzo's novel, he wants to be a mathematics professor). Charlie Allnut in *The African Queen* just wants to lazily drift downriver and swill from his stock of booze, rather than stick his neck out to help what he calls a "crazy psalm-singing skinny old maid."

Adventure is certainly important to entertainment. But, in most memorable popular films, the hero isn't looking for and doesn't heed a call — he's *coerced* into it.

CATHARSIS

FOR THE LAST 2,500 years, the most popular and memorable dramatic stories have tended to be filled with sex and violence. Some people have always been offended by this, and periodically throughout its history, theaters have been condemned, censored, and shut down as a result. Other have argued that, rather than being a danger to individuals and society, the depiction of these deep human impulses on stage and screen produces "catharsis."

The term was used a couple of times in Aristotle's *Poetics*, but what he meant by it has been debated for centuries. Aristotle's father was a doctor, and he may have had in mind the biological process of "purgation," or cleaning out the bowels. Or he may have meant the more metaphysical sense of "cleansing" or even "purification."

Whatever Aristotle and other ancients mean by "catharsis," there has always been a widely held belief that we are, both as individuals and as societies, auto-toxic. That is, our own systems generate bad things, whether of the body, mind, or spirit, and they must be flushed out of our systems because if they aren't, we will be poisoned by them.

Other scholars have argued for centuries that the process of "catharsis" is not what happens in art and entertainment at all. People, they argue, become *fascinated* with sex, violence, and other impure, unclean, or poisonous thoughts and emotions, and therefore the depiction of these noxious acts *increases* toxicity rather than purges it.

The term "fascination" stems from the Latin word meaning "to bind," and in recent history it gave us the word "fascism." Psychiatrists use the term "cathexis" to convey the notion of something that holds us in its grip. The two sides agree that individuals and societies generate impure thoughts and emotions; where they differ is in what should be done about it.

This argument has gone on for two millennia. People who create drama and stories generally side with Aristotle, but it is possible this is because they have a vested interest in doing so. This much seems clear: the most memorable, and popular, stories *do* fascinate, *do bind* us to them. But by the end of the story, they usually provide a sense of release, sometimes even of freedom and exultation. So, it may be possible that the most memorable films involve *both* catharsis and cathexis.

CAUSES

REBEL WITHOUT A CAUSE is a paradoxical title, because James Dean's character does, in fact, have a cause — one that we often find in memorable popular films: he wants people to tell the truth.

Tom Joad says early in *The Grapes of Wrath* "I'm just tryin' to get along without shovin' anybody, that's all." By the end of the film, however, he has dedicated himself to the cause of fighting injustice in the world. Early in *Casablanca*, Rick Blaine says, "I'm the only cause I'm interested in," but by the end, Victor Laszlo says, "Welcome back to the fight."

Most of the time, the villain has no cause but himself; in fact, his purely personal desire to impose his power over everyone else is what *makes* him a villain.

(See also: FANATICS; TRANSCENDENCE)

THERE ARE TWO basic kinds of change in storytelling: of circumstances and of character. In westerns such as *High Noon* and *Shane,* detective stories such as *The Maltese Falcon, Dirty Harry* and *Chinatown,* horror films such as *Frankenstein* and *Dracula,* and musicals such as *The Sound of Music* and *West Side Story*, the circumstances of the central character change, but by the film's end the characters are still essentially who they were at the beginning.

The central characters in *It's a Wonderful Life, Apocalypse Now,* and *The Godfather*, however, are not only in greatly changed circumstances by the end of the film — they are not who they were at the beginning. Early in *It's a Wonderful Life*, George Bailey says that he wants to get out of the crummy little town he was born in, but before the story is over, he has saved it, and, in turn, the town saves him. Willard in *Apocalypse Now* begins by saying he wants a mission, but by the end of his successful completion of one, he says he is out of the U.S. Army. Michael Corleone in *The Godfather* begins by telling his girlfriend he doesn't belong to his family, and by the end he runs it. Such changes of character are even more important than the changes of circumstances.

When the circumstances or the character of the protagonist are worse at the end of the story than they were at the beginning, the story is a tragedy in the Greek or Elizabethan mode — something American films usually avoid.

There are many memorable dramas and films in which heroes die or leave town, but this is compensated for by the fact that their spirit lives on in others. J. P. McMurphy has been smothered by the end of *One Flew Over the Cuckoo's Nest*, but his spirit lives on through Chief, who fulfills McMurphy's mission of escaping from the mental hospital. *Shane* leaves town at the end of the film named after him, but his example lives on in young Joey Starrett. The little fellow in *E. T.* goes back to his home planet far, far away, but he touches young Elliott on his forehead and tells him that he'll be "here" — in Elliott's memory — the one place immortality can be assured.

The highest form of change is a deification, in which the central character transcends his status as an ordinary mortal and becomes a symbolic force for good. *Gandhi* may be dead at the end of the film that bears his name, but his message and mission live on in the hearts of his followers and the audience. Similarly, Tom Joad's final speech in *The Grapes of Wrath* says he'll be wherever injustice and cruelty is being perpetrated, fighting for "the little guy."

As with everything else, there are exceptions to the "rule." The title character in *Citizen Kane* does not change; at his end, he is what he was at his beginning — a stunted, lonely, petulant being. His circumstances have certainly changed, but his character has not. What changes most in the film is the audience's perception of Kane. This can be the most memorable change of all.

(See also: CHARACTER, POWER; POWER; MISSIONS)

OFTEN, IT IS chaos, rather than evil, that is the enemy. Disorder and chaos are the conditions the hero fights against; unification, organization, and comprehension are the conditions the hero attempts to bring about.

CHAOS

Chaos and evil are not antithetical; in fact, where there is chaos, you will often find evil. And where there is evil, you will often find chaos, if for no other reason than that the human mind has difficulty distinguishing between chaos and evil.

Stories such as *The Exorcist* and many other horror films that set out to convince us of the reality of some evil usually first set up the "natural" world and then introduce an "unnatural" one that threatens it. This is why detective, horror, war films and much science fiction so often begin with scenes in middle-class homes, small towns, schools, parks, etc. They establish the ordered existence that defines what is "natural" in order to set up the contrast with the chaotic force that will then descend and threaten to destroy "normal" ordered existence.

CHARACTER, POWER

SINCE ALL DRAMA is about power, it is important to examine the *kinds* of powers characters can possess, and how power operates differently in film than in real life.

Institutional Power. If you are stopped by a police officer, the chances are good you will become nervous, awkward, and apprehensive. If the officer tells you to hand over your driver's license, you won't argue; if he tells you to get out of your car, you will probably obey. You are unlikely to argue with this officer of the law no matter how indignant you may be that he's stopped you.

If you are a student in a classroom and the teacher calls on you, you will also tend to become a bit nervous and will generally respond in a compliant manner. If a doctor tells you to bend over, you will obey just as quickly as you would if a judge told you to stand up.

Cops are called "police officers" and judges and lawyers are "officers of the court." Their titles demonstrate that their power does not spring from themselves as individuals but rather from the institution they represent.

Institutional power is usually indicated by some kind of uniform, whether it's the badge of the policeman, the black robe of the judge, or the white smock of the doctor. The "uni" form such people wear expresses uniformity, not individuality, which is why soldiers are told in the U.S. Army that one salutes the uniform, not the individual wearing it (see: ARMOR).

Thus, when Father Merrin, a "man of the

cloth" in *The Exorcist*, recites the formula for exorcism, he says, "It is the power of Christ that commands you." It is not *his* personal power. Significantly, at the end of the movie, after the ritual (another expression of uniformity) of exorcism has failed to produce the intended result, Father Karras demands, "Take me, damn you! Take *me!*" It is only then, when the institutional power that Karras represents has been replaced by his *personal* power, that the demon does as he is commanded.

Although institutional power is enormously important in real life, it is either suspect or inadequate in films. Institutions of government such as the military, police, courts, Congress, the White House, or CIA and institutions of business such as insurance, medical care, oil, and electricity are frequently the malevolent power in film stories. This is such a familiar feature of popular films that a character can simply say that "they" are engaged in a nefarious conspiracy, and audiences will understand that the reference is not to individuals but to some institution.

When a central character wears a uniform, the film will generally spend considerable time demonstrating that that he or she is not really one of "them" — that is, all the others who wear the same uniform. In fact, if the protagonist wears a uniform, he almost invariably has a conflict: on the one side, he struggles against some outside enemy; on the other side, he struggles against the suffocating, wrongheaded, corrupt, or evil hierarchy within the very institution he represents (see: BETRAYAL).

Physical Power. Personal physical strength has historically been the clearest and simplest form of power, as the mythical Hercules, the biblical Samson, Superman, and similar superheroes demonstrate. Because it's clear and simple, such power appeals to the young of mind, however old they may be.

In memorable movies, however, the strongest guy around is not likely to be the hero. In *The Godfather*, the strongest person in the film is Luca Brasi, who waits outside Vito Corleone's office during the opening wedding scene. He is also, perhaps not surprisingly, the first person killed by the Corleone family's cunning enemies.

The actor who won a world competition for his physique, Arnold Schwarzenegger, was transformed into a major movie star for his role in *The Terminator*, where he was unquestionably powerful. But he was also the villain in that film. Similarly, in the very popular series of films that began with *Alien,* the title character possesses enormous physical power but she is also the villain.

There is much talk in *Star Wars* and its sequels about "The Force," but it is clear that this does not refer to physical power or to *anything* physical. The characters who teach Luke Skywalker about higher powers are Obi-Wan Kenobi, an old man, and Yoda, a cute ugly gnome.

Children and adolescent males may think physical power is important, but in films aimed at more mature audiences, physical power is never *enough*.

Sex Appeal. There is another kind of physical power, which we often call "sex appeal." It is difficult to *write* a character with sex appeal — you need an actor who has it. This is why popular movies since the earliest days have been sold on the basis of the attractiveness of their stars. Paradoxically, while good looks get people cast in movies, no memorable *characters* succeed merely on the basis of their looks.

In life people with nothing more than "sex appeal" frequently acquire considerable wealth and power and live to a ripe old age, even maintaining a vestige of their good looks with the aid of various chemical and surgical procedures. In movies, however, a character who uses his or her sex appeal to gain power is likely to be left alone at the end — as is true for the title character in *All About Eve* and Mrs. Robinson in *The Graduate* — or dead, as in *Double Indemnity*.

Technology. If there's one thing Americans know, it's the power of technology. We built an economy on powerful automobiles; we consume more electrical and gasoline power than any nation on earth; we brought the power of computers into every home on the planet that could afford one. Our mass media, made possible by our technology, dominates the world's culture. Our weapons are the biggest, fastest, and best. Surely technology is power.

But that's only in real life. In our most memorable movies, technology is of limited value. Terry Malloy in *On the Waterfront* says to his one-time boss Johnny Friendly near the end of the film, "You take them heaters away and you're nothing, you know that ... you're nothing!"

A character who wins simply because he possesses superior technology is not likely to be a memorable character. In *Star Wars*, Obi-Wan Kenobi's advice to Luke Skywalker isn't to "Trust the light saber," but to trust the force that lies *within*.

Intelligence. In real life, children who score highest on intelligence tests are likely to be put in the highest classes, get into the most prestigious colleges, and be given the best jobs. There is no question that being smart gives you enormous leverage in the real world.

If you are smart, though, it is because you inherited good genes — *you* didn't do anything to deserve them. Therefore, like physical strength and sex appeal, mere intelligence is as likely to work *against* characters as for them, and in any case it is never enough. This may explain why there are so few memorable popular films in which the central character is super-smart. In fact, it is often the contrary. In *Rain Man*, Raymond Babbitt is an "idiot savant" in some ways, but he is totally lacking "smarts" in others; in *Forrest Gump* the title character is deficient in what the world calls "intelligence" but successful because he possesses other qualities (see: GOOFY).

Education. The power of education is part of the catechism of the American belief system. Many people become well-educated because they have the good fortune to have been born into a family with the means to educate them. But, like intelligence, a good education is not something the *individual* is totally responsible for.

In *The Dirty Dozen*, Major Reisman refers to his nemesis, Colonel Everett Dasher Breed, as "that West Point bum," reflecting the anti-elitist attitude that permeates American films. If a film introduces someone who has graduated from West Point, Harvard, Yale, or some other elite institution, he may, as in *The Dirty Dozen*, possess power at the beginning of the film because his education entitles him to it. But before the movie is over, he and the audience will discover that all that book learning hasn't prepared him to face real life. Education, powerful though it may be, is never *enough*.

Wealth. It is axiomatic that Americans aspire to wealth in real life, but you would never conclude this by looking at our most memorable popular movies.

In *Citizen Kane*, which deals with the man who inherited the world's third largest gold mine, Kane's flunky, Bernstein, says "It's no trick to make a lot of money ... if all you want is to make a lot of money." It is an attitude seen repeatedly in our most popular films.

When a character in a movie is only concerned with making money, it is a sure sign that something is wrong with that person. In *Rebel Without a Cause*, the parents of Jim Stark make their first appearance dressed in a tuxedo and an evening gown, having been summoned from a party at their country club to bail their son out of jail. We know immediately that such people can't be good parents to the boy. In *Sunset Boulevard*, Norma Desmond's enormous chauffeur-driven car, like the mansion she lives in, are portents of bad things to come. In *A Streetcar Named Desire*, the fancy clothes and gaudy jewelry of Blanche DuBois tell us there's something corrupt about her.

In *Schindler's List*, the opening scene immediately establishes Oskar Schindler's character by having him don an expensive shirt and expensive cufflinks as he prepares to go to an exclusive restaurant where he will buy the best champagne to bribe a Nazi officer. Schindler may be interested in wealth in the *beginning* of the film, but in his final scene he breaks down in tears as he realizes that his few remaining possessions could have been bartered for a few more lives.

Like Oskar Schindler, many central characters *start* by being interested in wealth, but by the end of all of the memorable films, there is confirmation of the line in Matthew 19:24 that it is easier for a camel to pass through the eye of a needle than for a rich man to enter the kingdom of heaven.

In memorable popular movies, institutional power, physical power, sex appeal, technology, intelligence, education, and wealth don't matter. However two kinds of power *do* matter:

1) The hero is better than the other people in the film, not because he possesses more of the kinds of powers described above, but because he possesses higher *principles*.

2) The hero is better than other people because he possesses more of what, in the final analysis, defines all heroes: *will* power.

(See also: POWER; PRINCIPLES; DECISIONS; JUSTICE; WEAPONS; ARMOR)

CHARACTER RELATIONSHIPS

WHAT MAKES MOST characters interesting is often not the characters themselves but rather their *relationship* with other characters. Characters are defined, not so much by what they are as by what they do, and what they do in drama is to interact with other people. *Casablanca* is a film in which the characters sit around doing an incredible amount of gabbing about causes and courage and it even deals with that most deadly of cinematic topics: political philosophy. At the same time, it also creates one of the most memorable and often-quoted set of characters in film history.

Rick, who runs a gin joint in an isolated and obscure corner of the world, doesn't *do* a whole lot. His first important line, after all, is "I stick my neck out for nobody," and for the first half of the film, he doesn't. The Letters of Transit, the McGuffin (see: McGuffin) around which the action revolves, are not something Rick has worked to obtain — they're *given* to him by Peter Lorre's sniveling weasel of a character, Ugarte, whom Rick disdains so much he doesn't lift a finger to save him. Throughout the film, this morally ambiguous character *responds* to others who come to him rather than initiating action on his own.

It is Rick's relationships that make *Casablanca* one of the most memorable popular films ever made. He becomes an interesting character through his interaction with Louis Renault, the police captain; Major Strasser, the sneering Nazi; Victor Laszlo, the Czech patriot. And what would Rick be without Ilsa Lund, the bewildered former lover who is inconveniently married to the only man

Rick really admires. Finally, who can forget Sam, the piano player who has very few lines in the film but sings the unforgettable, "As Time Go By"?

Even his relationship with minor characters helps develop Rick's character: Yvonne, the singer; Sascha, the bartender; Carl, the waiter; Annina, the Bulgarian immigrant; Berger, the member of the Free French underground; Signor Ferrari, the rival saloon keeper. Every character's *relationship* with Rick Blaine adds another brushstroke that helps reveal the portrait of one of the most memorable characters in film.

Michael Corleone relates with his father and his two brothers, the one who is too quick and the one who is too slow. His relationship with Kay doesn't become very interesting until the very end, when he betrays her, but his relationship with Sollozzo, the drug dealer and McCluskey the crooked cop, with Clemenza, the fat *capo* and Tessio, the tall, thin, *capo* are interesting and in constant flux.

Considered by himself, T. E. Lawrence is a bit of a prig and not all that interesting. Sherif Ali, Auda abu Tayi, Prince Feisal, General Allenby, Dryden the diplomat, and even the Turkish Bey he has a one-night stand with make his character interesting. If you lived next door to Benjamin Braddock (*The Graduate*), R. P. McMurphy (*One Flew Over the Cuckoo's Nest*), or J. J. Gittes (*Chinatown*), you'd probably say they were irritating nobodies — they only become interesting when they have someone to inter-relate with.

In a sense, we might say there is no such thing as an inherently interesting character — there are only interesting character *relationships*.

WHAT MEMORABLE FILM *isn't* a character study? In
the film industry, to call your work a "character
study" is sometimes the kiss of death, because it
is interpreted as, "Nothing much happens in this
story" — that is, it's boring. Being boring is to films
what being fat is to romance: some people may love
you despite what you are, but never *because* of it.
But there is nothing about well-done characterization that is boring.

Some films focus on developing the action;
others focus on developing the character. The best
develop both. There is no evidence that filmmakers
can't present emotionally engaging action *and* emotionally engaging character development. If a film
isn't a study of character, what's the point?

CHARACTER STUDIES

CHARACTER-IZATION

AFTER TWENTY-FIVE CENTURIES of western drama, it may be difficult to find new themes or plots, but there are an infinite number of new and memorable characters waiting to be created.

A film may succeed in its own time on the basis of plot, spectacle, special effects, hype, and scandal. But if it is to endure in our collective memories, it must contain great characters. (How many films can you think of in which you remember the film but don't remember the characters? How many in which you remember the characters but are hazy about the film?)

Whether you are trying to understand a film or to create one, the very first question to ask is: "Whose story is this?" When you look at films that didn't succeed, you will often find that the filmmakers never figured out the answer to this simple but absolutely fundamental question.

The simplest way to answer the question, "Whose story is it?" is to ask:

1) Who is there in the beginning?
2) Who is there at the end?

Dorothy in *The Wizard of Oz*, Scarlet O'Hara in *Gone with the Wind*, the title characters in *Lawrence of Arabia, Gandhi, Annie Hall, Tootsie, Shane, The Graduate,* and *The Godfather* are examples of this principle. In films such as *Butch Cassidy and the Sundance Kid* and *Thelma & Louise*, which are about a team, *Annie Hall,* which is about a couple, or *The Wild Bunch*, which is about a gang, the answer to the question, "Whose film is this?" is a social unit, but the principle is the same: the central character or characters are there in the beginning and they're still there in the end.

This is not something the motion picture industry invented. In *Oedipus Rex, Hamlet, Death of a Salesman* and other great works of western drama, nearly all of the scenes, actions, and lines of dialogue further the development of a single individual's character.

Ultimately, the function of characterization is care-actor-ization; that is, getting the audience to care about the characters. This doesn't mean they have to like the characters; it means they have to have an emotional investment in what happens to them.

Create an interesting character and he or she can sit in a rocking chair and the audience will still pay attention. Fail to create an interesting character, and he or she can walk on burning coals in the nude and everyone except nudists, firewalkers, and burn unit personnel will fall asleep. Memorable films — by definition — contain memorable characters.

(See also: CHARACTER RELATIONSHIPS)

CHARACTERS, STOCK

IT IS COMMON and easy to do, but the automatic denigration of stock characters ignores their importance to the history and art of storytelling. Stock characters were a staple of ancient Greek and Roman drama, and during the Restoration in England, stock character types were codified in the "Theory of Humors" that was influential for centuries, not only in the theater but also in medicine. The boastful Texan, the laid-back Californian, the mall-obsessed Valley Girl are all stock characters, and dentists, lawyers, professors, and other occupational groups are often treated as stock characters.

Filmmakers sometimes say they want to create a totally new character. But if a character were totally new, how could anyone understand it? As many memorable films demonstrate, the appearance of the new is often the result of bringing together stock elements that have not yet been brought together (see: BISOCIATION). As vineyards demonstrate, what is grafted onto the stock determines whether the result is something that rots the gut or something that gives added pleasure and meaning to life.

Michael Corleone is not just "a gangster" — he's the Godfather; that thing in the water is not just a big shark — it's "Jaws"; that drooling scissors job is not just a drooling insectoid — it's the Alien; those two women aren't just another ditzy housewife and waitress — they're Thelma and Louise.

There's nothing wrong with beginning with stock elements. The trick is to *transcend* them.

(See also: CHARACTER RELATIONSHIPS)

CHARACTERS: WHAT ARE THEY? WHO ARE THEY?

TO UNDERSTAND CHARACTERS, we need to ask the same questions about them that we sometimes ask about ourselves: "What am I?" and "Who am I?" We can be male or female, young or old, white or black, tall or short, fat or skinny. We can be Muslim or Buddhist, introvert or extrovert, funny or morose, mean or kind, corrupt or innocent, and an infinite number of other possibilities. But these are all "what" we are — our attributes (see: ATTRIBUTES AND APTITUDES). They are determined by Fate, and we personally deserve neither credit nor blame for them.

Who we are depends on two things: (1) the decisions we make and (2) the actions we take.

When we are young, we have not done much other than what our parents, teachers, peers, and society expect us to do, and thus our character has not yet had a chance to form. As we age, we begin to make our own decisions. It is only then that our character really takes shape.

It is the decisions we make and actions we take that define character — that determine "who" we are. And that determination — at least in drama — always comes from within.

(See also: ATTRIBUTES AND APTITUDES; CHARACTERS, STOCK)

CHASES

FROM THE STANDPOINT of structure, all that is required of a chase is a pursuer and a pursued. Physical chases have been a staple of film ever since Mack Sennett's Keystone Cops chased Charlie Chaplin all over Glendale, and American studio animation from Mickey Mouse and Bugs Bunny to *Toy Story* is almost totally devoted to chases.

But the structure of the chase is not limited to physical movement. Detective films involve the pursuit of wrong-doers and conventional love stories involve the pursuit of a girl by a boy. In biographies and a great many historically based films, the hero pursues the realization of a cause, truth, or scientific discovery.

At bottom, a great many memorable stories alternate between pursuing and being pursued.

(See: BUT)

CHILDREN ARE CREATED in films for the same reason they are created in real life: because they carry the future with them. If they exist, the tribe will continue to exist; if they die, the storyteller and the audience die. Thus, all of a society's hopes, fears, and its wildest fantasies of future existence are bound up in children.

People often confuse stories *about* children with stories *for* children. Shirley Temple, Judy Garland, and many child actors were enormously popular with adults, even though some kids their own age couldn't stand them. On the other hand, as every parent is well aware, the films that appeal to children can often be loathsome to an adult sensibility, or worse yet, boring.

Children are often allowed to consume children's television by themselves. But children who consume films in theaters generally do so in the company of adults, and thus a "children's film" must appeal to adults as well.

Just as there is much that appeals to adults that children are not attuned to, so is there much that appeals to children that passes over the heads of adults. As with every other genre, the key to memorability and popularity is to *transcend* the elements that are customarily associated with it.

(See also: AUDIENCES; ANIMATION; CUTE)

CHILDREN'S STORIES

CHIMERAS

THE ANCIENT GREEKS created a fire-breathing female monster that had the head of a lion, the body of a goat, and the tail of a serpent and they called it a *chimera* (pronounced ky-MIR-uh). Dragons, which are a specific kind of chimera, usually had scaly skin, the claws of a lion, the tail of a serpent, and the wings of a bird. In modern genetics, a chimera is the result of genetic engineering, the product of mutation, grafting, irradiation, fusion, or transformation of different life forms into a single organism. The Egyptian Sphinx was a chimera, as were the Greek centaurs and the Minotaur. One Christian interpretation of Satan followed the principles of chimera creation and gave him horns like a goat and a tail like a serpent, but also human features. An astonishing number of characters in mythology, folk tales, and other forms of storytelling around the world have been chimeras, and the fascination with combining different species and life or lifelike forms is widespread in modern films.

In earlier ages, chimeras were created by merging parts of men and beasts; in our own age, it is more likely to result from the merger of men made of parts from different bodies, as in *Frankenstein*, men mixed with other life forms, as in *The Fly* and the *Alien* series, and men and machines who have become indistinguishable, as in *The Terminator* and *The Matrix*.

Frankenstein's monster is an organism that has gone haywire; HAL in *2001* is a machine that has gone haywire. The Replicants in *Blade Runner*, and the life forms in the *Alien* series that are part insect, part reptile, and part human all exemplify the abiding appeal of the principles of chimeras. Without chimeras, many of the most memorable science fiction and horror films would have been impossible.

The appeal of chimeras reveals one of the most important creative principles: bring together elements that had been thought of as totally separate and find a way to unify them.

(See also: BISOCIATION; HORROR FILMS; ANIPALS)

CHOICE

IN ATHLETIC COMPETITIONS, the players get only three strikes, four downs, or some other limitation on their chances to succeed. Like drama and film, a limitation on options enhances the excitement and interest.

In many action films, the hero must deal with a time bomb by cutting the wire that will prevent it from going off, but he doesn't know which wire it is. If he makes the wrong decision, many — including the hero — will die.

In life, there may be many different choices one can make to accomplish a goal. In films, there is often only one, and the hero gets to show how smart he is by figuring out what it is.

(See also: TRAPS)

When people believe in Fate, it is easy to believe in coincidence, the bringing together of two people or events at a propitious moment. In life, coincidences often produce a sense of wonder and are sometimes taken as evidence that some unseen power directs our lives.

Coincidences

Coincidences frequently appear early in the development of the story. In romantic comedies, for example, the "meet cute" in which the boy and a girl bump into one another (often literally) is simply a way to get the story going. But, once it's well under way, coincidences in modern drama are less acceptable.

Drama depends on the assumption that things don't "just happen" but that individuals are *responsible* for what happens to them. Thus, the appearance of fate, coincidence, and divine intervention are seldom seen as evidence of good dramatic writing.

(See also: Destiny; Cute Meet)

COLLABORATION

ONE OF THE great clichés about film is that it is a collaborative art form. Just because it's a cliché doesn't mean it isn't true, but it's important to be clear about the ways in which this statement is true.

A painter generally works by himself, using materials that he has purchased out of his own pocket. So, too, do the poet, composer, playwright, and novelist. They can afford to be loners, and since they have put their own time, materials, and energy into their creation, they can demand to be the sole arbiters of what happens to their work.

But a screenwriter is like an architect: he will seldom have the money to actually bring to fruition the work he designs. Like architects, screenwriters are usually hired to produce a specific work. This is also true for nearly all the other people who work in film.

Collaboration, of course, requires compromise. But this goes against the predisposition of most young filmmakers who think of themselves as artists. An artist is usually thought of as someone who pursues his or her own vision, which often means struggling against compromise. How, then, can anyone working in a medium that requires constant compromise be considered an artist? It is a dilemma without easy resolution.

The production of music, whether it is a symphonic work for a great hall or a garage band, requires collaboration. But would we say the violinist *compromises* with the oboe player, or the guitarist compromises with the drummer? They work together to produce a unified collaborative work, which is what's supposed to happen in film. The musician who ignores the composer's score or plays out of synch with the other members of the group will soon find himself playing in his garage all by himself.

Collaboration in film, however, is not like collaboration in music. The band generally plays together simultaneously, but in film, many of the collaborators play in serial fashion, one after the other. The screenwriter may work before anyone else, and, in turn, may *finish* working on the film before anybody else. This is one of the reasons screenwriters have relatively little power — they surrender their creative contribution before most other people have even come aboard.

The major actors and the director also are involved early in the project, and without them the project is unlikely to obtain financing or get made. They also remain with the project the longest, since they are involved not only in production and post-production, but also in marketing as the film is introduced into theaters. The fact that they are involved the most is one of the reasons actors and directors are paid the most. Cinematographers, editors, composers, set designers, and other key personnel, on the other hand, are generally brought in after the actors and director are hired and are gone before the film is even finished.

Without compromise and without anticipating the needs of others working on the film, the result can be chaos. In filmmaking, compromise is not antithetical to creativity, it is what makes it possible.

The creative potential of genuine collaboration was demonstrated in the making of what has often been called the greatest American film: *Citizen Kane*. Orson Welles had passion, inventiveness, brilliance, and courage, but he was only twenty-five and had never made a feature film before. Herman Mankiewicz, the screenwriter who wrote almost all the dialogue and scenes, was a middle-aged cynic who had long since given up the hope of finding a vessel into which to pour his considerable wisdom, and he needed to have his creative prowess harnessed to a worthwhile end. Gregg Toland, the middle-aged cinematographer, was one of the great technological innovators in motion picture photography. His experience and vision, coupled with a determination to constantly probe the boundaries of the possible, made him a master guide who could help Welles realize his often impossible vision. Bernard Herrmann, the composer, was a temperamental young guy who turned out to be one of the most inventive geniuses in movie music.

Two younger men collaborated with two older and experienced artists. The young ones had no sense of the limits of the medium, but the older men knew how to go beyond them. Together, these four collaborators produced a unified work that was beyond anything each had produced before or would ever produce again.

When we look at the list of memorable popular films, we frequently find something similar — that the writing, directing, cinematography, music, etc. together produce a unified whole that transcends its parts.

(See also: ART VS. CRAFT)

COMEDY

ALTHOUGH THE MODERN sensibility demands that a comedy be funny, this was not always the case. For the ancients, a comedy was simply something that ended happily, while a tragedy was something that did not.

Dante's *Divine Comedy* is not likely to make anyone other than the most confirmed sadist laugh. The first two-thirds of the story takes place in Hell and then Purgatory, focusing in exquisite detail on pain and agony. Why, then, is the work called a "comedy"? Because at the end, Dante is reunited for the briefest instant with his beloved — but dead — Beatrice and he gets to glimpse the glories of Heaven.

Americans love to laugh, and they love those who make them laugh. A comedy that doesn't produce laughter is likely to be a flop. Comedies account for a large proportion of the most com- mercially successful films every year; yet, when Academy Awards are given out, few comedies win anything. We may love them, but we don't respect them in the morning.

This ambivalent love but lack of respect has always been the case. The Greeks cranked out a lot of comedies, but few have been preserved. When Aristotle gave lectures on the theater twenty-five centuries ago, they were compiled into two vol- umes, the *Poetics*, which dealt with tragedy, and another work that dealt with comedy. We don't even know the title of the other work, because the last known copy appears to have been destroyed when the great library in Alexandria burned early in the Christian era.

Perhaps, considering the history of theatrical works since, this was a blessing. One of the reasons writers who set out to produce tragedies frequently produce boring works is that everyone *knows* the rules of tragedy — they're all there, some say, in Aristotle's forty-page instruction manual.

However, because critics and other arbiters of taste have lacked a rulebook by which to judge comedic works, it has had the freedom to be chaotic. While it's hard to get away with breaking the rules of tragedy, in comedy it's not a problem because there *aren't* any rules.

Tragedy builds tension through rising action that culminates in an emotional climax. Comedy, on the other hand, builds tension and then releases it through laughter. As a result, comedy tends to have a looser, more episodic structure and the laughter can interrupt the performance without interrupting the thought.

This is one reason comedy so easily adapted itself to the requirements of television, while tragedy fared less well. As soon as there is a climax of laughter in a television comedy, you can cut to a commercial; but if you cut to a commercial during a tragedy, you risk destroying the emotional effect.

Because we are supposed to laugh, an audience constantly demonstrates how it feels about its experience *during* comedies. The creators and performers know instantly whether their work has succeeded with the audience — which is why there are virtually no comedies that were "before their time."

Comedy affirms the importance of feelings and

praises the fluid and the unconventional, even if
that means creating disharmony by breaking social
and other kinds of laws. Charlie Chaplin, Harold
Lloyd, Buster Keaton, Laurel and Hardy, the
Marx Brothers, Abbott and Costello, Jerry Lewis,
Steve Martin, and Jim Carrey all built careers in
which their characters were defiant, disobedient,
and created chaos.

Comedies charm us, warm us, and give us relief
from the pain of life. However, it is tragedy we
most often recall, perhaps because we recall pain
more readily than pleasure. Or perhaps it is because
tragedy reconciles us to our ultimate fate, which is
loss, decay, and death.

Comedy ignores or blocks our recognition of
the fact that the senile old man and the toothless old
hag that are so common in comedy are visions of
ourselves as we shall eventually be. Tragedy neither
avoids nor blocks this realization; it is, in fact,
obsessed by it.

Comedies usually begin with someone who
is out of a job, poor, broke, unemployable — a
"loser." By the end of the story, more often than
not, they're a "success." The course of comedy is
thus always an ascent to power.

The danger in comedy is that, at any moment,
it can become a tragedy. The danger in tragedy is
that, at any moment, it can become a comedy. In
watching films that play with this delicate balance,
it is useful to observe how the conversion of one to
the other is prevented from happening.

(See also: JOKES; LAUGHTER; TRAGEDY, BLOCKING, TRAPS)

Coming-of-Age Films

In one sense, all memorable stories are coming-of-age stories, if what we mean by the term is a story about someone who moves from one stage of development to a more advanced one. It isn't just films such as *The Wizard of Oz* and *To Kill a Mockingbird* that deal with "growing up" — T. E. Lawrence in *Lawrence of Arabia* and Mohandas Gandhi in *Gandhi* both "grow up" during the course of their respective films.

Films explicitly labeled a "coming-of-age story," however, are often about nothing more than someone's becoming aware of sex. But if this is all the film deals with, it probably has little chance of appealing to anyone other than teenagers. As is true for films in other genres, it is the films that transcend their genres, that go beyond them and are about *more* than the stock elements of the genre that stand a chance of being popular and ultimately memorable.

(See also: Individuation; Transformation; Genres)

It is often difficult to tell if your hero is committed or *ought* to be committed. The line between commitment, obsession, compulsion, and possession is more a matter of attitude and motivation than of overt behavior.

COMMITMENT

Villains are often said to be obsessed or even possessed, but we use such terms to express the fact that we don't *approve* of what they're committed to. This is because they're usually committed to *themselves* and their own self-aggrandizement and acquisition of power. We say the hero is committed, no matter how obsessive his behavior is, because he's usually committed to something *beyond* himself.

Frequently the hero and villain's actions look very much alike. It's what these actions are *for* that determines whether we think of the character as being obsessed or committed.

(See also: ATTITUDE; MOTIVATION)

COMMUNITIES

DRAMA IS A social art form in which a community speaks to itself *about* itself. It follows, then, that trying to construct a genuine community is important to memorable drama. A genuine community, which can be defined as a social group in which its members nurture one another, is one of the rarest and most valuable human structures, often yearned for but seldom obtained.

In the field of physics, scientists proved that bringing elements together — fusion — was a great deal more powerful than fission, the process of blowing elements apart. Similarly, in drama, while blowing things apart has a certain kind of power, fusing them together has the potential to be even more powerful.

The striving for oneness, wholeness, community, and family is a constant desire of the human heart and therefore a constant creation of the human imagination. This is why, by the end of many films, the community has discovered the importance of the hero, and the hero has simultaneously discovered the importance of community.

A sizeable number of the most memorable films deal with the hero's struggle to identify the true, rather than the false, community. The false community can be a corporation, as in *The Best Years of Our Lives, The Apartment, Network,* and *Alien.* It can be an institution, as in *Mr. Smith Goes to Washington, One Flew Over the Cuckoo's Nest,* or *Apocalypse Now.* It can even be one's family, as in *Rebel Without a Cause.* By the end of such stories, the protagonist frees himself from the false community and begins to form a new, better community. Willard in *Apocalypse Now*, for example, starts out as a good soldier yearning for a mission; yet, near the end of the film he says of the false community, "They were going to make me colonel but I wasn't in their fucking army anymore."

The title characters in *High Noon* and *Dirty Harry* save the communities they are part of, but at the end they reject them. Such stories follow the structural patterns of tragedy. On the other hand, the characters in *Some Like It Hot* and *Tootsie* are outside the community when the film starts, but by the end they have become part of it, which is the structural pattern of most comedy.

(See also: TEAMS AND COUPLES; SOCIETY)

COMPASSION

"PASSION" COMES FROM the same root as suffering, which explains why, when Christians refer to "the passion of our Lord Jesus Christ," or put on a Passion Play, they are not dealing with romance.

Compassion is not the same as pity or "feeling sorry for" someone who is less fortunate. In memorable films, we generally feel compassion for the hero, but it would be a profound misunderstanding to think of him as less fortunate than we are.

Compassion is directly connected to the process that underlies all successful storytelling: identification. It is not just a feeling — and certainly not a cheap one. It is as much a thought process, one that leads us to *understand* the character.

(See also: FEELINGS; IDENTIFICATION; PITY; SACRIFICE; WRITING WHAT YOU KNOW)

LIKE RELIGION, PEOPLE go to movies, not to see the world as it really is but to see a world that *compensates* for the one they know. If stories survive, it is because they help *us* to survive, because what we experience in life is not adequate to sustain us and because the desires we have for justice, truth, compassion, and excitement can often only be fulfilled in the world of the imagination.

(See also: JUSTICE; REALISM; REALITY FALLACY; ENDINGS, HAPPY)

COMPENSATION

COMPLETION AND RETURN

You CAN USUALLY predict where most films will end: where they began. In *Shane*, the title character enters the town at the beginning, and leaves it at the end; in *Dirty Harry,* the title character confronts a bad guy at the beginning and asks him, "Do you feel lucky, punk?" and at the end he confronts an even worse bad guy to whom he asks the same question. In *Forrest Gump*, the title character is sitting on a bench at the beginning and is there again at the end. In *Gandhi* the title character cries out, "God!" as he is assassinated, and the exact scene is repeated at the end.

This common structure may be called "Completion and Return." It is, however, not circular. By the end of the story, the central character or the situation or the audience — sometimes all three — have moved beyond where they were at the beginning. Like a piece of music that sets up a motif at the beginning and then resolves it at the end, the spiral structure of "Completion and Return" is very satisfying to experience.

It is the folly of youth to believe that everything is complicated, and the folly of age to believe everything is simple. Novels aimed at adolescents, comic books, soap operas, video games, and other works intended for relatively young audiences often owe a significant part of their appeal to the fact that they are *so* complicated that only young initiates can — or want to — follow them.

There is a difference between being complicated and being complex. Although many people think that good characters need to be complicated, this is not always the case. E.T., Sam Spade, Shane, the Wicked Witch of the West, Goldfinger, Jaws, Harry Callahan, Rocky, HAL, Dr. Strangelove, and Darth Vader are all characters whose essence can be conveyed succinctly.

Something full of complications resembles a large jigsaw puzzle laid out on the table — the challenge is to figure out how to put the many pieces together. Something complex is more like an old-fashioned watch, where all the pieces work together for a single purpose. Complications don't necessarily give depth to a work, but complexity often does.

(See also: ELEGANCE)

CONCEPTS

THERE ARE PEOPLE in the film industry who say that ideas are a dime a dozen, but this is almost invariably said by someone who has never had one.

The most commercially successful films are usually built around a concept that can be expressed 1) simply, 2) succinctly, and 3) vividly. Rather than thinking of these attributes as slick and simplistic tools used by Hollywood to capture an audience, it would be useful to recognize that the ability to express concepts quickly, simply, and vividly has *always* been one of the core principles of effective communication.

Consider the succinct, simple, and vivid concepts in Christianity ("Jesus is love; He died for your sins"); Islam ("There is only one God and Mohammed is his Messenger"); Marxism ("From each according to his means, to each according to his need"); Freudianism ("Where id is, let ego be"); Einsteinian physics ("E=mc2"); and American democracy ("We the People...").

The key to an effective concept is condensation and compression — finding a shorthand way of communicating the essential idea in a way that people can remember and, of equal importance, be able to repeat to others. An effectively stated concept captures the essence of a story, not in any detail, but in a way that causes people to say, "Tell me more."

It is not always possible to convey the essence of a story simply, succinctly, and vividly, but it's much more possible than many people think. The inability to do so often stems from not having thought enough about what's really important in the story.

(See also: ELEGANCE)

CONFLICT

It is axiomatic that drama depends on conflict, but this does not mean war is the only model for dramatic action.

The object in war is to destroy or weaken the other side so that it is without effective power. But what if the conflict is with oneself? Rick Blaine in *Casablanca* is in conflict within himself over his lost love, Ilsa Lund, which is why he gets drunk and tells Sam to play "As Time Goes By." Although he says he's trying to blot Ilsa out of his life, she is the best thing that ever happened to him. He repeatedly declares, "I stick my neck out for nobody," but when he does stick his neck out, it leads him to sacrifice Ilsa, which is against his own self-interest. If Rick is "at war with himself," then whichever way he turns, he will lose a part of himself. A very interesting situation.

What if one is "at war with nature"? The drought and ensuing dustbowl in *The Grapes of Wrath* cause the Joad family to lose everything they've worked for years to build; yet, nature is not the enemy. A satisfactory dramatic enemy has intention, desire, and will — all of which may be judged in moral terms. But nature is not concerned with morality; man is. This is why the true enemy in *The Grapes of Wrath* — as in virtually all films that seem to deal with conflicts with nature —is other human beings, in this case, the bankers in Oklahoma and the farmers in California who exploit their fellow human beings.

People tend to think only of war as the model for dramatic conflict for two reasons. First, inner conflicts are difficult to photograph and difficult to present precisely *because* they are inner. This sometimes leads films based on inner conflict to use the structure of *Dr. Jekyll and Mr. Hyde*, in which the "good" person suddenly and dramatically turns into the "bad" person, and then back again. This is seen in stories about alcoholics, drug addicts, wife-beaters, and child-molesters, but the danger of this structure is that the repetitive alternation soon becomes boring or even unintentionally comic, leading someone in the audience to call out, "Get some help!"

The second reason wars are so often used as a model for conflict is that a war between two individuals, teams, communities, or nations is easily seen and understood.

(See also: CHARACTER, POWER; WAR FILMS)

CONFLICT, SINGLE

LIFE IS ONE damned thing after another. As soon as you resolve one conflict, two more take its place, and only sometimes do they have any relationship to one another. But films, which may look like life but are seldom structured like it, usually revolve around a single conflict, and when that is resolved, the story ends.

When someone tells us about a film, our first question is likely to be, "What's it about?" This is seldom an invitation to recite the entire plot; rather, it is an attempt to understand what the film's *fundamental* conflict involves. If you can't tell what the central conflict is, the film is going to have trouble finding an audience.

This doesn't mean the central conflict has to be clear to the audience from the outset. Sometimes, it isn't until late in the film that the audience realizes what's really going on (see: MISDIRECTION). However, it helps if the people who *create* the film know what its central conflict is before the cameras start rolling.

(See also: HEROES, SINGLE; COMPLEXITY; ELEGANCE; SUBPLOTS)

CONSERVATIVE

THE PERSISTENCE OF the villain meets the resistance of the hero — more often than not, the villains wants to change things, and the hero wants to prevent change from taking place.

George Lucas, while writing *American Graffiti*, wrote a note to himself in which he asked, "Why can't things remain the way they are?" His film, like many another popular film, was an attempt to freeze into time the way things once were.

In *It's a Wonderful Life*, Mr. Potter is the character who wants to change things, while George Bailey is the guy who wants to keep them the way they are. In *The Best Years of Our Lives*, three GIs just want to go back to the life they had before the war changed everything. *Gone with the Wind*'s very title identifies its obsession with an order that has been disrupted.

In real life, the people we call heroes, such as Gandhi, Martin Luther King, Jr., and Nelson Mandela, frequently want to change the underlying nature of their societies. In our most memorable popular films, however, heroes seldom want to make fundamental changes in their societies. They may wish to restore what used to exist, they may want people to live up to what they say they believe, but they are seldom revolutionaries who want to bring about change in the *fundamental* nature of their society.

As tends to be true for all popular arts, the vast majority of films and their protagonists are inherently conservative. It is even possible they are popular *because* they are conservative.

ONE MEANING OF "plot" is "conspiracy," so it should not be surprising to find that many of the most memorable popular films contain conspiracies. The thrillers of Alfred Hitchcock and the comedies of Frank Capra are constructed around them, as are *2001, Alien, The Terminator, The Matrix, The French Connection, Chinatown, Double Indemnity*, and *The Maltese Falcon*. Action/adventure, detective, science fiction, gangster, and horror films frequently revolve around conspiracies. If a political or social institution is important to the story, as in *The Manchurian Candidate* and *One Flew Over the Cuckoo's Nest*, the institution conspires to overcome the individual.

CONSPIRACIES

Conspiracies are useful storytelling devices for at least two reasons. First, they replicate the way many of us see the world. Our enemies are often "them" — the government, corporations, the opposite gender, professional, ethnic, religious, or national groups or some other collective but amorphous "they."

Drama, of course, demands concrete characters. But very often the enemy that the hero struggles against is a representative of some larger force, as the many clones of Mr. Smith in *The Matrix* demonstrate. Nurse Ratched in *One Flew Over the Cuckoo's Nest* is not just a bitch who destroys lives; she represents a social institution — perhaps "society" itself. Such depictions follow an ancient tradition.

The second reason conspiracies are dramatically useful is that they increase the stakes. David and Goliath is often cited as a model for dramatic storytelling, but the trouble with such *mano a mano* conflicts is that, when one of the *manos* is defeated, the story is over. In modern stories, "Goliath" is either an institution or a collective group. Michael Corleone does not struggle against just Moe Green, Tattaglia, Barzini, and Cuneo; he struggles against all the other "Four Families" engaged in a conspiracy against the Corleone family.

Collective heroes are seldom found in drama or films, but collective villains abound. When our guy works with other people, he or she is engaging in teamwork; when "they" work together, they are engaged in a conspiracy. As with so many other aspects of storytelling, the difference between the good guys and the bad guys is not in what they do, but in how we value it.

CORRUPTION

CORRUPTION COMES FROM the same root word as "rupture." What is stretched and broken beyond repair when there is corruption is the social contract — the boundaries and bonds of behavior that make institutional, corporate, political, and social life possible.

When Captain Renault in *Casablanca* says, "I'm only a poor, corrupt official," we forgive him because he lives in a society controlled by Nazis for whom the audience feels no sense of loyalty, so his corruption is justifiable. But when there is a reference in *The Godfather* to the judges, politicians, and newspapermen the Corleone family keeps on its payroll, we are never allowed to *see* their corruption, because if we did, it would be harder to identify with the Corleones. Whenever we *are* allowed to see corruption in courtrooms, newspapers, schools, churches, police, government, or other social institutions, the corruptors become the enemy against which the central character must struggle.

(See also: INNOCENCE; LOYALTY; BETRAYAL; VIOLATION)

Courage

Heroes, in movies and life, do things that require courage, pain, and suffering. They face the threat of physical and psychological death and they do so knowing that their actions may go entirely unnoticed.

It is possible to have courage and not be a hero — the villain often has as much courage as the hero. In fact, what looks like courage may be merely compulsion. Differentiating between the two is how we distinguish the hero from the villain.

Most of all, the hero needs to have the courage of his convictions, which means, in turn, that he must have the will to overcome his constraints. Unleashing his inhibitions is one of the crucial moments in the progression of the story.

(See also: Commitment; Crisis Point, One-Hour)

IT IS OFTEN said that the Chinese ideogram for the word "crisis" brings together two concepts: "danger" + "opportunity." In theater, film, and most other forms of storytelling, the more crises there are, the more engaging the work is likely to be.

CRISIS POINT, ONE-HOUR

The hero must face danger because the confrontation gives him an opportunity to *prove* he's a hero. Of the many crises heroes face, the one that is generally the most important in memorable films occurs most frequently around one hour into the story. (This is an observation, not a rule. The important point here is not when the crisis occurs but that it *does* occur.)

In the vast majority of films that we as a society choose to remember, the hero or heroine is reactive for most of the first hour of the film. This does not mean they are passive; it merely means that what they do is a *response* to something someone else has done.

But at the One-Hour Crisis Point, the hero makes a decision — usually involving an ethical choice — that determines everything else that follows. It can be like the decision T. E. Lawrence makes in *Lawrence of Arabia* to go to Aqaba, which his Arab companions say is impossible; or it can be like the decision Michael Corleone makes in *The Godfather* to join the family business that he originally wanted no part of; or it can be like the decision Thelma makes in *Thelma & Louise* that she will go to Mexico without her boyfriend.

As long as they are simply *responding* to others, heroes and heroines are pushed from behind; once they seize control of their destiny, however, they have opened the door to the possibility of heroic behavior.

(See also: DECISIONS; DESTINY)

CRUELTY

THERE'S A SILENT film in which two men court the same young woman, and the director placed a kitten at the door of her house. As the first man knocks on her door, the cat snuggles up to him, and the young man responds by kicking it off the porch. Then, the second young man knocks on her door, and the cat snuggles up to him. He bends down and pets it gently and asks if the cat's having a good day. Without a word, audiences around the world knew which young man was the hero who would win the girl.

It pleases contemporary filmmakers and their audiences to think they are much more sophisticated than this, but cruelty continues to be the mark of villains, the thing that lets the audience know who they are supposed to be *against*.

But Harry Callahan deliberately steps on the open wound of the serial killer in *Dirty Harry*, Michael Corleone orders the garroting of his brother-in-law, Carlo, in *The Godfather*, and the title character in the two sequels to *The Terminator*, in which he is the good guy, exerts painful force on others. Why don't we turn against such characters? Because the people to whom they cause pain *deserve* it.

If, instead of a kitten, an aggressive tomcat had waited on the porch and had hissed and slashed at the first young man, audiences wouldn't have minded his being kicked off the porch. But if it's an innocent kitten, audiences mind very much. Innocence is - central to determining whether the behavior is cruel or not.

(See also: JUSTICE)

THE GREATEST CURSE you can place on fellow human beings is to cause them to lose faith in their own potential. This is why classic curses in myths and legends involve actions such as turning one of the main characters into a frog, or, as in *Snow White and the Seven Dwarfs*, imprisoning them in a state of suspended animation.

A curse is anything that prevents a person from being truly alive and able to fulfill his or her own potential. Being told you're not valued because you belong to a particular race, gender, class, religion, or occupation or being told you're too small, too fat, or too clumsy are all curses. Curses are intended to be traps. They usually occur early in the story so that there is time for us to see how the protagonist escapes from that trap.

(See also: GIFTS; BLESSINGS; TRAPS; INDIVIDUALISM; DESTINY; POWER)

CURSES

Cute

Some attributes are like sugar and caffeine — useful, even pleasurable, in small quantities, but dangerous and capable of negative side effects if consumed too often or in too large a quantity. Cuteness is one of these.

"Cute" is a sex- and age-linked word, more likely to be used by women and to be about the young. But "cute" is also used to diminish something that might otherwise be threatening. Teddy bears, lions, tigers, dinosaurs, and other animals are usually dangerous and scary when found in nature; when domesticated in a child's playpen or in an animated film, they are made to appear "cute."

Cute is a commodity; often a very profitable one, as Walt Disney discovered long ago. The relationship between cute and cloying is like the relationship between sentiment and sentimentality: both require restraint.

(See also: Goofy; Sentimentality)

As DON LOCKWOOD is racing to get away from his
fans in *Singin' in the Rain*, he literally drops into the
front seat of the car being driven by Kathy Selden,
who just happens to be driving by. This "Cute
Meet" (or, as it is called in Hollywood, the "Meet
Cute") is the traditional way in which lovers meet
in countless romantic comedies. There is no problem in the notion that lovers are "meant" to meet.
If your society doesn't do the prearranging of your
marriage for you, some deity or outside force will
do just as well.

The danger in what the industry calls the "Meet
Cute" scene is that the heavy hand of the filmmaker
will, like the shadow of the boom that holds the
microphone, be *seen* by the audience. Like so much
else in drama and film, contrivance works best
when it hides the process that produced it.

(See also: DESTINY)

CUTE MEET

D

Popular American films invariably encourage us to believe in destiny and to deny the existence of fate.

DEADLINES

DURING THE AMERICAN Civil War, a line was painted on the ground around the perimeter of the camps where captured Union soldiers were placed. If a soldier walked over this line, he was immediately shot. This line came to be called a "dead-line" and this spatial term came, in turn, to describe a temporal marker as well: if you don't finish by the deadline, you're a goner.

Because motion pictures move through real time, anything that makes us aware of the passage of time, that turns *time itself* into an element of the story, can increase dramatic intensity. This is seen most clearly in that film whose very title refers to time, *High Noon*, where the running time of the film closely parallels the fictional time of the story. In *Lawrence of Arabia,* the sun, the ultimate time-keeper, spells potential doom for Gasim, who is left behind in the desert when he falls off his camel. As Lawrence returns to the desert to search for him, the sun climbs higher in the sky, threatening to consume both Gasim and Lawrence.

Making us aware of deadlines is not, of course, unique to films. Athletic events, video games, chess matches, television quiz shows, and other contests use deadlines to increase tension and interest; in fact, if there were not a deadline, many of the games we play and much of the drama we watch would lose much of their power. Conversely, an otherwise ordinary story can take on urgency and excitement simply by creating a deadline.

(See also: TIME)

DEATH HAS BEEN the ultimate conflict and the ultimate resolution of stories ever since Cain slew Abel, Jehovah slew the Egyptians, and Oedipus slew his father. It should not surprise us, then, to find that *most* memorable popular films involve death or the threat of death.

DEATH

The struggle with death, however, is not concerned primarily or perhaps even principally with the preservation of the body; it is concerned even more with the death of the soul, of the self, of consciousness.

While men die with astonishing frequency in memorable popular movies, few women die. (Perhaps this compensates in some way for the fact that women don't get to be heroes very often.) When men die, it is usually at the hands of another man. When women die, it is hardly ever at the hands of another woman; rather, it is usually from diseases such as cancer, tuberculosis, or some other cause outside of human control (see: DESTINY).

Ultimately, as so many memorable popular films demonstrate, death is not the worst thing that can happen. In fact, as many legendary public idols demonstrate, sometimes death can be a good career move.

(See also: IMPOTENCE)

Deception

Plato wanted to banish storytellers because they told lies, which he defined as anything that is not true. Storytellers practice the art of deception in much the same way and for the same reason that magicians do: because it's fascinating. Henry Wadsworth Longfellow wrote a famous poem declaring, "Things are not what they seem," which could be said of all the world's most memorable art, and certainly of all memorable films.

A character who at the end is what he seemed to be in the beginning is probably a boring character. If we know in the beginning of a detective story that the butler did it, why watch? If the girl who tells the boy early in the film that she could never love him is telling the truth, where can the story go?

When we watch magicians perform, we expect and are entertained by deception, but for deception to be entertaining, certain principles must be followed. In detective films, for example, we demand that there be clues planted as the story unfolds. Even if we didn't see them at the time, we demand that they be there.

We don't mind being outsmarted by a film's creators, but we do not like to feel cheated — the creators must "play fair." When we realize the truth, let us say in a whodunit, we must have a sense of recognition; that is, re-cognition — that the evidence was there, but we didn't *see* it. Things may not be what they seem, but we must be *able* to see it.

(See also: Discovery)

THE WORD "DECISION" comes from the same root as "scissors." When people make decisions, they cut themselves off, not only from something that might lie ahead but also from a possible escape route that would allow them to back out of their decision. That is why making a decision can, in itself, be dramatic and memorable — in life as well as film.

DECISIONS

Oedipus decides to find the cause of the plague that is destroying Thebes; Macbeth decides to kill the king; Charles Foster Kane decides to stay with his mistress at the cost of losing the election and his family. Rick Blaine in *Casablanca* decides, after saying repeatedly he sticks his neck out for nobody, to do just that. Terry Malloy, in *On the Waterfront,* decides to tell the authorities the truth about mob boss Johnny Friendly; Michael Corleone, in *The Godfather,* decides to kill the drug dealer and the crooked cop protecting him; T.E. Lawrence, in *Lawrence of Arabia,* decides to attack the Turks and take no prisoners.

The most memorable dramatic actions are often decisions that involve ethical values. It follows, then, that the most dramatic scenes are often those in which ethical values are in conflict and the central character must choose between them.

(See also: ETHICS; VALUES)

DEFIANCE

THE HERO MUST not only have the courage of his convictions, he must also have the will to overcome his constraints. He does this most often through defiance of the rules or laws of his society. Defiance is the first requirement of the hero; in fact, it is difficult to think of any heroic figures — in life or in film — who are *not* defiant.

Charles Foster Kane engages in defiant actions when he takes over the newspaper, when he pushes Susan Alexander into a career as an opera singer, and when he continues to run for governor after his confrontation with Boss Jim Gettys. Harry Callahan, in *Dirty Harry,* defies the mayor of San Francisco when he is ordered to stop his pursuit of the serial killer, Scorpio. Benjamin Braddock in *The Graduate* defies Mrs. Robinson's prohibition against dating her daughter Elaine. R.P. McMurphy defies Nurse Ratched in *One Flew Over the Cuckoo's Nest.* Mohandas Gandhi defies the entire British Empire in the film that bears his name. In *The Godfather,* Michael Corleone's emergence as the hero of the story begins with his defiant question, "Where does it say that you can't kill a cop?"

Because defiance is so central to creating the character of the hero, stories often spend much of their time getting the audience to understand what the law is, and then getting them to *want* the hero to break the law.

Defiance, however, cannot be merely an attitude. It's not enough to just to stand up to something; the hero must stand *for* something. Defiance, if it is to be heroic, must stem from a moral position.

(See also: VALUES; POWER)

FRENCH DRAMATISTS AND dramatic theorists
of an earlier age used to speak of a *dénouement*
(pronounced day-noo-MAWN), which means
"unraveling" or "untying the knot." Sometimes,
the dénouement wasn't really necessary to the story;
it was, like the post-coital cigarette that was often
customary in films made during an era when lei-
sure time and smoking were all more prevalent than
they are now, a way to end with a bit of a flourish.
"Louie, this could be the beginning of a beautiful
friendship" in *Casablanca* and "The stuff that dreams
are made of" in *The Maltese Falcon* are examples.

In most recent American films, however,
dénouements have tended to be missing or are
severely truncated.

(See also: EPILOGUES)

DÉNOUEMENT

DESERTION

AT THE HEART of many of the most memorable stories, there is a deep-seated fear of desertion. *Snow White*, *Bambi*, and most of Disney's other central figures are left alone in a dark, menacing world they've never faced before. In *The Wizard of Oz*, Dorothy is swept away by the tornado into a strange and frightening land. Elliott, in *E.T.*, leaves the protection of his toy-filled room, and like Snow White and Dorothy, ends up in a dark, menacing forest. Simba is deserted in *The Lion King*; Buzz Lightyear is deserted in *Toy Story*; Nemo is deserted in *Finding Nemo*. These films demonstrate the ancient but seldom-admitted principle of entertainment that goes back at least as far as the days when the Romans enjoyed their afternoons at the Coliseum: we take our pleasure from torturing our characters.

What often feels like desertion, however, is sometimes a necessary stage in our — and therefore the hero's — development. Children must be weaned from their mothers, teenagers must leave home, and adults must try to give up whatever they use as a crutch if they are to learn to stand on their own two feet and become autonomous human beings. However the story arranges it , desertion is a test of character that determines whether someone possesses "the right stuff." What is important is not so much the desertion as how the character deals with it.

(See also: TESTS; TRIALS)

DESIRE

IN REAL LIFE, people desire to see a world in which effort is rewarded, innocence protected, guilt punished, love requited, hunger sated, truth triumphant, lies exposed, wars won, criminals brought to justice, inner strengths confirmed, power controlled, gasoline cheap, housing plentiful, disease curable, children happy, and beauty eternal.

But what we know about the real world is that many of these desires are never going to be fulfilled. So, we turn to popular motion pictures, where we find desires fulfilled — not necessarily those of the characters, but of the audience.

Early in *It's a Wonderful Life*, George Bailey tells his father, "I want to do something big, something important." Similarly, in *The Graduate* Benjamin Braddock tells his father, he wants his life to be "different." The title character in *Rocky* tells his lover, Adrian, "All I want to do is go the distance." Charlie Allnut, in *The African Queen*, declares to his new-found lover, Rosie, that there's "Nothing a man can't do if he believes in himself." Esther Blodgett, in the Judy Garland version of *A Star Is Born*, sees "The chance of being bigger — something I never even dreamed of." In *Some Like It Hot*, Marilyn Monroe sings, "I wanna be loved by you," a song that explicitly talks of desire. And that monument to innocent desire, *The Wizard of Oz*, contains a heart-rending line in "Somewhere Over the Rainbow," that says, "The dreams that you dare to dream really do come true."

(See also: DUTY; JUSTICE; SELF-DENIAL)

Despair

THERE ARE THREE things a memorable popular film is never about:

1) Unrequited love
2) Impotence
3) Despair

Because the gospel of popular entertainment is based on individualism — the belief that you can become anything you want if only you want it badly enough — anything that suggests otherwise is forbidden.

It's a Wonderful Life begins with George Bailey so deeply into despair that he tries to commit suicide. But that's not what the story is about. It's about *overcoming* despair, about realizing the value and potency of one's life — which is probably why the film has moved so many people for so many years.

In real life, people experience unrequited love, impotence, and despair all the time. But we go to movies seeking hope, the opposite of despair.

(See also: LOVE, UNREQUITED; IMPOTENCE; DEATH)

Though some dictionaries treat fate and destiny as synonyms, from the standpoint of character and the motivation of human behavior, they are quite different. In common English usage, we recognize this: If someone is killed in an accident, we refer to it as a "fatal accident," not a destined accident. In American history, on the other hand, the term "Manifest Destiny" was used to justify the country's expansion from the Atlantic to the Pacific oceans, but no one called it "Manifest Fate."

Destiny

You *seek* your destiny; you *succumb* to your fate. Destiny originates within the self; fate comes from outside. Fate is the force that lies beyond individual will and control; it pushes you from behind. Destiny is the attracting force in front of you that acts like a magnet and that you *choose* to acquire.

Popular American films invariably encourage us to believe in destiny and to deny the existence of fate — if they didn't, they wouldn't be popular. The idea that you *can* seize control of your destiny is the central tenet of America's unstated state religion, Individualism. It is the ideology that the United States exports to the rest of the world, and perhaps more than any other single factor, explains the ongoing appeal of American films.

At their most powerful, American films are sacred dramas for a secular society. What is most sacred in American society is the faith Americans have, which we see in virtually every popular film, that each individual possesses *within himself* the power to control his destiny.

Jewish, Christian, and Islamic fundamentalists see human behavior as being determined by a single outside force — their conception of God. Freudians and other psychological schools that say people act the way they do because of "the unconscious" or "instinct," place the motivating force deep inside, where the individual can neither know nor control it. Marxists, Fascists, and other political theorists who say that all power comes from the state similarly locate the power-that-matters outside the individual. Adherents of all of these belief systems tend to be lousy dramatists, because drama is predicated on the belief that *the individual* creates — *and is thus responsible for* — his destiny.

In real life, if the result of a decision is good, we are likely to attribute what happened to destiny, that is, something we *chose* to do. If our decision leads to a bad or ineffective end, however, we are likely to attribute it to fate. Drama does not have this luxury.

(See also: INDIVIDUALISM)

PSYCHOLOGISTS USE THE term "circumstantiality" to describe the annoying practice of telling far more than is necessary to know about the details of an experience or event. Circumstantial people feel it necessary to tell us who was married to whom, where they came from, what they did before, what time of day it was, what the weather was, who else was there — and never seem to get to the *point* of their story.

And yet, details are often what give a story authenticity and make it real and convincing. If you witness an accident and are called to testify, any good lawyer will help you prepare your spontaneous testimony carefully. If, for example, they plan to ask you to describe what you saw, and your initial response is, "Well, this white car was going very fast, and it slammed into the black SUV and I heard a crash," they will stop you. How fast was "fast"? Thirty-five miles an hour ... forty-five ... sixty-five? Precisely where did the white car hit the black car — and in what part of the intersection? What exact sounds did you hear? Breaking glass? Crumpling metal? Providing details in such a context help make your version of the story credible.

It is not the details themselves that are necessarily important; it is the precision used in telling the story that helps make it credible and interesting.

(See also: ELEGANCE)

DETECTIVE FILMS

THAT TOUCHSTONE OF western drama, *Oedipus Rex*, is a detective story, and so are, at bottom, a good proportion of the world's most memorable and popular stories created in the 2,500 years since Greek drama flourished.

Much of the logic and structure of "detective films" can be found in other works that have nothing to do with gumshoes, cops, and *femmes fatales*. Films such as *Lawrence of Arabia*, *Gandhi*, and *Citizen Kane* pose a question the story seeks to answer, but instead of "Who did it?" the question is "Who is this person?" or "Why did he do what he did?" One of the things that makes the detective story structure so satisfying is precisely that it asks a single fundamental question, and when the answer is revealed, the story is over.

Detective stories are obsessed with corruption, which is identified with the antagonist. In one strain of the detective genre exemplified by British stories such as those of Agatha Christie or the American television series *Murder She Wrote*, the protagonist is an innocent; that is, someone who is not and never will be corrupted, and the focus of the story is on finding the guilty person.

In another strain of detective stories, often seen in American films, the protagonist is attracted to the corruption and becomes complicit in it, as in *Double Indemnity*, or is already so enmeshed in it that it is difficult to say who is corrupt and who isn't, as Jake Gittes in *Chinatown* and Sam Spade in *The Maltese Falcon* demonstrate.

Detective stories are inherently conservative — the detective wants to *restore* order. In detective stories the villain is often a kind of scapegoat — if it weren't for the villain, the community would be tranquil, and once he is removed, it will become so again. In more recent films, especially those involving serial killers or perpetrators of terrible crimes such as *Chinatown* and *Silence of the Lambs*, however, the world remains corrupted.

(See also: DISCOVERY; DECEPTION; MISDIRECTION; MYSTERY; SUSPENSE; CONSPIRACIES; FISH OUT OF WATER; HABITUATION)

DEUS EX MACHINA

THE GREEKS INVENTED a stage device they called the *theos ek mechanes*. The Romans, who conquered and then copied the Greeks in so many things, called it a *deus ex machina*, a "god from a machine." A kind of crane appeared at the end of certain plays, bearing an actor playing one of the Greek gods who decides at the last minute in the story to descend from on high to save the hero from a trap he couldn't otherwise escape from.

Even among astute Greeks, this device was considered lazy dramatic writing. The filmic equivalent of the *deus ex machina* is seen when at the last minute the cavalry comes to the rescue. While John Ford got away with it in *Stagecoach*, it is not a device to be recommended unless all else fails.

(See also: DESTINY)

DIALOGUE

WHEN SOUND WAS introduced into American motion
pictures in the late 1920s, film studios imported
every playwright they could seduce into coming
west. Playwrights, after all, knew how to write
dialogue, especially the kind of "realistic" dialogue
that, it was claimed, films required. But if you listen to those early sound films written by esteemed
Broadway playwrights, you will see that what is
"realistic" for one generation can be seen as stagy
and artificial for another.

What is called "realistic" dialogue in films
could not, in fact, be more artificial. Film uses
short phrases that might leave the astute observer
to wonder if its characters are one step shy of
being catatonic. Films alternate dialogue back and
forth like Ping-Pong balls. Film dialogue bears
little relationship to the way people speak to one
another in real life. Real speech is filled with
hesitations, stuttering, half-completed sentences,
repetitions, and irrelevancies. No screenwriter who
wants to continue being employed would dare
imitate *real* speech.

In real life, people often utter long speeches
that would, if placed in a screenplay, fill several
pages — and be condemned as amateurish. (Greek
and Shakespearian drama were filled with long
monologues that would invariably be truncated or
thrown out in a contemporary film.)

The screenwriter faces an enormous creative
challenge, since he is hired to produce words — but
not too many of them. The famous speeches in films,
such as "Frankly, my dear, I don't give a damn,"

"We'll always have Paris," "I'll make him an offer he
can't refuse," "I'll be back" or "Plastics," are almost
always fewer than ten words in length.

In no other written art form is the writer
required to use as few words as possible. While few
producers and critics think of them this way, screenwriters know that the challenge they face is similar
to that of poets. Although screenwriters are forbidden to use lofty or "poetic" language, their goal
is very like that of the poet: to say much in as few
words as possible.

A FILM THAT is only about a disaster is likely to be one. Disasters are, by definition, "natural" events such as tornadoes, earthquakes, floods, or fires. But nature, by itself, is an inadequate dramatic antagonist. This is, in part, because nature is not a character but an impersonal force. It is also because nature is not concerned with morality, and the most memorable dramas are all morality tales.

DISASTER FILMS

Disaster films have an inherent structural problem: if there is a catastrophic disaster, when does it occur? If it is early in the story, the risk is that the rest of the film will feel anti-climactic. If it is late in the story, the risk is that the earlier parts of the film will feel boring and the audience will want to "get to the good stuff."

To deal with the dramatic inadequacies of man versus nature, disaster films generally add some kind of love story. This can involve a man and a woman, a parent and child, or both. In addition, many disaster films juxtapose nature and human technology, usually to demonstrate the inadequacy of the latter. *Titanic* combines both a love story and technology, perhaps because an iceberg is a relatively unexciting force of nature that requires a single, brief encounter.

The line often associated with horror films, "Don't fool with Mother Nature," is often applicable to disaster films. There is almost invariably some know-it-all character or corporation, as in *Jurassic Park, Titanic,* and *Towering Inferno,* that at first dismisses the threat, then foolishly confronts the force of nature without understanding what it's up against. The protagonist, as in horror films, survives because he does his homework — carefully studying his adversary and not acting until precisely the right moment (see: DEADLINES).

Disaster films, like war films, are usually structured around multiple battles. The danger is that these encounters will become repetitive. How many storms, falling trees, floating or flying houses can, for example, a film dealing with tornadoes show before the audience says, "Enough already"? What usually prevents the feeling of repetitiveness is the dramatic requirement of rising action, in which the pace, scale, and emotional impact of each battle becomes greater as the story progresses.

(See also: REPETITION; GENRES; WAR FILMS)

AN INTERESTING STORY is one in which we go through a constant process of discovery. Of what? In a great many memorable films: the truth.

It is not as important for the filmmaker to reveal the truth as for the audience to discover it. Nor is it absolutely necessary for the characters in the story to be the ones making the discovery. In *Citizen Kane*, for example, none of the characters in the film ever does learn the meaning of Kane's dying word, "Rosebud," even though it is the question around which the entire film revolves. The *audience* alone learns its significance, but that is enough.

Filmmakers are often tempted to tell the audience things. Far more powerful is letting the audience *discover* them.

(See also: DECEPTION; IRONY; DETECTIVE FILMS; MYSTERY)

DOCUMEN-TARIES

EVERYONE CAN DEFINE what a fiction film is, and that definition has not changed for many years. But defining a documentary has varied with the times, fashions, economic realities, changing audience tastes, developing technologies, and theories of its makers.

Despite these changing definitions, what remains consistent about a documentary is that its structure is centrifugal, whereas a drama's is centripetal.

A documentary is about something *outside* itself — an individual, culture, institution, historic, or current event. Therefore, like a centrifuge, its energy is directed outward, toward the thing in the real world that the film is about.

A dramatic film, however, spins inward, towards its own center, centripetally, inviting the audience to forget what they know about the real world in order to enter the make-believe world created by the filmmakers (see: SUSPENSION OF DISBELIEF).

Audiences — and sometimes even filmmakers — believe that a documentary has an obligation to tell the truth about the real person, event, or issue — or to present at least "both sides" (as if there were only two sides).

Drama, however, is concerned with an inner truth, and seldom worries about the "other" side of the story. If it did, we would realize how often one person's comedy is another person's tragedy.

(See also: PROPAGANDA)

DUALITY

DUALITIES ARE NOT contradictions. A contradiction exists when one thing refutes or cancels out the other, which is why when we face a contradiction we feel it necessary to pick one or the other. But men and women coexist (or at least try to). Day and night, past and present, summer and winter, up and down do not contradict each other, they are different stages or elements of a whole, and you cannot understand one unless you also understand the other.

All drama is constructed on a dualistic foundation. Often one side represents the good and desirable and the other represents the bad and undesirable. The relationship in *Star Wars* between Darth Vader and Obi-Wan Kenobi is typical.

But from the standpoint of drama, the good side *needs* the bad side; without it, there would be no story. Dr. Frankenstein has his monster, Van Helsing has Dracula, and Father Karras in *The Exorcist* has the demon.

It is possible for the hero to be attracted to the dark side, but few villains are ever attracted to the idea of becoming good. Some of the most memorable characters are those who contain within themselves the potential for both good *and* evil, and the possibility that the protagonist will move from one to the other can create a powerful dramatic tension. *Dr. Jekyll and Mr. Hyde* is the classic example of this, but so are Harry Callahan in *Dirty Harry*, Willard in *Apocalypse Now* and Oskar Schindler in *Schindler's List*.

Wherever the light shines the brightest, it creates the darkest shadows. It is often not the brightness that makes characters interesting, but rather the darkness.

(See also: PARADOX; BISOCIATION; INCONGRUITY)

IN MANY OF the most memorable stories, the central character is torn between desire and duty, between what the self seeks and society demands. The inner voice whispers, "I *want*..." but the outer voice responds, with an echo-chamber resonance, "You *must*...."

In *The Maltese Falcon*, Sam Spade tells Brigid O'Shaughnessy, "When a man's partner's killed, he's supposed to do something about it," and when she pleads with him to spare her because she knows he loves her, he responds, "I won't because all of me wants to, regardless of consequences."

Everyone knows that great cliché, "A man's gotta do..." and everyone knows that what a man's got to do is his duty. At the end of *Casablanca,* Rick Blaine tells Ilsa Lund, "I've got a job to do .... Where I'm going you can't follow." In *It's a Wonderful Life*, George Bailey and his bride are on their way out of town, planning to use the savings he's scrubbed together over several years for a honeymoon, when the rush on the bank starts. George uses his savings to rescue the bank, and he never *does* achieve the desire he repeatedly voiced earlier in the film to get out of Bedford Falls. The reason he doesn't fulfill his desire is because he's done his duty. He is but one of a great many memorable protagonists who do so.

Whenever push comes to shove, we're on fertile dramatic ground, which is why the conflict between desire and duty is so powerful. In *On the Waterfront*, Terry Malloy speaks to his brother of the duty Charley *failed* to fulfill: "I could've had class. I could've been a contender. I could've been somebody, instead of a bum, which is what I am. Let's face it … It was you, Charley."

Terry Malloy, in contrast to his brother, stands up to the union boss, Johnny Friendly, by telling the truth, and while he's beaten to a pulp, he rises at the end, the victor.

The duty of the hero is not merely to stand up; he must stand *for* something. It's not something he *desires*; it's something he's *got* to do, something that is his *duty*. Poor guy.

(See also: DESIRE; JUSTICE)

E

The press, audiences, and filmmakers themselves all seem to believe that, to be a success, a Hollywood film must have a happy ending. Like so much else that "everybody knows," this is false.

ELEGANCE

A FILM ONLY needs two elements to become memorable: originality and elegance. Achieving these qualities, however, requires more time and effort than most people are willing to expend, which is why we see them so seldom.

Film aspires to the condition of poetry — saying as much as possible with as few elements as possible. When this happens, scientists, mathematicians, and artists alike call it "elegant," which is justly considered the highest form of praise.

(See also: COMPLEXITY; HEROES, SINGLE)

Question: What do these memorable popular films have in common?

- *Amadeus*
- *American Graffiti*
- *Annie Hall*
- *Apocalypse Now*
- *Bonnie and Clyde*
- *The Bridge on the River Kwai*
- *Butch Cassidy and the Sundance Kid*
- *Casablanca*
- *Chinatown*
- *Citizen Kane*
- *A Clockwork Orange*
- *The Deer Hunter*
- *Doctor Zhivago*
- *Double Indemnity*
- *Dr. Strangelove Or: How I Stopped Worrying and Learned to Love The Bomb*
- *E.T., The Extra-Terrestrial*
- *Easy Rider*
- *Frankenstein*
- *The French Connection*
- *From Here to Eternity*
- *The Godfather*
- *The Godfather: Part II*
- *Gone with the Wind*
- *The Grapes of Wrath*
- *High Noon*
- *King Kong*
- *Lawrence of Arabia*
- *The Maltese Falcon*

- *The Manchurian Candidate*
- *Midnight Cowboy*
- *Mutiny on the Bounty*
- *Network*
- *On the Waterfront*
- *One Flew Over the Cuckoo's Nest*
- *Patton*
- *Platoon*
- *Psycho*
- *Pulp Fiction*
- *Raging Bull*
- *Rebel Without a Cause*
- *Schindler's List*
- *The Searchers*
- *Shane*
- *The Silence of the Lambs*
- *A Streetcar Named Desire*
- *Sunset Boulevard*
- *Taxi Driver*
- *To Kill a Mockingbird*
- *The Treasure of the Sierra Madre*
- *Unforgiven*
- *Vertigo*
- *West Side Story*
- *The Wild Bunch*

Answer: None of them has a "happy ending."

The press, audiences, and filmmakers themselves all seem to believe that, to be a success, a Hollywood film must have a happy ending. Like so much else that "everybody knows," this is false.

Endings must be happy for the audience, but not necessarily for the characters. More often than not, the central characters in the film have gone through such trauma, loss, pain, sacrifice, and suffering that calling their final state "happy" would be a bitter, maddeningly insensitive joke. They have *survived*, but no person should envy them.

What is required for the ending of a film is not happiness; it is justice. The bad force may not totally overcome the protagonist, but it always takes its toll. The endings of the vast majority of memorable popular films are, in fact, Pyrrhic victories (see entry).

The Declaration of Independence and every politician who invokes it may speak of the "pursuit of happiness," but happiness has nothing to do with being a hero; in fact, happiness is something heroes learn to live *without*. It is one of the reasons why, in real life, we seldom seek to be heroes.

(See also: JUSTICE; WILL POWER; BEGINNINGS AND ENDINGS)

EPICS

ONE OF THE things that defines an epic is its length, but this has led some filmmakers to think that length alone would give their work epic proportions, when often all it does is cause it to gain weight. The word epic comes from the Greek for "song," and what is sung in an epic are the praises of its heroes and heroines. Epics usually tell a tale of some bygone past when people behaved more courageously, with more conviction, determination, and altruism than, it is felt, animates the contemporary listener of the tale.

Like length, scale is also associated with epics, which is why the American West or some other frontier is so often the stage upon which the action occurs. While heroes are mandatory, it is not so much individuals whose destiny is determined by the action in epics as it is nations, religions, followers of an idea, and civilizations. In epics, the individual represents one of these larger forces.

Although epics are customarily set in the past, science fiction films owe much of their appeal to being epics set in the future. In *2001*, Dave Bowman is consciously intended to evoke the epic Greek hero, Odysseus, as the full name of the film, *2001: A Space Odyssey*, demonstrates. What is at stake in this film is the future evolution of mankind itself. *The Terminator* is also concerned with the future of our species. *Star Wars* goes even further: the future of the entire galaxy rests in Luke Skywalker's hands.

IN THE SIXTIES , with the release of the movie *Z* in France and *The French Connection* and *American Graffiti* in the United States, it became increasingly common for filmmakers to append to their films an epilogue, a device that was much seen in Elizabethan drama but had largely disappeared by the time film became popular.

EPILOGUES

Epilogues are not to be confused with dénouements, which clean up the loose ends of the story. The epilogue goes *beyond* the story — usually to some point in the future. In *Z, The French Connection,* and *American Graffiti*, we are told what happened to the major characters.

Notice that we are *told* what happened in epilogues and dénouements. Since the greatest truism of film is "show, don't tell," these are devices that are generally used sparingly and briefly.

(See also: DÉNOUEMENT)

ETHICS

ETHICS AND CHARACTER are inextricably connected. When we speak of a person "of good character," we are not making a statement about their psychology but about their ethics. Ethics is often thought of as a kind of philosophy, which is why Terry Malloy in *On the Waterfront* says, "You want to know my philosophy? Do it to them before they do it to you."

Such overt statements of ethical philosophies are, however, rare in memorable films because personal philosophies, like motivation, are things that are better acted upon rather than stated. For example, one hour into *Schindler's List*, Oskar Schindler and a female companion are having pleasurable horseback rides when, from the top of a hill, he happens to come across the Nazi troops savagely clearing the Jewish ghetto below. Although no words are spoken and there is little expression (see: ACTING), the camera lingers on Schindler's face for a long time after he sees a little girl in a red coat. This forces us to read into his expression the ethical conflict going on in his mind. In subsequent scenes, we see him treating his Jewish employees with respect and care, and we realize he has made the ethical decision to help them.

In *Citizen Kane*, the title character is threatened with the loss of his family if he does not pull out of his self-aggrandizing political race against Boss Jim Gettys. He refuses and in so doing fails his ethical test, and the rest of the story is downhill from there. In *Apocalypse Now*, when Willard kills Kurtz, the natives he rules are obviously prepared to anoint Willard as their new king. But he renounces

the power that he holds in his hands and leaves. In
The Godfather: Part II, Michael Corleone's brother,
Fredo, pleads with him to accept him back into
the family that he has betrayed. Michael appears
to forgive him, but after their mother has died, he
has Fredo murdered in a boat on Lake Tahoe. Rick
Blaine in *Casablanca* and Rhett Butler in *Gone with
the Wind*, after saying they look out only for themselves, join a war. Harry Callahan in *Dirty Harry*
decides to bring the serial killer to justice, even
though it will cost him his career. Will Kane in *High
Noon* and Shane in his eponymous film both decide
they must once again do what they had renounced
in order to save their communities. In *The Exorcist*,
Father Karras agrees to perform the exorcism ritual
even though he fears he has lost his faith.

It is not just actions that make a scene memorable; often, it is the ethical decisions that lead
to them.

(See also: DECISIONS; VALUES; POWER)

EVIL

FOR THE ANCIENT Greeks, a *daemon* was usually some form of divine presence, often located within one-self, and often associated with one's lot or fortune in life. In Christianity, demons became exclusively evil, and were usually projected outward — a force "out there," rather than within oneself.

Among the explanations for bad or evil behavior, these four are most frequently used:

1. Possession: The Devil made me do it. "Temporary insanity" pleas are contemporary examples of this, as well as everyday excuses such as, "I was overwhelmed with anger" and "I wasn't myself." (To which one might respond, "If you weren't yourself, who were you?")

2. A foreign substance made me do it. "I was drunk, high on drugs, sugar, caffeine, etc."

3. Society made me do it. (Bad friends, racism, poverty, etc.)

4. I'm bad.

Our greatest fear, of course, is the last. It's much more satisfying if the evil is caused by possession (*The Exorcist*), a failed scientific experiment (*Frankenstein*), bad child-rearing (*Psycho*), or some other external force that relieves the person who does evil from *responsibility* for it.

In Elizabethan drama, the existence of evil was taken for granted. Many modern people, however, have difficulty believing that evil actually exists, which is why *The Exorcist* devotes the entire first half of its running time to establishing the reality of the demon or demons that possess the young girl, Regan.

True evil makes no excuses, cops no pleas, and apologizes for nothing. Lucifer, according to Dante and most Christian theology, knew exactly what he was doing when he challenged The Dominant Authority. Today, if a film wanted to tell such a story, much time would be spent "explaining" Lucifer's motivation, background, economic deprivations and perhaps even his childhood wounds. But the simpler the explanation, the more powerful the evil seems.

Jaws and *Alien* deal with malevolent forces of nature; *Frankenstein, The Terminator,* and *Robocop,* malevolent forces of technology. *Dracula, Rosemary's Baby,* and *The Exorcist* deal with malevolent supernatural forces. Once we know what kind of evil force is involved, no further explanation is needed.

EXILE

HAVING PREPARED HIMSELF to die, the warrior/hero often finds it difficult to *live* in the society that sent him forth. This is in part because that which has the power to save also has the power to destroy.

Heroes can be dangerous people to have around once you no longer need them, and it's best if, as in *High Noon, The Searchers, Shane, Lawrence of Arabia,* and *Apocalypse Now*, they depart once their job is done.

The "Exile of the Hero" has been an important element in most heroic stories since *The Iliad* and *The Odyssey*. Heroes are not something society wants — it *needs* them. But when that need has been fulfilled, it's time for the hero to head into the sunset.

ALL ART SEEKS the exotic, to make the strange familiar or the familiar strange, to create worlds we have never seen or to introduce us to characters we have never imagined.

Although everything that is exotic has some component of the foreign, something that is merely foreign is not necessarily exotic. Writing that someone has "an exotic beauty" is not the same as writing that they have "a foreign beauty." In the first case, the connotation of "exotic" is that the person comes from a tribe that is not ours, but we respond positively to their unfamiliar attributes. In the second, the connotation is simply that the person is from some other tribe but remains "other."

Filmmakers have constantly sought exotic locales for their films, whether they are the American West, Paris, the Amazon, or anywhere else that their audiences have not yet seen. The desert in *Lawrence of Arabia*, the jungle in *Apocalypse Now*, Transylvania in *Dracula*, the ritzy homes in *The Graduate* and *Chinatown*, the lower-class dives in *Midnight Cowboy* and *Taxi Driver* all have elements of the exotic.

Time periods can also be exotic. As the narrator in the film based on L. P. Hartley's novel *The Go-Between* says, "The past is a foreign country. They do things differently there." The 1930s in *Bonnie and Clyde* and the year *2001* in Stanley Kubrick's film are exotic, and a significant part of the appeal of costume dramas and "period pieces" is their exotic look and customs.

The opening scroll of *Gone with the Wind* says of the world we are about to enter, "Look for it only in books, for it is no more than a dream remembered, a Civilization gone with the wind...." The scroll that opens *Star Wars* tells us that we are about to enter "a galaxy far, far away."

In memorable films, the more familiar the characters are, the more likely it is that they will appear in an exotic setting. Conversely, the more familiar the setting, the more likely it is be populated it with exotic characters.

(See also: INTERMEDIARIES)

EXPOSITION

IN *STAR WARS*, Princess Leia says to Obi-Wan Kenobi, "General Kenobi, years ago you served my father in the Clone Wars." This is an example of exposition, in which one character tells another something he already knows, and the line is delivered not for the sake of the character but for the sake of the audience.

A second kind of exposition is demonstrated in *Raiders of the Lost Ark*, when we are told that the Ark of the Covenant that held the Ten Commandments was stolen from Jerusalem by an Egyptian pharaoh and taken to the city of Tanis and the pursuit of the ark then consumes the rest of the film.

A third kind of exposition, which is usually thought of as part of the dénouement, occurs at the end of *Psycho*, when a psychiatrist gives a long-winded explanation to the police chief of what happened in Norman Bates' past and why he had such a hang-up about his mother.

In all three cases, exposition is an *explanation* for something that has happened or is about to happen. Exposition often creates a problem for the film-maker. As the word itself suggests, exposition takes us away from the "position" we are currently in — the present time and place of the characters — and takes us somewhere else, often backwards.

Exposition risks losing the audience because it stops the forward progression of the story. Exposition usually consists of information, facts, and data the audience needs to know; but it is usually *knowledge*, not emotion, they get, and it is therefore inherently undramatic.

Exposition that is merely informative can be redundant or irrelevant. When it is integrated into the dramatic action, however, it can serve a useful function. In *The Terminator*, James Cameron needed to give the audience a great deal of information about what had occurred in the past and why events are now happening the way they are in the present. Rather than give us introductory expository information or flashbacks — the usual devices — Cameron *interwove* brief bits of information during the film's exciting and memorable chase scenes. If there must be exposition — and sometimes there really doesn't need to be — it's best, as *The Terminator* demonstrated, if the audience isn't aware that it *is* exposition.

IN ART, "EXPRESSIONISM" is usually defined as the exteriorization of an interior state. When screenplays contain directions such as," He thinks to himself...." or "He is torn between...." they are attempting to define an *interior* state of mind. This works in literature; but in film there is nothing *but* exteriorization — what the audience sees and hears. Ultimately, all film is expressionist.

(See also: ACTING)

EXPRESSIONISM

F

It is feelings *that lie at the heart*
of all memorable popular films.

FAILURE

IN LIFE, WE dread failure and do what we can to avoid it. Albert Einstein failed high school math, couldn't get into the college of his choice, and failed to achieve his dream of becoming a mathematics professor; thus he was forced to work as a technical assistant in a Swiss Patent Office. Abraham Lincoln failed repeatedly in business and politics until, surprisingly, he was elected president.

We *love* stories of failures who became successes, perhaps because so many of us feel it is the story of our lives. In the real world, the pain of failure is so great that most people give up rather than allow others to label them a failure. Many people may dream of being a movie star, athlete, painter, writer, or explorer but most "get over it," become "realistic," and settle for some job that is within easier reach.

In drama, the question is not whether there will be failure — without it, the story lacks interest and has no place to go. The question is: what will the hero do in *response* to his failure? Call a lawyer? *Cry?* The only solution for the hero is to pick himself up, dust himself off, and keep going. Failure is what gives heroes an opportunity to prove that they *are* heroes.

In *Lethal Weapon*, Martin Riggs is strung up on a hook, doused with water, and zapped with high-voltage electricity; he chases the villain through every dangerous corner of the city, totally demolishes every vehicle he can get his hands on, loses every weapon he can beg, borrow, or steal — but do you ever believe he's finished, defeated, that he'll end up failing? Of course not. That's the "downbeat" ending everyone dreads and only the most refined tastes can tolerate in a film.

Comedy is the story of a failure who achieved success; tragedy is the story of a success who achieved failure. Many of the most memorable films are about someone who achieved one kind of success but failed to achieve another.

(See also: SUCCESS; ENDINGS, HAPPY; PYRRHIC VICTORIES)

FAMILY

"SOCIETY" IS AN abstraction. It didn't exist until relatively recently in human history and its members are impossible to define, let alone see in the flesh. The idea of the family, however, is something that everyone sees and experiences. Families are *tangible* and thus far more emotionally involving than society.

The most memorable films demonstrate an astonishing focus on families. In doing so, they are merely continuing the 2,500-year-old history of the theater, which produced *Oedipus, Medea, Hamlet, Macbeth, King Lear, Othello,* and a host of other family stories.

The family is the matrix of identity ("matrix" comes from the same root as "mother.") Most of what we will ever know about love and hate, jealousy and desire, compassion and tenderness, cupidity and fear, respect and loathing, are learned within the family, so it is only natural that fictional families are such fertile ground for the development of dramatic material. Basing a film on a family is, in fact, the quickest way to appeal to multiple constituencies — young and old, men and women, parents and children.

If we were lucky in the family fate gave us, we could predict that our parents would care about us as well as care *for* us. We could predict when meals would be served, when people would sleep, wake up, what they would watch on television, read, and to a large extent what they would say and do. Predictability is a major part of the attraction of families, and is one reason they are omnipresent on television, which thrives on the familiar (which, of course, comes from the same root as family).

The family is also where we first experience the tensions and conflicts between the needs of the individual and the needs of the group, between desire and duty, the most fundamental conflict of all (see: Duty).

It is a mistake to take the concept of the family too literally. *Casablanca* has no biologically related individuals, but it is clear that Rick Blaine is the patriarch of a surrogate family whose members come from all over the earth to "Rick's Place."

In *The Godfather*, "the family" refers not just to the Corleones but also to the extended gang family. It is possible to see the popularity of the gangster family in American films as an indication of the failure of many biological families to nurture and sustain its members, who then seek an alternative form of family identity.

Where there is a family, there are age and gender differences, and both provide rich veins of dramatic potential, since ageism and sexism stem from a competition for power, and power is, of course, at the core of drama.

(See also: Teams and Couples)

6

6 2

FANATICS

A FANATIC IS someone engaged in the unprincipled pursuit of a principle. Fanatics will stop at nothing to reach their goal, no matter whom they have to hurt along the way. They are often found in politics, religion, business — and movies, where their fanaticism helps make them fascinating.

Heroes sometimes may *seem* at times to be fanatics, but it is their adherence to a higher principle that distinguishes them from villains. In *The French Connection*, for example, Popeye Doyle's mad chase after the killer on the elevated train comes close to making him a fanatic; but when he swerves to avoid hitting a woman wheeling a baby carriage, he reveals his observance of some other principle than catching the killer. Had the bad guy been driving that car, he would have kept on going, and his callous disregard for innocent bystanders would have confirmed his villainy.

FANTASY COMES FROM the same root as "phantom," meaning something that isn't there. In a fantasy, the attitude is: "Wouldn't it be nice if....?" The conditional verb, however, expresses a wish that you don't seriously expect to be fulfilled.

FANTASY

Fantasy sells, perhaps better and more predictably than any other genre. Nearly all animated films from *Snow White and the Seven Dwarfs* to *Toy Story, Finding Nemo,* and *Shrek* have been fantasies. *E.T., The Lord of the Rings,* the *Harry Potter* series, *Jurassic Park, Ghost Busters, Back to the Future, Batman, Superman, Spider-Man,* and many others testify to how profitable and popular fantasy films can be.

During the late twentieth and the early years of the twenty-first century, there have been several years in which *nearly all* of the top-grossing films coming out of the U.S. film industry were fantasies of one sort or another. Some might shudder to think what this might indicate about the - United States.

FEAR

FEAR IS A terrific motivator in life and can cause people to do all kinds of things they wouldn't otherwise do. But it's a totally inadequate motivator in film. The hero may be afraid, but he never lets that fear stop him from doing what he must do.

Three kinds of people are allowed to express fear: children, women, and men who will come to an unfortunate end. In all three cases, fear is a weakness that either requires someone else to do the job or is a kind of fatal flaw.

I'm singing in the rain
Just singing in the rain
What a glorious feeling
I'm happy again

> — Don Lockwood (Gene Kelly) in the most
> famous song in *Singin' in the Rain*

I see, it's *you* that this is being done to! It's not me at
all. Not how *I* feel. Not what it means to me.

> — Susan Alexander (Dorothy Comingore) to
> Charles Foster Kane (Orson Welles) as she
> walks out on him and he destroys her room,
> picking up the glass ball that causes him to say
> "Rosebud" in *Citizen Kane*

You want to feel sorry for yourself, don't you?
There's so much at stake. All you can think of is
your *own* feeling.

> — Ilsa Lund (Ingrid Bergman) to Rick Blaine
> (Humphrey Bogart) the night she comes back to
> him in *Casablanca* and they rekindle their love

I first became aware of it, Mandrake, during the
physical act of love ... Yes, a profound sense of
fatigue, a feeling of emptiness followed. Luckily I
was able to interpret these feelings correctly....

> — Col. Jack D. Ripper (Sterling Hayden) to
> Group Captain Lionel Mandrake (Peter Sellers),
> explaining how he came to realize the necessity
> of all-out nuclear war in *Dr. Strangelove*

He's smart. He communicates through Elliott.
Elliott feels his feelings.

> — Michael (Robert MacNaughton) explaining the
> relationship between Elliott (Henry Thomas)
> and the title character in *E. T.*

Now I know what it feels like to be God!

> — Henry Frankenstein (Colin Clive), in the 1931
> version of *Frankenstein*

I just feel like if I didn't get away, I'd bust.

> — George Bailey (Jimmy Stewart) in his last con-
> versation before his father's death in
> *It's a Wonderful Life*

Who are you kidding? You have no feelings to hurt.

> — Roger Thornhill (Cary Grant) to Eve Kendall
> (Eva Marie Saint) in the art gallery scene in
> *North by Northwest*, when he realizes she is the
> villain's mistress

Toto, I have a feeling we're not in Kansas anymore.

> — First words of Dorothy Gale (Judy Garland)
> after the tornado has taken them to Oz in
> *The Wizard of Oz*

He'll feel a lot better after he's robbed a couple of
banks.

> — Butch Cassidy (Paul Newman) to Etta Place
> (Katharine Ross) about the Sundance Kid
> (Robert Redford) in *Butch Cassidy and the
> Sundance Kid*

Boy, if, if I had one day when ... when I didn't have to be all confused, and didn't have to feel that I was ashamed of everything ... If I felt that I belonged someplace ....

> — Jim Stark (James Dean) explaining what's
> troubling him in *Rebel Without a Cause*

There's not a day in my life that I don't feel like a fraud.

> — The first words spoken by Father Damien
> Karras (Jason Miller) in a conversation over-
> heard by Chris MacNeil (Ellen Burstyn) in
> *The Exorcist*

I can't feel the inside ... I'm going to die.

> — Wyatt/Captain America (Peter Fonda), during
> the LSD scene in the New Orleans cemetery in
> *Easy Rider*

I feel pretty, oh so pretty...

> — Maria (Natalie Wood), in a key song in
> *West Side Story*

Announcer: Ladies and gentlemen, let's hear it — how do you feel?

Audience: We're mad as hell, and we're not going to take this any more!

> — The scene in *Network* in which Howard Beale
> (Peter Finch) dies

I feel awake. Wide awake. I don't remember ever
feeling this away ... You feel like that, too. Like you
got something to look forward to.

> — Thelma Dickinson (Geena Davis) to Louise
> Sawyer (Susan Sarandon), in *Thelma & Louise*

Let go of your conscious self ... and act on instinct
... your eyes can deceive you. Don't trust them.
Stretch out with your feelings.

> — Obi-Wan Kenobi (Alec Guinness) to Luke
> Skywalker (Mark Hamill) in his first training
> session to be a Jedi Knight in *Star Wars*

Look, maybe you don't care if you live or die. But
everybody's not like that! Okay?! We have feelings.
We hurt. We're afraid. You gotta learn this stuff,
man, I'm not kidding. It's important.

> — John Connor, age 10, to the Terminator
> (Arnold Schwarzenegger), in *Terminator 2:
> Judgment Day*

Some memorable popular films have great acting; others have great direction or great special
effects or great action scenes. Still others have great
camera movement, editing, lighting, music, costumes, or set design. But it is *feelings* that lie at the
heart of all memorable popular films, and quotes
such as those above can be found in nearly all
memorable popular films. When the feelings of the
filmmakers, the feelings of the characters, and the
feelings of the audience come together, there is the
opportunity for greatness.

IN AMERICAN LIBRARIES that use the Dewey Decimal System, all of human knowledge expressed in books is organized into two simple categories: Fiction and Nonfiction.

Librarians could have used a system that divided books into "truth" and "non-truth," but this would offend those who believe fiction contains its own kind of truth as well as those who object to certain books being labeled "truth." "Nonfiction" was a far safer way to describe the second category of books.

But the division into "fiction" and "nonfiction" suggests that we are clear about what fiction is, but the best we can do with everything else is to label it as not belonging to that category.

In film, "fiction" is the norm, the mode that defines everything else. Unlike libraries, in the commercial film world there is little interest in non-fiction. When screenwriters, directors, producers, actors, critics, and audiences speak about "truth," or "reality," in films, they are not referring so much to the exterior world, where truth or falsity can be tested; they are talking about a kind of artistic truth, which is difficult to define and even harder to prove.

Stanley Kubrick tried to be scrupulously faithful to the realities of what was known about the realities of space travel when he made *2001* in 1968 — a year before anyone had gone to the moon. Kubrick knew that, because there is no air in space, his spaceship did not need to be aerodynamic; because there is no sound, most of the film is without dialogue; and because there is no gravity, movement is awkward and "unnatural."

George Lucas's first *Star Wars* film was released eight years after space travel had become a reality. Yet, Lucas chose to make what could be considered an anti-science film that respected none of the most elemental facts. There is earth-like gravity wherever the characters go, the most famous battle scenes are true to the aerodynamics of earthbound airplanes but not to what was by then well known about how ships actually would move in the vacuum of space. Kubrick respected the facts; Lucas couldn't have cared less. The relative popularity of the two films demonstrates how little audiences care about facts and how much they prefer fiction.

FILM NOIR

FILM NOIR IS the only genre to have been invented by critics. The makers of films in the 1940s and 1950s such as *Double Indemnity*, *The Big Sleep* and *The Lady from Shanghai* that were later called "film noir" thought at the time that they were making detective films, cop films, heist films, or "thrillers." So, too, did the studios that marketed them and the audiences that came to see them. It was only years later that a small group of French critics decided they knew better — that such filmmakers had created an entirely new genre: "film noir" (variously translated as "black" or "dark" films).

The French and the American critics who adopted this view focused to a large extent on the style and attitude of this disparate group of films. But this style had long before been associated with Expressionism, the manifestation of the inner feelings of a character through exterior visualization. A high-angle shot looking down on a character, for example, can be used to express feelings of powerlessness, or the camera can be tilted in a "Dutch angle" to express a skewed or off-center way of looking at the world. Lighting can use an old trick of classic horror films such as *Frankenstein, Dracula,* and *The Wolf Man*, inverting the source of the light, which usually comes from above, and placing it below the characters.

Unlike clearly defined genres such as westerns and gangster films, where elements of style, character, and content are quite consistent, "Film Noir" is more a critical catchphrase, especially among people who have attended film school.

(See also: EXPRESSIONISM; ATTITUDE; GENRES)

FISH OUT OF WATER

IT IS WIDELY recognized that the protagonist in comedy is almost invariably a "fish out of water," a "stranger in a strange land" —somebody who doesn't really belong.

What is less often recognized is that the protagonist in *tragedies* is also usually a person who doesn't belong. The difference is that, in comedy, the stranger is usually trying to get *into* the strange land, whereas in tragedy he's trying to get *out*.

Michael Corleone in *The Godfather* insists early in the film, "That's my family, Kay, not me," and Willard in *Apocalypse Now*, after succeeding in his mission, declares late in the film that he no longer belongs to the U.S. Army that wants to promote him. Michael was a fish out of water at the beginning, and Willard jumped out of the water at the end.

In almost all memorable stories, you could say of the hero, "He didn't really belong." A character who does belong, who is *not* a fish out of water, is not likely to be very interesting.

(See also: INTERMEDIARIES)

FLASHBACKS

CASABLANCA FLASHES BACK to Paris twice to give us the "backstory" between Ilsa Lund and Rick Blaine — how they fell in love, and then how she subsequently deserted him at the train station when they were about to go away together.

There was a period near the beginning of the 1960s when it was said by many in Hollywood that the flashback was a passé device akin to the iris shots of D.W. Griffith. But by the mid-'60s flashbacks began to return to American films, and eventually become as prevalent as they had been in its earlier years.

The reason flashbacks came back was that they are not merely stylistic flourishes, like iris shots; they are necessary tools that, so far, cannot be replaced by others.

The available devices for moving from present time into a flashback are limited, and have been clichés for many years. The camera moves into a tight closeup of a character's eyes; they glaze over and we hear an echo chamber voice, and perhaps see heat waves distorting the image, or the camera going slightly out of focus. *Citizen Kane*, *Casablanca*, *Lawrence of Arabia* and both versions of *The Manchurian Candidate* all use such effects because no one has come up with anything substantially better.

(See also: BACKSTORIES; TIME; NARRATIVES AND NARRATIONS)

FLOW

WHEN YOU'RE WATCHING a movie and you have to ask someone, "What did he say?" what happens to the movie? It flows on, and the chances are good you'll miss something else that is important while you're asking the question or listening to the answer.

A movie flows through real time, like a river carrying you toward your destination. If you ask a question or think about something other than the movie, you're out of the river and up on the bank — out of the flow. This is seldom good.

(See also: TIME)

FOILS ARE POISED around the hero like spokes in a wheel. They are necessary to support the force and the momentum of the story, but the center of gravity and power needs to lie at the center, in the person whose story it is

Foil characters exist to fulfill a particular need of the story, which is usually to reveal something, not about the foil, but about the central character. In *High Noon*, for example, the teenager, the middle-aged man with a wife and children, the town drunk, and even the deputy sheriff who volunteers to join Will Kane in the coming gun battle, each reveals different aspects of Will Kane's character: fatherly tolerance, compassion, resoluteness, and righteous anger. In *Schindler's List,* Helen Hirsch serves the function of revealing tenderness in Schindler that was not evident in his behavior earlier in the film.

(See: CHARACTER RELATIONSHIPS)

FOIL CHARACTERS

FORE-SHADOWING

IT IS SOMETIMES said, "Don't telegraph," that is, give away what's going to happen. But great dramas have frequently done this.

If the foreshadowing tips the audience off as to *exactly* what's going to happen and the audience knows early in the film that "the butler did it," the sense of discovery that is so important to audience satisfaction will be lost. If, on the other hand, the audience knows *something* is going to happen, but doesn't know exactly what it is, as when it sees a vulture flying overhead in *The Bridge on the River Kwai*, or when it sees Sonny Corleone angrily rushing out of the family compound in *The Godfather,* the result is an increase in tension, which is always desirable.

We might notice that these two examples, one visual, and one accompanied by ominous music, demonstrate that foreshadowing is often accomplished through something other than words.

(See also: FLASHBACKS; PREDICTION)

Fourth Wall

In the groundbreaking play *Our Town*, Thornton Wilder created a character called "The Stage Manager" who spoke directly to the audience. This broke the "Fourth Wall" that had been a staple of drama for centuries, but as is so often true for a well-conceived violation of an artistic convention, the effect was powerful and satisfying.

When we sit in a theater, whether it is devoted to plays or film, we are like an omniscient deity that sees all but is not seen. In the real world, there would be a wall blocking the audience's view; in the theater, the "Fourth Wall" is like an imaginary one-way mirror — while the audience can see the actors, the pretense is that the actors cannot see the audience, which is why actors do not look directly at audience members. Thus, when the actor playing Hamlet recites the famous "To Be or Not to Be" speech, the theatrical convention often has the actor move downstage so that he faces the audience, but he doesn't generally make eye contact with them.

Wilder's Stage Manager in *Our Town* brought to the theater a device that was customary in novels — the omniscient narrator. *Platoon*, *Apocalypse Now*, and many other films use the same device in "voice-over" narration. Even here, though, the "fourth wall" retains its power — the audience is seldom directly addressed, and it is often never clear to whom the narrator is speaking.

(See also: Narratives and Narrations; Acting)

FRONTIERS

WAR STORIES ARE set on fronts, while westerns and science fiction films are set on frontiers. Both are places of danger, death, and transcendence. They are the perfect setting for drama because they provide the hero with the opportunity to *be* heroic.

(See also: INTERFACE; TRANSCENDENCE)

G.

America has not produced movements;
it has produced genres.

GANGSTER FILMS

FROM THE STANDPOINT of political structures, the gangster world is a fascist entity, organized hierarchically around a single figure who ruthlessly punishes transgressions, especially disobedience and disloyalty. The gang fights like an army, but not on behalf of any principle, community, or nation but for the self-aggrandizement of its leader and, secondarily, of its members.

There are several gangster films in which a member of the gang says he's got his eye on a farm or ranch out west, where he plans to get married and settle down. Anyone familiar with gangster films knows upon hearing this speech that this character will be dead before the story is over. Once you're in the gang, you're trapped, even if you're its leader. Perhaps *especially* if you're its leader. As Michael Corleone says in *The Godfather: Part III*, "Just when I thought I was out, they pull me back in."

Gangster films are inherently tragic. Like many classical Greek and Shakespearian tragedies, the gangster film frequently deals with both the rise and fall of its protagonist. The original 1932 *Scarface* and its 1982 remake, for example, both begin with a lower-class boy who fulfills what some see as The American Dream — but then he is crushed by it.

The protagonist in gangster films often begins outside the gang. In *The Godfather*, Michael is the only Corleone boy who is *not* a member of the gang, and it isn't until one hour into the film (see: CRISIS POINT, ONE-HOUR) that Michael takes over the family business, not by bumping off the existing boss as in *Scarface* and many other gangster films, but because he's just trying to save his father's life. Much of the appeal of *The Godfather*, in fact, stems from Michael's desire to save his family, rather than enhance his own power.

It takes a long time for the gangster hero to come into his power because he must prove that he *deserves* to be the boss by demonstrating courage, intelligence, ingenuity, and unstoppable will power. (In this, he is like most heroes.)

The gangster film faces the same structural problem as the horror film: as much as we may be fascinated by the behavior of the protagonist, he can be allowed to prosper only so far. We may admire their cleverness and courage, we may seek to understand them, we may even learn to have a certain compassion for them, but we can't ignore the fact that they represent a threat to society; that is, to you and me. And so, through whatever plot devices are necessary, the memorable popular gangster films, like memorable popular horror films, arrange things so that, at the end, the central character is safely locked away or dead. Like fascism, it is fascinating to watch, but having seen naked power in action, it is time to dispose of the evidence.

(See also: GENRES)

GENRES

THE HISTORY OF motion picture production in most countries is marked by film movements that have borne names such as Surrealism (France), Socialist Realism (Soviet Union), Neo-Realism (Italy), and the New Wave (France). America, however, has not produced movements; it has produced genres.

Movements, in film, politics, religion, or other areas of life, usually define themselves by what they are *against*. If you belong to a movement, the answer to the question, "What holds our side together?" is to a large extent "their side."

Nothing unites human beings more solidly than having a common enemy. In motion picture history, ever since the late 1920s, there have been two kinds of films: 1) Hollywood, and 2) the rest of the world. It is not surprising, then, that movements such as Italian Neo-Realism and the French New Wave were explicit in their rejection of the "Hollywood Model."

The American film industry has been so powerful for so long that it hasn't felt the need for a film movement — what would people in the industry be moving *against*? Since filmmakers can't categorize (and sell) films on the basis of what they are against, they divide them into genres.

Genres are to film what ethnicity is to restaurants — we feel in the mood for a war film, comedy or romance the same way we feel in the mood for Chinese, Italian, or Mexican food.

Categorizing films according to genres also helps critics and audiences decide what they *don't* want to see. Just as some people never consume

Mexican or Chinese food, some people never consume a horror film, science fiction, war film, or romance.

As the separate entries in this book for various genres demonstrate, each genre defines itself by an implicit contract with its audience. The story will contain familiar ingredients served up in a certain order and a certain way. We hope at the same time to experience something new, but we don't want it *too* new. You may like hamburgers, but you don't go to a Chinese restaurant to get them, nor would you expect to find an Italian restaurant with bagels on its menu. Similarly, a western that does not end with man-to-man combat, a horror film without up-close-and-personal gory deaths, or a science fiction film that doesn't involve technology would be disappointing and probably unsuccessful.

From an artistic standpoint, genres can be constricting precisely because of the implicit contract between filmmaker and audience. A contract, by definition, requires you to act in a predictable manner; but predictability is the enemy of art. The trick with genre films is to be predictable, but in some way unpredictable as well.

For more than fifty years, one third of all films released in the United States were westerns. They could be made cheaply, and a certain proportion of the male population could be predictably counted on to see them. Horror films, which were not identified as a popular genre until the 1930s, became a predictably successful genre in the 1960s. Like the western and every other genre, the primary audience consisted of a certain segment of the population — adolescent males.

Having a predictable audience is, of course, good for business, and as long as the cost of making the films can be controlled, genre film production can provide a steady source of income. The problem, however, is that most clearly defined genre films quickly use up their potential audience segment, which is why horror films often do good business the first week or two in theaters and then disappear.

Unless a genre film *transcends* its conventions, its potential audience will be limited. If audiences saw *The Exorcist* as just another horror film, *The Godfather* as just another gangster film, *Star Wars* as just another science fiction film, or *Saving Private Ryan* as just another war film, the audience for these films would have been only a fraction of what they were.

The Exorcist is, on one level, surely a horror film. Yet it's *also* about the salvation of a family whose most innocent member is tortured, which is why the audience for the film included millions of women who ordinarily wouldn't go near a conventional horror film.

Some of the studio executives who put *The Godfather* in production saw it as just another gangster film, which was, in fact, why Francis Ford Coppola initially didn't want to direct it. But *The Godfather* is *also* the story of a family's survival in the midst of great dangers (see: FAMILY).

Lawrence of Arabia appealed to that segment of the audience that loved action/adventure epics; but the film also dealt with geopolitical events that shaped the modern world and contained a character study of a fascinating and paradoxical man that carried it far beyond the usual limitations of the action/adventure genre.

The most memorable popular films have rarely been *good* examples of their genre. People who considered themselves true fans of the western originally disdained *Shane* and *High Noon*, and true fans of gangster or horror films may feel that *The Godfather* and *The Exorcist* are aberrations from the genre — and they are right.

The challenge in working in a genre is to fulfill the terms of the implicit contract with the fans of that genre, but at the same time to transcend those elements so the film can reach a much wider audience. As in so many other ways, popular films operate much like popular politics.

(See also: ACTION; DETECTIVE FILMS; FANTASY; FILM NOIR; GANGSTER FILMS; HORROR FILMS; ROMANCE; SCIENCE FICTION; WESTERNS; WAR FILMS)

GIFTS

LOVERS, TEAMMATES, PARTNERS, and members of genuine communities engage in an exchange of gifts.

What age gives to youth is wisdom and experience; what youth gives to age is energy and hope. In movies where the central character is accompanied by a "sidekick," the main character provides strength and ability, while the side character provides laughs and sometimes common sense.

In movies such as *Butch Cassidy and the Sundance Kid* or *Thelma & Louise*, the exchange of gifts often swings from one character to the other. In the first half of *Thelma & Louise*, the older Louise uses her knowledge and experience to lead. Halfway through the film, however, she succumbs to despair, and Thelma becomes the leader.

The exchange of gifts is most clear in romantic relationships. In fact, if there *isn't* an exchange of gifts, there is no reason for the relationship to exist. In countless love stories, the man is good at rational thought and analysis while the woman is good at understanding and expressing feelings. Each gives the other qualities they lack or brings out of the other their latent potential.

Gift-giving is an inherent part of all social relationships, and involves an unspoken obligation: If you accept the gift, you are expected to reciprocate. In movies, as in life, the exchange of gifts is what holds the lovers, teammates, partners, and members of the community together.

(See also: CURSES; TEAMS AND COUPLES)

YOU WOULD PROBABLY not buy a jigsaw puzzle in a plain white box, sight unseen. You would want to know what you were going to get before you got it, which is why they put a picture of the completed puzzle on the box. Film audiences don't get a picture of the motion picture on a box, but neither do they buy it sight unseen. They already know a number of things about the film through advertising, trailers, interviews, reviews, and word of mouth.

They also know the principles of storytelling. What the poet Coleridge called "the willing suspension of disbelief" allows them to pretend they don't know that the lovers will come together or the killer will be caught. But they have an implicit picture in their mind before they see the film, and when it is finished, what was on the screen had better match at least part of that image or they will feel cheated.

And yet, audiences also want to be surprised, want to make discoveries, and want to feel that something in the film is new. Only a hack settles for giving people *only* what they want. But only a fool fails to be aware of what that is.

Knowing what the audience's expectations are and how to simultaneously give that to them but also surprise them is an attribute of genius.

(See also: DISCOVERY)

GIVE 'EM WHAT THEY WANT

GOD

POLLS SHOW THE vast majority of Americans profess to believe in God, but you will not find any significant evidence for this in memorable films. This is one of the major reasons the orthodox branches of Judaism, Christianity, and Islam revile popular motion pictures.

Aside from *The Ten Commandments*, *The Passion of the Christ*, some versions of the Joan of Arc story and a few others, when in the history of popular films is God addressed, or for that matter, even referred to? In what films does the hero say, when talking about the future — as orthodox believers ritualistically do — "If God wills"?

Drama is not about God's Will; it's about the will of the central characters. The nearly total absence of deities in popular films does not necessarily correlate with what filmmakers and audiences believe or don't believe; it correlates with a requirement of drama since the Greeks.

The fundamental rule of memorable popular films — like the drama of the past 2,500 years that preceded them — is that what happens to a character is the result of what he or she *chooses* to do. People in their daily lives may believe that what happens to them stems from God, luck, coincidence, fate, or other forces outside their control (see: DESTINY). In popular films, however, character is destiny and divine intervention is against the rules.

(See also: INDIVIDUALISM; DECISION; DESTINY, DEUS EX MACHINA; COINCIDENCES)

MANY OF AMERICA's memorable popular films have at their core a goofy character. A particularly American word that is difficult to translate into other languages, "goofy" can mean bumbling, eccentric, loveable, and much else besides. Whatever words one uses to define goofy, they are not likely to be the conventional terms we associate with heroes.

GOOFY

The central characters of all of Frank Capra's films, among the most-loved in American history, were certainly heroic but they were also all goofy. Many of the major male stars of the classic period of American film, the 1930s through the 1950s — Gary Cooper, Jimmy Stewart, Spencer Tracy, etc. — played one goofy protagonist after another. In modern times, Dustin Hoffman, Eddie Murphy, and Mel Gibson have played a string of goofy characters. Even our superheroes tend to be goofy, as Clark Kent/Superman and Peter Parker/Spider-Man demonstrate.

Perhaps this is because "goofy" so often goes with "loveable." Or perhaps it is part of the American tendency to bend over backwards to avoid being pretentious. In American culture, goofy is good.

(See also: CUTE; VULNERABILITY; WISDOM)

GROSS

THE WAY TO get a gross is to be gross. This brings consternation to parents and guardians of good taste, but pleasure to millions of others.

Animal House and other films based on gross humor follow a tradition that goes all the way back to the ancient Greeks. In Greek theatrical celebrations, there would be a cycle of three tragedies, followed by a satyr play or other comedy in which fart jokes, feces-throwing, giant erections, and bosoms were all incorporated in a way that would make any fourteen-year-old male die with laughter.

Such gross comedies offended the subsequent trustees of the West's cultural heritage, and the result was that while lots of tragedies were preserved, hardly any complete raunchy Greek comedies survive to this day. Even Aristotle's book on comedy, which was the companion to his work on tragedy, was allowed to disappear from the face of the earth. (See: ARISTOLATRY)

Gross comedy has always been disreputable, which was why it was relegated to vaudeville, music halls, and prime time television, where it continues to appeal to people who don't read books like this.

H

The hero doesn't become a hero
simply because he takes a stand against
the villain; he becomes a hero because
he stands for something.

HABITUATION

THE PRINCIPLE OF habituation helps explain why movies get louder, more violent, and maybe even longer: We quickly habituate or become used to sensations, so, to produce the same level of arousal, we either need more of the same stimulus, or we need to repeat it more frequently. If there is not an increase in level or frequency, the original response is diminished, and sometimes we fail to respond at all.

The struggle to overcome habituation lies behind nearly every aspect of modern art, commerce, education, philosophy, and religion. It is manifested in that word that is ubiquitous in the modern world: "New."

(See also: NEW; ORIGINALITY; BISOCIATION)

HAPPINESS HAS NOTHING to do with being a hero. The need for happiness is, in fact, one of the things the hero has *transcended*. This is one of the reasons ordinary people aren't interested in becoming heroes in real life. Parents in democratic societies don't say, "I want my child to grow up to be a hero"; they say, "I want my child to grow up to be happy." It is *society* that wants heroes, not the people who love them.

HAPPINESS

Heroes are usually the most honorable of people, but they are seldom the most successful or the happiest. Success is something the hero no longer aspires to, and happiness is something the hero no longer is concerned with, or perhaps even capable of.

To choose heroism is to choose pain, sacrifice, loss, and sometimes even death. What sane person would do this? When we hear a character say to the hero, "Are you crazy?" it is often a reasonable question. Heroes are like saints: they die for our sins, and happiness is beside the point.

(See also: ENDINGS, HAPPY; SUCCESS; HEROES, SINGLE; HEROINES; COMMITMENT)

HEROES

In 1898, GERMAN chemists synthesized a new psychoactive substance that inflated the user's personality, giving him a grandiosity that led him to do reckless and foolish things — to act like a hero. Thus, the scientists called their substance "heroin."

Like heroin, heroism can be addictive. However, it can also be boring to watch because the behavior it produces is so predictable. Heroes have to *act* like heroes — what a narrow range of behavior that is!

Villains, on the other hand, can act any way they choose, and that's why they are often more interesting than the hero. Darth Vader in *Star Wars* is certainly a more interesting character than Luke Skywalker, just as Hannibal Lecter in *The Silence of the Lambs* is more interesting than Clarice Starling.

When people hear the term "hero," they often think of Superman and other characters that strut around the screen rescuing one person after another. This kind of hero can be traced back to the bold and brave characters in the epic poems of Homer and countless Greek myths. Yet, as popular as such heroes were in poetry, folk tales, and religion, this kind of hero seldom appeared in ancient Greek *drama*.

Oedipus, Medea, Antigone, Lear, Hamlet, Macbeth, and many other great protagonists in world drama are flawed, vulnerable, vacillating, and contradictory characters. None of them bears any resemblance to Superman. Nor do the most memorable film characters such as Rick Blaine in *Casablanca*, R. P. McMurphy in *One Flew Over the Cuckoo's Nest*, or Michael Corleone in *The Godfather*. In memorable popular films, heroism is not a lifestyle; it consists of a few heroic *acts* (see: ANTIHEROES).

Filmmakers know, as their predecessors did, that heroes are almost invariably defiant and incapable of fitting in. But sometimes they lose sight of the importance of the hero's reluctance. Perhaps this is because many producers and studio executives in our time insist that the hero be "proactive," which they think means he needs to be in control early in the film. But this is not consistent with the history of memorable heroes.

The person who rushes into battle and storms to the top of the hill is certainly being proactive, and he may seem to be heroic. But he is also likely to be dead by morning. Heroes are reluctant because no person in his right mind *volunteers* to be a hero.

The villain was a villain long before the hero arrived on the scene, and the hero had no part in turning him into a villain. Nor, if the hero disappeared, would the villain cease to be a villain.

While heroes do not turn people into villains, villains turn people into heroes— it is the hero's *reaction* to the villain that makes him a hero, and when the villain disappears, there is nothing left to be heroic about.

In *High Noon*, Frank Miller decides to return to Hadleyville after being released from prison, which forces Will Kane to save the town. In *The Godfather*, Sollozzo tries to kill Vito Corleone, which forces Michael to save his father's life. In *2001*, HAL sabotages the spaceship and kills its crew, which forces Dave Bowman to take charge. In these and almost all other memorable films, the hero is not proactive; he is *re*active.

The hero doesn't become a hero simply because he takes a stand against the villain; he becomes a hero because he stands *for* something. This can be justice, a cause, his family, friends, community, or nation. Invariably, while the villain stands for himself, the hero stands for something *beyond* himself.

Drama has always involved a dialogue between the individual and society, dealing with the conflict between desire and duty (see: Duty). Heroes don't do what they do to achieve success, win approval, or reap material benefits; they do it because it's "the right thing." Invariably, what is required of heroes is that they sacrifice themselves for some transcendent value.

(See also: Heroes, Single; Heroines; Defiance; Transcendence)

NEARLY ALL LISTS of the most memorable classical plays include *Oedipus Rex, Medea, Antigone, Hamlet, King Lear,* and *Macbeth.* In American theater, *Death of a Salesman* is usually ranked among the most memorable modern plays. In American movies, *Citizen Kane, Lawrence of Arabia,* and *The Godfather* are invariably listed in the top ranks. What do these works, spanning 2,500 years, have in common?

Each is the story of a single individual, who is referred to in the title, and around whom all the important action, all the major scenes, and all the other characters revolve. It is the strongest dramatic structure ever conceived.

One reason for the power of the single-hero story is that it is the most economical and concentrated way to tell a story. It may also be an analog of our own psychology, since many of us see life as having one major, central, character: ourself.

Because there is much power in this structure, it is always important to ask of a film, "Whose film is this?" Often, when a film does not work, it is because the creators of the film have failed to figure out the answer to this simple but fundamental question.

(See also: TEAMS AND COUPLES; CONFLICT, SINGLE; HEROES; HEROINES; STRUCTURE)

HEROES, SINGLE

HEROINES

WHEN ASKED TO name the great heroines of history, the first response is often, "Joan of Arc." When asked what Joan did that made her heroic, most people reply that she was burned at the stake. Often that is the only thing they know about her.

When asked who has been the most depicted woman in western painting, the answer anyone familiar with art will give is: the Virgin Mary. When asked what she is doing in those paintings, the answer is either that she is holding the dead body of Christ, "The Pietá," which comes from the word "pity," or she is suckling the infant Jesus.

Women nurture. This is good for society, but bad for drama. When a woman is depicted as a heroine, however, she is supposed to do what all heroes and heroines do — *suffer.*

It is clear from the history of film that, while females in the audience are interested in seeing male heroes, males are not as interested in seeing female heroes — especially if the audience members are young. How do filmmakers get an audience interested in female heroes? *Thelma & Louise,* which is usually cited in discussions of "strong women" in film, provides an important clue. Halfway through the film, Louise's boyfriend tracks her down to the motel where she is staying and urges her to let him come along. If she had allowed him to join her, it would have been the boyfriend who confronted the leering truck driver, the sheriff's deputy, and the other males who threaten the two women. But

because Thelma refused to let her boyfriend come
to her rescue, she and Thelma have a *chance* to act
heroically.

Men can—and usually do — act heroically when
a woman is present. One way for women to emerge
as heroes, therefore, is to get rid of the men.

(See also: HEROES; HEROES, SINGLE)

HISTORICAL FILMS

EVERY SO OFTEN in its history, Hollywood decides not to make any more historical films. Usually, this has been after some big flop, such as *Cleopatra*, which nearly bankrupted Twentieth Century-Fox and caused a regime to fall.

Yet, a third or more of the memorable popular films on most lists are historical works such as *The Birth of a Nation, Gone with the Wind, Ben-Hur, Spartacus, The Bridge on the River Kwai, The African Queen, Lawrence of Arabia, Schindler's List*. The western, which accounted for a quarter of all movies made in America until the early 1960s was, by definition, an historical film, and a good proportion of the most popular musicals were historically based.

But history is expensive. The filmmakers have to build or remake streets so they don't show telephone poles and satellite dishes, they have to make expensive costumes, the hairstylist bills are frightening, and doing all that research to ensure accuracy (assuming the filmmaker cares about it) is time-consuming and expensive.

Some stories must be set in a specific time period because they wouldn't work if they were set in the present. Sometimes, however, there is no particular or compelling reason why the story *has* to be set in the past.

The elements of an historical film that are most likely to win Academy Awards are its set and costume design. But while the authenticity of the drapes, mahogany armoires, bustles and hoops receive favorable comments from critics and fellow workers in the industry, they are seldom the reason

most members of the audience come to see historical movies, so the costs of authentic reproduction
do not automatically translate into higher box
office receipts.

Some historical periods have provided very rich
ground for filmmakers: the American Civil War,
the American west in the decade between the end
of the Civil War and the turn of the century, World
War II, the period of Greek myth, and occasionally
the biblical period.

Other historic periods, however, have not fared
well with audiences. As important as the American
Revolution was to the United States, no one seems
very interested in watching George Washington and
Thomas Jefferson prance around in powdered wigs
and waistcoats. And, as important as the 1960s were
to recent American history, few seem to want to
revisit it — *Easy Rider* strikes many people today as a
movie from a galaxy far, far away. In fact, it may be
that *most* of the historic periods since World War II
seem far removed.

Historical tales work best with audiences if they
feel relevant to our own time. That will be achieved,
not in sets and costumes, but in characters.

(See also: EPICS; EXOTIC; FANTASY)

HOLLYWOOD

HOLLYWOOD IS A mythical kingdom that millions of people seek to enter but once they do, will never admit they're a part of.

THE HOOK IS what gets people into the film. In
E. T., little humanoids from a spaceship are explor-
ing a suburban community when government
officials frighten them and they take off so rapidly
that they leave one of their members behind. In
The Terminator, thunder and lightning accompany
the sudden appearance of a totally naked Adonis
from the future. In *Dr. Strangelove*, an ethereal
American B-52 bomber is seen refueling in mid-
air as if engaged in some kind of erotic coupling.
The "hook" is what causes people to say, "Tell me
more." At its best it's not just a gimmick, but rather
an inherent part of the story.

(See also: CONCEPTS)

HOOKS

Horror Films

Horripilation is the term for the hair on the back of the neck that stands up when we are seized by intense fear. Raising those follicles is the goal of all horror films.

Like comedies, we can tell while it's running whether a horror film is succeeding by the reactions it provokes in the audience. Just as the object in comedy is generally to produce laughs, the object in horror films is to produce screams. Both forms of release are satisfying, but while people continue to laugh throughout their lives, they do not generally feel comfortable screaming beyond a certain age.

As long as production costs are contained, it is hard for filmmakers to lose money making a horror film. This is because there is always a segment of the population who are self-declared "horror film freaks." The problem is that this niche audience is quickly used up.

The horror film is a genre aimed largely at pubescent and adolescent youth — the same people who love to scream on roller coasters and look for out-of-control sensations elsewhere in their lives. Attracting people who are not part of this constituency is often difficult. *The Exorcist* and *Rosemary's Baby* did so by dealing with families in a serious way — something the mostly young audience for horror films isn't especially interested in seeing.

The titles of memorable popular horror films tend to follow the patterns observable in much of the most memorable dramatic works: they are about a single character, around whom all the important action revolves and for whom the film is named.

In the many versions of the stories of Frankenstein, Dracula, Freddy Kruger, and other legends of horror, the audience knows that the main character must die or be removed before the end of the film. While these characters fascinate, they cannot continue, or, to be more precise, they must not *appear* to continue — until the sequel explains how they managed to survive or managed to produce offspring.

Many horror films could correctly be called "Supernatural Films," but this might reveal more than we care to acknowledge about the religious origins of so much horror. (As Dante demonstrated in his poetry and Hieronymus Bosch depicted in his painting, no place is more horrible than Hell.)

The origin of horror can come from whatever lies beyond death (*Dracula*), demonic forces (*The Exorcist*), or fooling around with Mother Nature (*Frankenstein*). Or the horror can be supernatural in a different sense, without religious connection but still not what we customarily think of as "natural." It can, for example, be the super science of *The Terminator* or the biological horror that seems "unnatural" in *Alien*. Sometimes, what's unnatural is merely a warped mind, as in *Psycho* and *Friday the 13th*.

(See also: FANATICS)

HUBRIS

WE LOVE TO see the effects of *hubris*, the ancient Greek term usually translated as "excessive pride." When presidents, captains of industry, billionaires, movie stars, television evangelists, rich and famous athletes — well, *anybody* rich and famous — gets too big for their britches, we just love to see them come tumbling down, to see their uppity noses ground into their feet of clay.

There are lots of stories about the rise of someone to great prominence; the stories we remember, however, are much more likely to be about someone's rise *and* fall (see: BUT). Take the legendary *Citizen Kane*. One hour into the film, Charles Foster Kane yells at the politician who opposes him in his run for governor, "I'm Charles Foster KANE!" and from that hubristic moment, the film is all downhill.

Humility, the opposite of hubris, is what we require of heroes. When they are possessed by *hubris*, they are no longer heroes.

(See also: HUMILITY)

HUMILITY

THE OLD TESTAMENT prophet Micah asked, "What does the Lord require of you but to do justice, to love kindness, and to walk humbly with your God?" Theology aside (see: GOD), these three attributes are found in a great many memorable heroes.

In *High Noon*, after the famous clock strikes twelve and the tension is at its highest, Will Kane pauses as he leaves his office for the final shootout in order to open a cell door and let the town drunk go home. It is a kindness that is totally unnecessary but reveals something important about the character of the man.

Ever since Greek tragedy, whenever a character boasts of his power, it can be predicted that he will lose it. Humility is one of the principal requirements for heroes; if they lose it, they lose us.

(See also: JUSTICE; HUBRIS; POWER)

I.

*In the United States, where belief
in the power and importance of the
individual is the unstated State Religion,
heroes thrive in the realm of fiction
but wither in the realm of reality.*

IDENTIFICATION

IDENTIFICATION IS A crucial process in dramatic and film experience, yet it is paradoxical.

Imagine you are watching a cop show and the familiar "lineup" takes place. This process involves the "identification" of the one person standing in the row who the witness says is the unique person the police are looking for.

The process of identification in drama and film, however, works just the other way around: the audience is presented with a single unique individual, and they are asked to see not only his uniqueness but how much he and they are alike.

It's common for teachers to point out that there is a difference between sympathizing and empathizing and to insist that one is appropriate for dramatic identification and the other is not. The trouble is, many people can't remember which is which.

What's important about the audience's relationship with a character is not whether they sympathize, empathize, or even whether they actually identify with the character. What's really most important is that they identify with the *situation* the character is in.

(See also: SITUATIONS)

IT IS NOT death we fear so much as it is impotence. This is why *Oedipus Rex* has often been the model of western drama and formed the basis of one of Sigmund Freud's key concepts. In this story, there is a curse upon the land and as a result the crops have stopped bearing fruit and the women have stopped bearing children. If these conditions continue, the city will wither and die. This "plague upon the land" is often seen in the beginning of many memorable stories, and its power stems from the apparent impotence of everyone in the story.

IMPOTENCE

Chinatown, for example, begins with the death of the man who has brought water to the Southern California desert. Something now threatens that water supply, without which the city will wither and die. *Amadeus* focuses on Mozart's rival, Salieri, who curses God for not giving him the power to create great music. *Dirty Harry* and *High Noon* both deal with a mad killer who has paralyzed an entire town.

On one level, all memorable drama deals with the conflict between power and impotence, fecundity and sterility, generation and degeneration. On its simplest and most overt level, this is the struggle between life and death. When this struggle takes place on the psychological and spiritual level, it is more subtle than one that takes place on the physical level, but it can be just as compelling.

(See also: POWER; DEATH; LOVE; DESPAIR)

Incongruity

INCONGRUITY RESULTS FROM the juxtaposition of two actions, characters, moods, or other elements that at first feel like they don't belong together. What's that ape doing on top of the tallest building in the world in *King Kong*? What's that shark doing having that beautiful girl for dinner? What's that demon doing inside that cute little kid in *The Exorcist*? How can Rhett tell Scarlett he doesn't give a damn when he's just spent four hours mooning over her? How can Rick send Ilsa away with Victor when he — and we — know how desperately he loves her?

When filmmakers lead us to understand and *accept* incongruity, contradiction, and duality, the effect can be very powerful.

(See also: PARADOX; BISOCIATION; DUALITY)

IN THE UNITED States, where belief in the power and importance of the individual is the unstated State Religion, heroes thrive in the realm of fiction but wither in the realm of reality. Anyone who reaches a position of power in politics, entertainment, sports, business, or anywhere else is immediately subjected to an intense scrutiny that aims to prove that he or she really is no better than ordinary people and is perhaps even worse.

On the other hand, in Nazi Germany, the Soviet Union, China under Mao, Cuba under Castro, Iran under the Ayatollah Khomeini, Iraq under Hussein, and a host of other countries that denied the power and primary importance of the individual, people were presented with what was purported to be a real-life hero, but there were few such heroes in fiction. Bearing names such as "Fuehrer" and "Supreme Leader," these real-life heroes were proclaimed to be the font of all wisdom — which, of course, means they subsumed all power. The very *idea* that ordinary human beings have within themselves the capacity to be heroes — let alone *should* be in control of their destiny — was unthinkable (see: DESTINY).

In such systems, the people looked to the real-life leader/hero to rescue them. In individualistic societies such as the United States, however, people bear the responsibility for rescuing themselves.

Rather than propagate the belief that there is only *one* hero, who is ordained by God, history, the Party, or some outside force that works in ways ordinary people must not challenge, America's

INDIVIDUALISM

most memorable popular films propagate the belief that heroism is within the reach of every individual human being — "You, too, can be a hero."

This is one of the reasons ideologues and true believers in politics and religion frequently express disdain or even hatred for American popular movies — such movies threaten their beliefs about where power lies or where they *want* it to lie.

(See also: HEROES; HEROINES; POWER)

INDIVIDUATION IS THE term Jungian psychologists use for the process of becoming an autonomous mature adult. It is a process that lies at the heart of most memorable stories.

In real life, we are all the product of our parents and families, our communities, our biological inheritance, and our times. The hero in fiction, however, is not merely the sum of all these parts; he must *transcend* them, find an authentic self. The hero is autogenic — in some important way, he creates himself. That is partly *why* we consider him a hero.

(See also: TRANSFORMATION; COMING-OF-AGE FILMS; MISSIONS; HEROES)

INDIVIDUATION

INGENUITY

INGENUITY IS ESPECIALLY treasured by Americans, but it has also been one of the requirements of heroes since ancient times.

In *Raiders of the Lost Ark,* Indiana Jones finds himself cornered in a bazaar by a swordsman wielding a scimitar. He's holding his favorite weapon, his whip, but he thinks a moment and then pulls out his gun and plugs the swordsman. As the scene demonstrates, ingenuity is often closely allied with wit. Both are the result of being able to "think on your feet," of being flexible and courageous enough to rely on your gut instinct.

Tests of ingenuity are frequent in popular films because it's one of the ways in which the central character can prove he has what it takes to *be* a hero.

(See also: TRAPS; BISOCIATION; INCONGRUITY)

DRAMA IS, OF course, based on conflict. Many of the most memorable dramatic works deal with an individual whose conflict is not merely with the outside world but within himself. In works such as *Hamlet, Othello, Macbeth,* and *Death of a Salesman,* the central character's inner conflict may be even more important than his outer conflict.

But film focuses on what we can see and hear — the exteriorization of thoughts and feelings (see: EXPRESSIONISM). A novelist may write, "He argued with himself over…." and the reader accepts the oppositional feelings, attitudes, or thoughts that are then expressed.

But what can the filmmaker *show* that would reveal a character arguing with himself? What would the audience *hear*? In some films, the actor talks to a mirror, or some other gimmick is found to express the contradictory voices in his head, but it is difficult to think of a scene in which such devices did not feel stagy and ineffective.

One way to express inner conflict is to use a voice-over narration, in which the narrator talks *about* the character's interior struggles, but we do not actually see anything that would lead us to understand the conflict (see: ACTING). Sometimes, the narrator is one of the central characters, who reveals the inner conflicts that he could not at the time reveal, as when Walter Neff dictates a long memo to his boss Barton Keyes in *Double Indemnity.*

In other cases, the narration is directed towards a character who never actually enters the film. *Amadeus* conveys the inner conflict of Salieri,

INNER CONFLICTS

the actual central character of the film, through an ongoing dialogue with God. In *Platoon*, Chris Taylor writes letters to his grandmother. *Apocalypse Now*, like many other films with narrations, is held together by the voice-over narration of the central character. But he's not talking to God, nor to his grandma — who is he talking to?

The answer is, of course, the audience. *Apocalypse Now* demonstrates what is true of all narrations used to express inner conflicts: there doesn't necessarily *need* to be a concrete second party because the narration consists almost entirely of exposition, in which a character *talks* about things that are dramatized on the screen.

Herein lies the danger of inner conflicts: since they *remain* inner, they defy the primary injunction of film, "Show don't tell."

(See also: Narratives and Narrations; Exposition)

As THE TWENTIETH century drew to a close, librarians across America were asked to name the best novel of the century. *To Kill a Mockingbird* placed first. When the American Film Institute conducted a poll to determine the top fifty film heroes, the film's central character, Atticus Finch, placed first. But, while Finch is the active agent in both the novel and film, the story is seen through the innocent eyes of his six-year-old daughter "Scout," who recollects the events years later in a voice-over narration. *To Kill a Mockingbird, Snow White and the Seven Dwarfs, The Wizard of Oz, Bambi, E.T., The Lion King,* and a host of other memorable popular films involve youths struggling with a crisis in which they will lose their innocence. When the character is an adolescent, as in *Rebel Without a Cause* and *American Graffiti*, we label it a "Coming-of-Age" story. But there are also many memorable popular films about a grown-up who goes through a similar process. Tom Joad in *The Grapes of Wrath* is certainly a mature adult, but what he goes through is similar to the other films mentioned: he loses his innocence. The loss of innocence is one of the great themes in fiction (and life).

Innocence comes from the Latin root, *nocence*, from which "noxious," or poisonous, also derives. Since its prefix negates what follows, someone who is innocent has not been poisoned … yet.

Parents and society try to shield children from things that they fear will corrupt or poison their bodies and mind, which is the rationale for keeping them from alcohol, tobacco, caffeine, pornography,

INNOCENCE

certain kinds of music, video games, and movies. But these prohibitions have the result that children are innocents, not because of their own choice, but through lack of opportunity.

Innocence often evokes a sense of loss (see: Loss), but we might note that sometimes innocence is not lost, it's given up — people *want* knowledge, even if it threatens to poison them.

The audience loves innocence, which is why so many child actors and child characters have been favorites. It also loves actors that seem to maintain a sense of innocence despite being full-fledged adults, such as Audrey Hepburn, Doris Day, Julia Roberts, and, as often been observed, even Marilyn Monroe.

(See also: CORRUPTION; COMING-OF-AGE FILMS)

INTELLIGENCE

IN DRAMA, INTELLIGENCE consists mostly of the ability to meet the unknown or the unexpected, what in another context is called "street smarts." No dramatic hero ever learned anything important in a book or in school.

So, what are you doing reading this book? Your answer demonstrates that the principles we follow in movies are not the principles we follow in life.

(See also: POWER; INGENUITY)

INTENTIONALITY

A CHARACTER IS waiting for a bus in an endless expanse of cornfields somewhere in the American Midwest. He's bored and impatient. The noise of an airplane is heard on the soundtrack. He notices it; we notice it. The sound continues and gets louder until finally the man looks up and expresses alarm as a crop-dusting plane comes right at him. He looks around for a place to hide but there is none and so he starts running for his life. It's one of the most memorable and exciting scenes in Alfred Hitchcock's *North by Northwest*.

Now imagine that two lovers are walking through a park and we hear birds chirping and children playing and, then, barely audibly, there is the sound of an airplane. It doesn't get louder, and many people don't even notice it, but the sound is noticed by a man wearing earphones who is off camera and paying careful attention to such things, and he signals a man standing next to the camera that is filming the two lovers. The director shrieks, "CUT!" and curses the wasted time and money the passing airplane caused.

Imagine that you go up to the director and point out that planes fly overhead everywhere in America and everybody knows this, hears them, but pays no attention, so there really was no need stop in the middle of an expensive scene. He may, in turn, ask you what planet you are from.

The director yelled "Cut" because he knows that fictional films are based on the Principle of Intentionality: *everything* has meaning, and *nothing* "just happens." If he allowed the sound of a passing airplane on the soundtrack, the audience would assume it *did* mean something.

It's the same logic that forces studios to pay considerable sums to extras to walk or drive down the street in the background, even if they're out of focus and don't say a word. In the world of movies, unlike life, there are no accidents or inadvertencies, and the contract between filmmaker and audience states that *everything* we see and hear is there for a purpose.

(See also: ACCIDENTS; FOURTH WALL)

INTERFACE

As ANYONE WHO uses a computer, drives a car, works with other people, or has a family knows, most of the problems we experience in life are the result of the interface between two or more elements.

This is why television dramatic series generally involve people in hospitals, police forces, the military, law firms, and schools — institutions where many different people interface with one another over a crisis in their lives. The more people interface with one another and with institutions, the more conflict there will be and the greater potential for telling interesting stories.

(See also: FRONTIERS; CONFLICT; TELEVISION VS. FILM)

THE HERO IS almost always an intermediary, someone who mediates between different social groups, between man and nature, man and God, or some other constellation of forces. Moses, Jesus, Mohammed, The Buddha, Prometheus, Joan of Arc, Lawrence of Arabia, Gandhi, Michael Corleone, Luke Skywalker, and Oskar Schindler were all intermediaries, people who did not belong totally within the family or community they were originally a part of, and were, partly as a consequence, able to *go between* their original group and some other.

INTER-MEDIARIES

Intermediaries are powerful because they are useful — *because* they can go between different communities. Villains, by contrast, are usually well-integrated into their communities, and are often members of its power structure. *They* belong; heroes don't.

Intermediaries, as most of the examples above demonstrate, are often viewed as outsiders by the groups between which they mediate. To be an intermediary is to always be lonely, because you never truly *belong*.

One of the recurrent paradoxes of heroes is that they so often successfully mediate between contending cultures or value systems, but they often cannot mediate between contending forces within themselves. Lawrence of Arabia wants to help the Arabs recapture their former glory, but as the story unfolds, he also wants his own personal glory. Luke Skywalker wants to be a Jedi Knight but he is also attracted to the dark side that his father succumbed to. Oskar Schindler likes the power and wealth he gets when he is embraced by the Nazis, but he struggles with his conscience when he begins to realize what they are doing to the Jews. The intermediary is almost invariably trapped *between* the contending forces — which, for purposes of drama, is just fine (see: TRAPS).

Many people have had the experience of being intermediaries in that most mythical, powerful, and vividly remembered of places: the family. Because of the biological process that led to our creation, each of us mediates between two different, often contending people: our parents. All of us are also caught in the middle of three different, contending generations — the one that came before us, our own generation, and the one that will come after us.

In the modern world, many people feel the loneliness and inner conflict of being intermediaries, that they don't really belong to their families, their society, their nation or, most anguishing of all, to themselves. This emotional quandary explains why we so easily identify with people who are trapped between contending forces: ultimately, we are all intermediaries.

(See also: INNER CONFLICTS; FAMILY; HEROES, SINGLE; HEROINES)

FILM IS PERHAPS the most intimate medium ever
invented. The closeup can produce an image that
fills the visual field in a way that is analogous to
the experience of a child at its mother's breast or
of two lovers in bed. Slow motion creates a sense
of intimacy by enabling us to see more clearly the
relationship between time and space and between
people or objects as they move within them.
Multiple camera angles allow the audience to see
relationships between characters and objects in ways
that are not possible in real life.

Intimacy works on a psychological as well as
a perceptual level. The conventional coverage of
violence and death in war, gangster, and science fiction films is usually through long or medium shots.
In horror films, however, intimacy with violence is
crucial to the effect of horror, which is why deaths
are almost invariably shot "up close and personal"
— people are killed through the use of knives, stran-
gulation, or, as in *The Exorcist,* through that most
intimate and horrifying of acts, possession.

As Charles Foster Kane whispers his dying
word near the opening of *Citizen Kane,* we are as
close to the central character as it is possible to be.
In *The Godfather,* Luca Brasi is strangled close up
and the corrupt cop, McCluskey, is shot in the face
at point-blank range; Michael's brother-in-law,
Carlo, is strangled from behind within the con-
fines of a closed automobile sitting in Michael's
driveway. In *The Wild Bunch,* which introduced
slow-motion violence to American audiences,
a man on horseback crashes through a window,

and we watch the glass shatter in slow motion. Throughout the film we see closeup spurts of blood as bullets tear their victims' flesh, and near the end, a slow-motion telephoto shot zooms into the villain's face as a bullet hits him between the eyes.

The ability of film to create intimate effects is complemented on the level of storytelling by devices such as voice-over narration, and, of course, by music. Intimacy, however it is obtained, can be very powerful, and it is no wonder that so many films strive for it on as many levels as possible.

INTUITION AND INSIGHT stem from the same linguistic root and are psychologically related qualities, referring to the ability to see what's important, to recognize the true nature of things. Some people seem to have a lot, and others don't, so where does it come from?

INTUITION AND INSIGHT

Obi-Wan Kenobi and Yoda in the *Star Wars* series are both exemplars of intuition and insight. But these are not qualities they were born with or acquired in books or in the classroom. They were acquired "the hard way" — from experience. It is one of the lessons in the *Star Wars* series — and in many another memorable popular film.

(See also: WISDOM)

IRONY

AT THE END of *Dr. Strangelove*, Major T. J. "King" Kong uses old-fashioned American ingenuity and perseverance to free a stuck nuclear warhead at the last possible moment. It plummets to earth with Major Kong riding it like a bucking bronco and reaches its detonation point over a Russian city, unleashing the "Doomsday Machine" that will explode nuclear warheads around the world and lead to the destruction of civilization. As the gigantic mushroom cloud rises, we hear Vera Lynn singing the famous sentimental ballad from World War II, "We'll Meet Again." At the end of *The Silence of the Lambs*, the cannibal, Hannibal Lecter, has escaped and calls Clarice Starling to chat, ringing off by saying he must go because "I'm having an old friend for dinner." These are two of the great ironic moments in film history.

Irony is the art of saying one thing and meaning another. The problem is, how do we *know* someone is saying one thing but really meaning another? This is especially difficult in film, in which the truism is "Show, don't tell." How is it possible to *show* one thing and *mean* another?

Much of what we call art and intelligence involves understanding hidden or ambiguous meanings. Poetry depends on it, and so does religion. A good proportion of the most powerful communications we create as individuals and as a species relies on saying one thing but meaning another.

(See also: PARADOX; DUALITY; BISOCIATION; DECEPTION; MISDIRECTION)

J

*We don't go to films just to see
the world; we go to see a just world.*

JOKES

IN REAL LIFE, we laugh with our ears infinitely more often than with our eyes — verbal humor is perhaps ten times as common as visual humor.

There are three basic kinds of verbal humor:

1) the single sentence, wisecrack, quip, or pun;
2) the gag; and
3) the joke or comic story.

Jokes have a minimum of two elements:

1) The situation or setup, which, in itself, often isn't funny.
2) The punch line, which is.

For example, in *Casablanca*, Ugarte comes to Rick Blaine with the famous "Letters of Transit," which he hopes will impress Rick. Ugarte says: "You despise me, don't you?"

To which Rick responds: "If I gave it any thought, I probably would."

Jokes frequently have a three-stage structure. When Captain Renault asks Rick Blaine what brought him to Casablanca Rick replies: "My health. I came to Casablanca for the waters."

Renault replies: "The waters? What waters? We're in the desert."

To which Rick shrugs and says: "I was misinformed."

The reason jokes so often have a three-stage structure is that it takes a minimum of two elements to establish a pattern, and the third element, the "punch line," reverses the progression, surprising us and making us laugh.

There are many jokes in *Casablanca*, as there are in a great many memorable popular films. The frequency with which jokes appear is, in fact, one of the distinguishing features of popular memorable American films.

(See also: COMEDY; BISOCIATION; INCONGRUITY; DUALITY)

JOURNEYS

MANY MEMORABLE FILMS — like memorable stories
throughout history — involve a journey. While they
often involve physical movement (the art form, after
all, is called motion pictures), even more important
is the movement in psychological or spiritual terms.
2001 is about a physical journey through space; but
on another level, Dave Bowman's actions prove
that the human race is ready to take the next evo-
lutionary step. Early in *Gandhi*, the title character
begins a journey to the sea, which marks his nation's
long march to independence. The Joads journey to
California to search for a new life in *The Grapes of
Wrath*. In *Thelma & Louise*, the title characters go
on a journey seeking to escape male domination.
Willard goes on a journey up the river in *Apocalypse
Now* that leads to his confrontation with "the horror." Luke Skywalker journeys across space and, in
the process, learns to trust The Force.

The journey of the central character can stretch
all the way across the solar system, as in *2001*, or it
can be as short as the trail from the ranch into town
in *Shane*, or the few blocks from Terry Malloy's
home to the docks in *On the Waterfront* where he
confronts union boss, Johnny Friendly. What is
important in the journey is not the physical distance
but the moral distance the central character covers.

(See also: MISSIONS; MOTIVATION; CALL TO ADVENTURE)

WE DON'T GO to films just to see the world; we go to see a just world.

If, in the beginning, a character has inherited wealth or power that he tries to use as a weapon against other people, we can be sure it will be diminished or lost by the end of the film. If, on the other hand, the character is poor and powerless in the beginning but tries to help people other than himself, we can be sure he'll acquire power before the end. If a woman is alone but is a nice person or is easy on the eye, we can be sure she'll find someone to love her by the end. Movies are one of the few places in modern life where things constantly work out the way we *want* them to work out.

One of the things that bind us to the Corleone family as we watch *The Godfather* is that Vito Corleone from the very beginning demonstrates his concern for — and understanding of — the concept of justice. In the first scene, an undertaker tells Vito about two young men who have beaten his daughter and "tried to take advantage of her." When Vito asks what the undertaker wants him to do, the man whispers something into his ear, but Vito responds, "That is not justice."

Justice is usually portrayed as holding scales because justice requires a sense of proportion —the punishment must fit the crime. As Vito points out, "Your daughter is still alive," so the request for the death of two young men is out of proportion.

In *High Noon*, *Dirty Harry*, *Casablanca,* and countless other films that climax with the death of the villain, that death is well-deserved and justice has been served.

In westerns, war, horror, science fiction, and other genres with a lot of death, the bad character kills people. But so, too, does the hero. So, what's the difference between them? The villain does it for his own power, self-aggrandizement, or fulfillment of some dark inner need. The hero, however, does it for other people, a cause, or the community. The villain is a killer; the hero is an executioner.

To be memorable, a film does not have to have a happy ending. It does, however, require a just one.

(See also: SUSPENSION OF DISBELIEF; ENDINGS, HAPPY)

In movies, nothing useful
ever comes of time spent in school.

KNOWLEDGE

AMONG THE POWERS a character can possess are education, knowledge, intelligence, intuition, and wisdom. In real life, people get as much education as they are capable of, can afford, or can stand, and the pedigrees that are awarded upon completion of an M.B.A., Ph.D., law school, med school, or other discipline generally entitle one to enhanced income, prestige, desirability as a mate, and power in the community.

In movies, however, nothing useful ever comes of time spent in school, which is why the only professor to be a lead character in a very popular film was Indiana Jones in *Raiders of the Lost Ark* — and he gets out of the classroom about twenty minutes into the film.

In the gangster film, the fancy lawyer or shrewd accountant is a necessary tool of the gang boss, but he's a corrupt, sniveling fool who neither gets nor deserves any respect. In war films, the kid with the West Point education may lord it over the GIs, but he invariably is taught a lesson and either ends up dead or wises up in the trenches, where he has to *earn* his right to lead.

It goes without saying that the hero is intelligent, but the kind of intelligence he displays is not the kind that wins high scores on SATs. Terry Malloy in *On the Waterfront* and Rocky Balboa in *Rocky* would not strike any college admissions committee as promising material, but each has "street smarts" and insight. Terry demonstrates this in the famous taxicab scene when he realizes both what his brother has done to his life, and that he himself has become a bum with a "one-way ticket to palooka-ville." Rocky, when he's first offered the chance to fight Apollo Creed, declines and wisely says, "I'm not that kind of fighter." Both Terry and Rocky possess self-knowledge, the most valuable knowledge of all — the kind the second lieutenant and a lot of other educated hotshots never seem to have.

(See also: POWER; WISDOM; INTUITION AND INSIGHT)

L

*A very large proportion of America's most
memorable films are permeated by loss.*

LAUGHTER

WE LOVE TO laugh and we love people who make us laugh. This is why so many business and political leaders often begin a speech with a joke, and why the most popular presidents in American history were the ones noted for their sense of humor.

The same principle applies to the creation of memorable popular characters. Some people in the audience may not especially like Margo Channing in *All About Eve*, but her wit binds them to her. Harry Callahan in *Dirty Harry*, the title character in *The Terminator,* and a host of other characters who never smile are nonetheless loved by their audiences because they make *them* smile.

Laughter is the most powerful tool for producing empathy ever invented. There is no such thing as a film that has too many laughs.

(See also: COMEDY; JOKES; IDENTIFICATION)

LENGTH

IN THE 1920s, feature films were often only an hour long and for the next fifty or sixty years, they averaged ninety minutes. In the latter part of the twentieth century, they grew to an average of 120 minutes. It would be impossible to claim, however, that as films got longer, they got better.

D.W. Griffith made two films that were considerably longer than the average of their day — *The Birth of a Nation* (1915) and *Intolerance* (1916) were both around three hours long. The first was an enormous success, the second a failure, and while few said *The Birth of a Nation* was too long, many people complained that *Intolerance* seemed interminable. Erich von Stroheim destroyed his career in part by making *Greed* (1924) eight hours long, and then when he couldn't get away with that, cutting it to four and insisting he couldn't cut any more. On the other hand, *Gone with the Wind* (1939) was four hours long and still stands as the film with the highest box office in history when you adjust for the value of the dollar.

When *Lawrence of Arabia, The Godfather*, and *The Godfather: Part II* did very well at the box office, some filmmakers seemed to conclude that longer is better, which may explain why the average running time of American films grew by thirty minutes in the period after them.

But the most memorable films nearly always adhere to the Principle of Parsimony, using no more lines, characters, scenes, and time than are absolutely required. Some stories are, to be sure, so complex, rich, and dense that they require more time. But consuming more time has no relationship to achieving timelessness.

(See also: ELEGANCE)

HEROISM IS NOT the same thing as leadership. The
hero is, in fact, most often a loner, which is not
very good training for leadership. Leaders do not
necessarily get in front of people and urge them
to follow; rather, they are often like generals who
stay behind and urge people forward. Heroes, on
the other hand, are the people at the front of the
line, yelling, "Charge!" and hoping people will
follow them.

LEADERS

In real life, such people are often dead by morning. In film, they're usually still alive, but like Will
Kane, the sheriff in *High Noon*, they're *still* alone.
Loners can't be leaders, But then, if you're a hero,
you don't need to be.

(See also: HEROES, SINGLE)

LOSS

THE SACRED TEXTS of all three major western religions are obsessed with loss, as are a good proportion of the world's memorable poems, novels, and films.

The loss of something important is often the true beginning of the film's story or it ends the story — often both. Like Paris in *Casablanca*, loss is often the backstory (see: BACKSTORY) that propels the present action. *Citizen Kane,* as the reporter Thompson says at the end of the film, is the story of "a man who got everything he wanted, and then lost it."

The introductory scroll of *Gone with the Wind* sets up the story we are about to see: "Look for it only in books, for it is no more than a dream remembered, a civilization gone with the wind...." Sam Spade at the end of *The Maltese Falcon* says to his lover, Brigid O'Shaughnessy, as he turns her over to the police, "I'll always remember you." Alvy Singer's story in *Annie Hall* is all about his loss of the title character. Early in *Lawrence of Arabia*, Lawrence reminds Prince Feisal that his people were once great, and when Feisal says, "Nine centuries ago," Lawrence responds, "Time to be great again, my lord." But by the end of the film, the greatness Lawrence hoped to bring the Arabs is lost.

Star Wars begins "a long time ago" and constantly evokes the sense of loss, referring back to a golden age when all Jedi Knights owed allegiance to the good side of The Force. Even before he did *Star Wars*, George Lucas was obsessed with loss. While working earlier on his screenplay for *American Graffiti* — that testament to the irrevocable passing of youth — he wrote, "Why can't things remain the way they are?"

E.T., *The Wizard of Oz*, *Snow White and the Seven Dwarfs*, *Bambi*, *Pinocchio*, *Peter Pan*, *The Lion King*, *Toy Story*, *Finding Nemo,* and virtually every other memorable children's story deal with parents, friends, or other valuable things the central characters have lost. Atticus Finch in *To Kill a Mockingbird* is a widower left to raise his children all alone, which is also true for Captain von Trapp in *The Sound of Music*. Forrest Gump spends his whole life yearning for Jenny, but as soon as he gets her and they produce a child, she dies, leaving him haunted by her memory. Mozart, in *Amadeus*, grieves over the loss of his father; Rose Sayer in *The African Queen* grieves over the loss of her brother. All three of the tough guys at the center of *Dirty Harry,* *Lethal Weapon,* and *Unforgiven* grieve over the loss of their wives.

Loss and memory go together, and the number of memorable films that evoke or are explicitly *about* memory is astonishing. This is because memory itself deals with that which is lost; if something is still present, there is no need for memory. On the other hand, if we lose our memories, who are we? The recognition of the crucial role memory plays in defining our humanity explains why Alzheimer's is often considered the worst of diseases.

A very large proportion of America's most memorable films are permeated by loss. It is the great universal theme, the emotion that everyone can identify with and be moved by.

(See also: LOVE; SACRIFICE; TRIALS; TESTS)

FRANK CAPRA ONCE said that all the world's great stories are love stories, and as long as we don't take that too literally, he may well have been right.

Love doesn't have to be sexual, although there are critics who insist on looking for it in every close-knit team in film history, especially if they are of the same gender. There are other kinds of love, equally powerful. The early parts of *It's a Wonderful Life* and *The Godfather* present sons who dearly love their fathers; *The Grapes of Wrath* has at its core the love of mother and son; *E.T.* is about the love of an earthling and a spaceling.

The paradox of love is that, the more you give away, the more you have to give — a lesson that George Bailey learns at the end of *It's a Wonderful Life* but that Charles Foster Kane never learns in *Citizen Kane*, which is why the film is a tragedy.

Something dies, though, in the act of love, which is why the French sometimes refer to a sexual climax as *le petit mort*. What is lost in love is a sense of the self as an autonomous being; what is born is a sense of a new self that is a part of a whole. People who are totally wrapped up in their own egos and are afraid to surrender themselves have reason to fear this strange and new state of being.

Love stories need to be distinguished from romances. In films, as in much of the world's literature, love stories frequently end with loss caused by the separation or death of the lovers, whereas romances, perhaps by definition, end with their unification (see: ROMANCE).

We have "a love story" when the participants
enrich each other's lives. We have its opposite, a
"war story," when the participants diminish each
other. The relationship between Adam and Carl
Trask, the father and son in *East of Eden*, and of
Stanley Kowalski and Blanche DuBois in *A Streetcar
Named Desire* seem to resemble other love stories,
but the relationships between the characters is one
in which each diminishes, rather than enriches,
the other.

People sometimes think their problem is that
they are unloved, when the real problem is that they
are unable to love. Scarlett O'Hara in *Gone with The
Wind*, Michael Dorsey in *Tootsie*, Clyde Barrow in
Bonnie and Clyde, and Charles Foster Kane in *Citizen
Kane* all demonstrate the dramatic potential of being
trapped inside oneself (see: NARCISSUS).

Before an audience can believe that two characters have fallen in love with each other, it must first
itself have fallen in love with the characters. *Gone
with The Wind*, *Casablanca*, and *Annie Hall* are on
many people's list of memorable love stories because
people find something to love in both the male and
female protagonists. The failure of certain love stories and romances are sometimes explained as being
due to the lack of "chemistry" between the two
actors; more often, however, it is lack of chemistry
between the characters and the audience.

Because romantic love is commonly thought of
as an attraction, chemical or magnetic analogies are
often used. As we know from physics and chemistry, the commonest way to prevent a chemical

or magnetic bond from forming — or to disrupt it once it has — is through a third force. The same principle holds true for storytelling, which is why love stories so often involve three-way relationships. *Gone with the Wind*'s triangle places Ashley Wilkes between Rhett and Scarlett. In *Casablanca*, Victor Laszlo is the third force that prevents Rick Blaine and Ilsa Lund from permanently bonding.

But the oppositional force that creates the triangle doesn't necessarily have to be another person. Lovers can wrestle with a social force that keeps them apart (*West Side Story* and *Guess Who's Coming to Dinner)*, with career and professional aspirations (*A Star Is Born* and *Annie Hall*), with a dark secret (*Chinatown*), or with the psychological (but never the physical) incapacity of one of them (*Bonnie and Clyde*).

Often, a character is pulled on the one hand by his love for another person and on the other by his need to do "what a man's gotta do." The best-selling theme song of *High Noon* repeats over and over again the dilemma of many heroes who love: he's "torn twixt love and duty."

Underlying all love stories is the exchange of gifts. In *Harold and Maude*, for example, Maude offers Harold wisdom and balance, while Harold offers Maude a sense of hope that she will have contributed to something that will outlive her. Lovers don't merely give one another gifts; love is *about* the exchange of gifts.

(See also: GIFTS; ROMANCE; LOVE; LOSS; LOVE, UNREQUITED)

LOVE, UNREQUITED

UNREQUITED LOVE EXISTS when one person loves another, but the person who is loved never returns the feeling. It is always a painful experience, and while it is often seen in life, it is almost entirely absent from any list of memorable popular films. The lovers may die, as in *Love Story* and *West Side Story*, or separate as in *Casablanca* and *Annie Hall*, and while this may be sad, it is not unrequited love because the love *was* returned.

When someone says, "I love you" and the other person says, "Drop dead, you jerk!" it is invariably early in the film; when the character repeats the line at the end of the film, it is invariably the prelude to falling into each other's arms. Rhett Butler tells Scarlett O'Hara early in *Gone with the Wind* that he hopes some day to hear her declare that she loves him. He waits nearly four hours for her to finally say it, but when she finally does near the end of the movie, his response is, "Frankly, my dear, I don't give a damn." However, *Gone with the Wind* is not about unrequited love — it's about love that takes a long time to be requited. Unrequited love is, to repeat, a love that is never returned — and it is almost entirely absent from memorable popular films.

What we frequently see in popular movies is not unrequited *love* but unrequited *sex*. In comedies such as *Some Like It Hot*, *The Graduate*, *Tootsie*, and a host of others, the laughter does not revolve around people falling in love; it revolves around people falling into bed.

It is not love that is funny; it is sex. If this is true, then we might expect to find the opposite is true for tragedy — and we do. There are few "sex tragedies" but there are many "love tragedies" as *Medea, Othello, Romeo and Juliet, A Streetcar Named Desire* and many other memorable plays, novels, and films demonstrate.

(See also: LOVE; ROMANCE)

LOYALTY

FRIENDSHIPS AND OTHER intimate relationships are based on two precepts: love and loyalty. Where there is love, there is automatically loyalty. Where there is only loyalty, there is seldom love. This is why gangs such as the Corleones and the gangs that sometimes run countries spend so much time worrying about loyalty — when loyalty stems from fear, it is not likely to last.

The fabric of all human alliances is woven from trust, and once that trust is broken, the foundation of the family, marriage, community, or society begins to crumble. That's why the relationship between loyalty and betrayal is so important in memorable films such as *Gone with the Wind, Casablanca, Star Wars, The Sound of Music, E.T.*, and *The Godfather*.

When there is a story dealing with a team, whether they are partners, lovers, warriors or some other close social unit, much of the first half of the story is customarily devoted to the *formation* of that team, to their learning to trust one another.

Loyalty is one of the highest of human achievements; it is the bedrock of any relationship between individuals or between individuals and institutions, community, and country. That is why its development is so important to so many memorable stories.

(See also: BETRAYAL; TEAMS AND COUPLES)

M

In films as in life, we only raise questions of motivation when something doesn't happen the way we think it should have happened.

MANIPULATION

WE DON'T USUALLY complain about manipulation when we find a comedian who makes us laugh, when a magician astonishes us, when a religious or political leader inspires us, or when a teacher opens our eyes.

When we complain about manipulation, what we are usually saying is that we have successfully *resisted* what the comedian, magician, leader, or politician was trying to get us to do. Often, it as much a comment on us as it is on them.

The arrival of the cavalry at the most desperate moment in *The Birth of a Nation* and *Stagecoach* excited audiences in their day, but now seem unduly contrived. The "Meet Cute" — when a boy and a girl who don't know each other bend over to pick up something they've dropped and then fall madly in love as soon as they look up into each other's eyes — can produce a groan because the manipulation is so clichéd.

Knowing how to manipulate an audience is far more important than knowing how to manipulate the technology of film. This is why so many of the most creative film directors — Griffith, Eisenstein, Welles, and Coppola, for example — came from the theater. Theatrical training didn't prepare them to use the tools and techniques of film; it did, however, prepare them to think in terms of audience responses, to understand that drama is based on manipulating hearts and minds.

(See also: SENTIMENTALITY)

ALFRED HITCHCOCK COINED the term "McGuffin" (which has been spelled several different ways) to describe what others have called "the weenie" — a plot device whose function is to get the action going, but which may be forgotten or become irrelevant by the end of the story. Marion Crane in *Psycho*, for example, steals money from her employer early in the film, and this leads her to go on the lam, which is what brings her to the Bates Motel. But the money — and Marion — disappear halfway through the film, and by the end, nobody knows or cares about what happened to the money. In *North by Northwest*, the McGuffin is the non-existent government spy, "George Kaplan," who has something to do with "government secrets."

MCGUFFIN

The term "McGuffin" has sometimes been applied to any object that triggers the plot of a film. *The Maltese Falcon*, for example, is centered on the battle to acquire the statue referred to in the film's title, even though at the very end it turns out to be a worthless fake. "Rosebud" in *Citizen Kane*, the "letters of transit" in *Casablanca*, the Ark of the Covenant in *Raiders of the Lost Ark* are all objects pursued by all the characters in these films. But Hitchcock's point about the McGuffin is that it *starts* the story and is then forgotten or turns out to be insignificant. In the examples just cited, the objects remain important until the very end of the film.

MECHANICAL BEHAVIOR

THE FRENCH PHILOSOPHER, Henri Bergson, formulated an influential theory of comedy that contended that humor is based on "the mechanical encrusted on the living." When human behavior begins to resemble that of a machine, he said, we find it funny.

The principle characteristic of a machine is that it is supposed to do the same thing in the same way over and over again, that is, "mechanically." A machine that does *not* do the same thing in the same way, would, by definition, be a bad machine. However, a human who acts "mechanically" is a ripe subject for humor.

The parent, teacher, boss, or other authority figure who uses the same gestures or clichés over and over again, the dirty old man who can't stop leering at every passing female long after he's lost the ability to do anything about it, the drunk who staggers the same way and slurs his words when he overindulges, all provide examples of mechanical behavior. Charles Chaplin, Buster Keaton, Harold Lloyd, the Marx Brothers, Laurel and Hardy, and many other popular comedians in film and television relied on mechanical behavior. Dr. Strangelove's mechanical arm that rises as he screams, "Mein Fuehrer!" is one of the most famous examples of a human being who acts like a machine.

The mechanical encrusted on the living, however, can also be a source of horror. Dracula behaves mechanically when the sun sets, and the Wolf Man and other victims of lycanthropy become raging beasts whenever the full moon comes out. Norman

Bates in *Psycho* "can't help himself" and becomes
a cog in a horrible psychic machine. The shark in
Jaws, the dinosaurs in *Jurassic Park*, the creatures in
Alien, the title character in *The Terminator*, and the
long list of serial killers in modern films all demonstrate what can happen when the mechanical
becomes encrusted on the living — and how it can
be used *either* for humor or horror.

MENTORS

MENTOR WAS AN actual guy — well, at least that's what Homer said in describing the wise and trusted friend that Odysseus relied on to raise his son in *The Odyssey*. "Mentor" and "mental" come from the root meaning "to think" and this is what mentors in storytelling urge their mentees to do instead of being haphazardly heroic. Obi-Wan Kenobi is Luke Skywalker's mentor in the first episode of *Star Wars*, and Yoda, who embodies that sure-fire combination of ugliness with cuteness, is his mentor in *The Empire Strikes Back* and later episodes in the series. As he had done with Luke's father, Yoda teaches Luke the ways of the Jedi Knight.

In Oliver Stone's *Platoon*, Private Chris Taylor is, like Luke Skywalker, torn between two mentors, Elias, who represents the good side, and Barnes, who represents the Dark Side. In Oliver Stone's *Wall Street*, Bud Fox is torn between two mentors — Gordon Gekko, whose motto is "Greed is Good," and his father.

Putting an innocent young person (see:INNOCENCE) between two mentors and forcing him to choose sides is a common device because it does what drama always seeks to do: trap the central character and force him to make a decision (see: DECISIONS).

Mentors are usually parents, surrogate parents, or even lovers (see: PYGMALION). In *Titanic*, Jack Dawson is the good mentor to Rose DeWitt, and he helps her reject her bad mentors, her mother, and her fiancé.

Mentors are handy to have around in films and in life. But why do Obi-Wan Kenobi in *Star Wars*, Barnes in *Platoon* and Jack Dawson in *Titanic* all die?

Because, as long as the mentor is around, the danger is that the mentee will remain a student and not become a hero.

The first job of heroes is to stand on their own two feet. In *High Noon*, Marshall Will Kane knocks on the doors of several people he thought were his friends looking for help in the coming gunfight with the bad guys. But no one gives it, not even his mentor, the previous sheriff. Of course not; how could Gary Cooper's character *become* the hero he does if he had help?

The true test of whether mentors, parents, teachers, or other helping characters have been effective occurs not when they're mentoring but when they're no longer around. At the end of *Star Wars*, when Luke is in mortal danger and appears about to be destroyed by Darth Vader, Luke's memory of the words of Obi-Wan Kenobi come back to him: "The Force, Luke. Trust the force." It is only because he has *internalized* Obi-Wan's lesson that Luke lives on to make five sequels.

(See also: FOIL CHARACTERS)

MISDIRECTION

FILMS OFTEN USE one of the principles of magic: misdirection. When the magician instructs the audience to watch carefully as he performs some feat, what he is directing the audience to pay attention to is not where the actual trick will be; it will occur where they are *not* watching. In *The Maltese Falcon*, most of the characters and the audience are paying attention to the question of who has the statue that gives the film its title. Sam Spade, however, is focused on finding the person who killed his partner, Miles Archer, in the first scene of the film. In most Hitchcock films, the central character and the audience reach one conclusion after another about who's done what and on whose behalf, but a lot of it is proven wrong. Misdirection is a frequent and powerful storytelling device. In the most interesting stories, things are never what they seem.

(See also: DECEPTION; MANIPULATION; McGUFFIN)

MISSION COMES FROM the Latin word meaning "to
send out," so when someone sees himself or is seen
by others as having a mission, that person is obeying
orders from a higher power — which is why missions are so often found in religions and war.

A mission is something outside the self, something *greater* than the self. Gandhi had it, but Charles
Foster Kane didn't — which may explain why
Gandhi died surrounded by people and Kane died
alone. Tom Joad didn't have it at the beginning of
The Grapes of Wrath nor did Terry Malloy at the
beginning of *On the Waterfront* or J.P. McMurphy
in *One Flew Over the Cuckoo's Nest*, but by the end,
they all had one. When we first meet Father Karras
in *The Exorcist,* he is telling a fellow priest that he
fears he's lost his faith, but by the end he's not only
regained it, he sacrifices his own life for another.

Missions in war films are not self-generated.
The title characters in *The Dirty Dozen* and the
squad sent out in *Saving Private Ryan* didn't ask for
and certainly didn't *want* their missions, yet most of
them die because of it.

If a character is going to become imbued with
a mission, he usually declares early in the film that
he's only looking out for himself — as the central
characters in *Gone with the Wind, Casablanca,* and
It's a Wonderful Life demonstrate. If, on the other
hand, the character *begins* the film with a mission,
the chances are good that he will, as in *Apocalypse
Now*, *High Noon*, and *Dirty Harry,* reject the group
that inspired it in the beginning.

(See also: RELUCTANCE; CALL TO ADVENTURE;
JOURNEYS; PARADOX; MOTIVATION)

MISSIONS

MODULATION

ANYTHING THAT MOVES through time, whether it is music, a vacation, sex, or a movie, requires modulation, an alternation from fast to slow, from exciting to quiet, from hard to soft,

There are many theories regarding how often modulation needs to occur in films and even what kinds they ought to be. There are those, for example, who say there needs to be a chase or "Big Bang" every seven minutes or some other interval. But when dealing with what is popular — and what is memorable — there are no formulas. All that we can say for sure is that, in films that work best, nothing *stays* the same for very long.

(See also: HABITUATION)

MONSTERS

"THE MONSTROUS IS inimical to the tragic pleasure,"
Aristotle wrote. Maybe so, but there are other kinds
of pleasure. The several versions of *Frankenstein,*
Dracula, King Kong, Jaws, The Terminator, and *Alien*
have all revolved around monsters, and they give
immense pleasure to their audiences, even if, in
Aristotle's terms, they are not tragic.

Human monsters are especially popular.
Hannibal Lecter appeared in two other films besides
The Silence of the Lambs; and *Nightmare on Elm*
Street's Freddie Kruger and *Friday the 13th*'s Jason
Voorhees appeared over and over ... and over ...
again. We never seem to get enough of monsters.

Monsters fascinate audiences, but because they
cannot be allowed to survive, there is often a sense
of pathos surrounding the endings of their stories.
King Kong's last line, "'Twas Beauty killed the
beast," is one of many that express the twinge of
regret we have over the demise of the film's central
character. Perhaps that is why we are so ready to
see them return.

The ancient Hebrews performed a yearly ritual
in which the sins of the tribe were symbolically
loaded onto the back of a goat that was then driven
into the desert. Monsters are often analogous to this
"scapegoat" — they die or are driven out in order
that the community might live.

We don't usually call monsters "heroes" but,
like heroes, monsters are usually intermediaries.
They can be "the undead," like mummies and the
innumerable vampires and versions of the Dracula
story that have been made into films. Such creatures

are not "alive" in the usual sense, but neither are they dead in the usual sense — they live someplace *between* the two.

In the original 1931 version of *Frankenstein*, the monster's creator famously exclaims "It's alive — it's alive!" Frankenstein's monster consists of the parts of several different men, and is doomed because its creator "fooled around with mother nature." The dinosaurs in the *Jurassic Park* series are also the result of fooling around with Mother Nature.

Monsters such as The Wolf Man, who is half-man and half-beast, and The Terminator, who is a machine that is indistinguishable from a man, express the duality and paradox that is found constantly in horror (and religion). If characters like Superman, Spider-Man, and other popular superheroes were not on the side of good, we would recognize that they are in many ways like monsters — part human and part The Other.

(See also: CHIMERAS; ANIPALS; BISOCIATION; DUALITY)

MONTAGE

Pioneers in the medium, such as D.W. Griffith, Dziga Vertov, and Slavko Vorkapich, demonstrated that the montage was one of the most unique and powerful techniques available to filmmakers. Comparable to the collages that artists in the early years of the twentieth century were experimenting with, montages compress a quick succession of multiple images and sounds to cover a long period of time, a sequence of actions, or simply to evoke the feeling and mood of complex events.

Near the end of *The Godfather*, Michael Corleone assumes the duties of a godfather in the baptism of his sister's baby. As he renounces Satan, we see intercut with this sacred ceremony a montage of assassinations that Michael has ordered. Montages are generally assembled in the editing room, rather than written into a screenplay.

(See also: Acting)

MOOD

THE MOOD OF a story is closely related to its attitude (see: ATTITUDE). Mood and attitude do not exist solely within the film itself; if they accomplish their goal, they create a mood or attitude in the audience as well. Comedies, which are usually brightly lit, convey a mood and attitude toward their stories and characters that are quite different from the dark lighting of horror and gangster films, which tend to use a multitude of shadows. The ways in which lines are delivered and scenes directed and edited all contribute to a film's mood and attitude. The music on the soundtrack is almost entirely intended to enhance the audience's mood and attitude. In memorable popular films, moods and attitudes are constantly changing. Filmmakers may want to cause the audience to be fearful, depressed, and/or anxious as the story unfolds, but they do not generally want to *leave* them there.

(See also: ATTITUDE)

MOST DRAMATIC WORKS, like most psychological, philosophical, and political systems of thought, deal with the problem of human causality: Why do we act the way we do? Is the origin of motivation to be found "out there" — in our society, our parents, our race, our class, our sex — in other words, in things over which we have no control? Or is it to be found "in here" — deep inside ourselves?

The search for motivation assumes that human action has a purpose, and if we can figure out what that purpose is, we can understand the action. How often in our own lives have parents, teachers, policemen, and spouses asked us, "Why did you do that?" Is what we might call "The M Question" (for motivation) a genuine search for information, or is it a thinly disguised accusation? We don't ask someone "Why did you do that?" if we approve of what they have done; we only ask the question when we *dis*approve of their behavior.

In films as in life, we only raise questions of motivation when something doesn't happen the way we think it *should have happened*.

(It might be noted, by the way, that we have a thousand theories in the modern era to explain what motivates people to do bad, but very few to explain what motivates them to do good.)

In film, questioning a character's motivation usually indicates something *else* in the film isn't working. It may be that the filmmakers didn't sufficiently prepare the audience for what a character does or the action appears to be "out of character."

But is consistency an absolute requirement of human behavior? Any student of history or psychology knows that human beings are potentially capable of almost anything. Effective films do not necessarily require that great amounts of screen time be devoted to childhood traumas, psychological complexes, character traits, or any of the other ways people try to "explain" motivation.

Little time is spent in *The Godfather* explaining Michael Corleone's motivation. The title characters in *Butch Cassidy and the Sundance Kid* do what they do, but there is no deep explanation for it. The reasons why the members of the gang in *The Wild Bunch* decide to engage in a futile and suicidal rescue at the end are never explored. Popeye Doyle's relentless pursuit in *The French Connection*, Michael Vronsky's return to Vietnam in *The Deer Hunter*, Wyatt and Billy's voyage in *Easy Rider*, the bonding between the central male characters in *Midnight Cowboy* are all crucially important, but they are not "explained."

In most memorable popular films, motivation is not talked about in advance or explained afterwards; it is implicit and integral — something that doesn't *need* explanation. If motivation *does* need to be "explained," there is probably something wrong with the story's structure.

(See also: Backstories; Attitude)

IN NO GENRE is the plot less important than the
musical. In no genre are characters less important
than the musical. This is why, when the American
Film Institute conducted an extensive poll to determine the fifty top heroes and fifty top villains in
American film history, none were from a musical.

The genre called "Westerns" is named after
the geographic location of the story; "Horror
Films" after the emotional effect produced in the
audience; "War Films" after the kind of conflict.
The Musical is the only genre named after one of its
artistic elements.

But the mere presence of music does not make
a film a musical. If it did, nearly every film made
in the United States would have to be considered
one, since even during the Silent Era films were
customarily accompanied by live music when they
were exhibited. Nor does the appearance of songs
necessarily make a film a musical. What makes
a film a musical is the *combination* of orchestral
music, songs, and — in the majority of memorable
musicals — dance.

The importance of dance to the musical is
proven by the fact that, at the top of all lists of the
great stars of musicals are Fred Astaire and Gene
Kelly — people noted for the perfection of their
dancing, not their singing. Conversely, hugely popular singers such as Bing Crosby and Frank Sinatra
had their greatest success in films, not in musicals,
but in other genres.

In no film genre is energy and exuberance as
important as in the musical. Nor is any other genre

as much *fun* as the musical. That is why people who are able to let themselves enjoy something that is not "serious" often find that high at the top of their list of favorite films are one or more musicals. (My own is *Singin' in the Rain*.)

(See also: GENRES; LOVE; ROMANCE)

WITHOUT MYSTERY, IT is almost impossible to tell a
memorable story.

MYSTERY

In storytelling and life, there are two kinds of
mysteries: those that deal with the past and those
that deal with the future. In the most obvious kind
of mystery stories — detective films and thrillers
— the mystery about the past concerns "Who done
it?" and the mystery about the future concerns
"Who's going to be done in?"

Annie Hall, Amadeus, Chinatown, Citizen Kane,
and *Doctor Zhivago* all focus on the mysteries of
the past. In *The Best Years of Our Lives, Casablanca,
The Godfather, The Godfather, Part II, The Maltese
Falcon, The Matrix, One Flew Over the Cuckoo's
Nest, Psycho, The Searchers, Shane, Silence of the
Lambs, Star Wars, A Streetcar Named Desire, Sunset
Boulevard, Unforgiven, The Wild Bunch,* and a host of
others, the past haunts the present and it isn't until
we discover what happened that we fully understand the major characters.

Even when there is no mysterious past, our
interest in the story is maintained by the question,
"What's going to happen next?" If we can predict
what that will be — if there is no mystery — the
story is boring.

There is great power in mystery; conversely,
the powerful seek to clothe themselves in mystery. A mystery, by definition, requires that we be
aware that some powerful knowledge exists that we
do not possess. Mysteries, therefore, deal not with
things that are totally hidden, but with things that
are *obscure*.

The most powerful mysteries are often embodied in words. The Greeks demonstrated this in the Eleusinian Mysteries, rituals that were performed once a year and revealed the secrets of life and death but could never be spoken of. The Hebrews demonstrated this at the Temple, where only the high priest was allowed, once a year, to pronounce the hidden name of God.

The Greek root for the word "mystery" refers to closing one's mouth, which prevents words from being spoken. The word "mustache" may have come from the same root — a mustache obscures the lips that pronounce words, and in popular culture the "man of mystery" has often sported a mustache.

For women, the analog of the mustache may be the veil, which obscures the eyes, which are often referred to as "the window of the soul." Even women who think of themselves as totally modern may don a veil at weddings and funerals, the rituals that mark the entrance into the greatest and most powerful of life's mysteries.

Although all mysteries lead to questions, all questions do not lead to mysteries. What we often call "Mystery Stories" are, in fact, usually "Question Stories," and once we have an answer to the question, the "mystery" disappears.

A true mystery, no matter how much we analyze it, *remains* a mystery. Great films, like all great works of art, are often like that — the more we learn about them, the more we realize that the mystery of their power remains.

(See also: PARADOX; DUALITY; MISDIRECTION; DETECTIVE FILMS; REPETITION)

N

The Echo/Narcissus story elements are
clearly there, just beneath the surface,
for anyone who cares to look.

NAMING

WHEN SOMEONE ASKS, "Who are you?" your first response is usually your name. Names have great power, affecting how people see you. Sean Aloysius O'Fearna changed his name to John Ford, and Schmuel Gelbfisz became Sam Goldwyn. Marion Morrison turned into John Wayne, Archibald Alexander Leach into Cary Grant, and Norma Jean Dougherty into Marilyn Monroe. People never looked at them the same way again.

But renaming also changes how you see yourself. A name can take on the aura of the sacred, which is why in the Hebrew Bible, there is much mystery about God's name, and people's names change when they get involved with the divine, as when Abram is changed into Abraham and Sarai into Sarah. This tradition is carried on in the Christian Bible, where Jesus of Nazareth became The Christ ("The Anointed One") and Saul of Tarsus became Paul. Siddhartha Gautama became The Buddha ("The Enlightened One"), Muhammad ibn Abd Allah became The Prophet, and Mohandas Karamchand Gandhi became Mahatma ("Great Soul") Gandhi.

In the modern era, Nguyen That Thanh changed his name to Ho Chi Minh ("He Who Enlightens"), the founder of modern Vietnam. In Russia, Vladimir Ilyich Ulyanov changed his last name to Lenin (after Lena, the peaceful Siberian river of his exile) and Iosif Vissarionovich Dzhugashvili changed his name to Stalin ("Man of Steel").

Taking a new name is not the same as being given one, so *how* one's name is changed says a great deal about someone's power. Christ, The Buddha,

The Prophet, and The Mahatma had their names *bestowed* upon them by their followers. Ho Chi Minh, Lenin, and Stalin, however, changed their *own* names. The first kind of change demonstrates moral authority, since it is willingly granted by others, the second, merely power or the desire for power.

Because memorable popular films tend to be morality plays, name changes often signal that a character has transcended his former state. In *Lawrence of Arabia*, when Lawrence comes back from having rescued Gasim, Sherif Ali and other Arabs confer on Lawrence a new name, "El Aurens." While that may sound to outsiders merely as the Arabic pronunciation for the protagonist's last name, it is in fact, an honorific.

When someone's name changes during the development of a story or in real life, it invariably connotes a change in moral value and power.

(See also: TRANSCENDENCE)

Narcissus

Most people know that Narcissus was a handsome Greek youth who fell in love with his own image. But if they knew how he got that way, people would recognize that it is a story seen frequently in motion pictures — and in life.

In *Metamorphosis*, the Roman poet Ovid tells us there was once a beautiful nymph named Echo, whom a goddess had cursed by making her incapable of initiating speech — the thing which makes us most human. Echo was only able to *repeat* what others said.

One day, Echo saw Narcissus from afar and immediately fell in love with him. Sensing that someone was present, Narcissus shouted, "Is anybody here?" Echo, poor thing, could only answer back, "Here … here!"

Narcissus tried again, yelling, "Come, come!" but the cursed girl could only echo back, "Come, come!" Like so many other heroes with a high regard for himself, Narcissus was accustomed to giving orders, not taking them, and he became infuriated that this stranger was commanding *him*, so he spurned her.

Echo was so overcome with humiliation and grief that she retreated to a cave, where she wasted away until the only thing left was her voice, which was forever doomed to repeat the words of others.

To punish Narcissus for his excessive pride, or *hubris*, another goddess placed a curse on Narcissus: he would fall in love with his own image in a pool of water but would never find gratification in it. Like Echo, he wasted away from unfulfilled longing and desire.

The tragedy of Narcissus is that the self cannot reach out to another, that the lover is *both* the subject of love and its own object. (Reputedly a common affliction in stories about males.) The tragedy of Echo is that she can only return what comes from outside herself, that she cannot express what lies within her. (Reputedly a common affliction in stories about females.)

Echo and Narcissus are a perfect tragic team. Echo cannot send out anything that is authentically hers, and Narcissus cannot genuinely *receive* anything that is not his. The result for both is sterility — which is always the greatest curse.

The Echo/Narcissus story has not overtly been told in memorable popular films, but its underlying elements are clearly there, just beneath the surface, for anyone who cares to look. It appears in the relationship between Charles Foster Kane and Susan Alexander in *Citizen Kane*, between Michael Corleone and Kay Adams in *The Godfather*, between Alvy Singer and Annie Hall in *Annie Hall* and in a great many other memorable films involving relationships between men and women. Beneath the surface of many a hero there lurks the familiar face of Narcissus, fixated by his own image and unable to hear the voice of anyone else.

(See also: Pygmalion; Love; Romance)

THE POWER OF FILM HOWARD SUBER   273

NARRATIVES AND NARRATIONS

SOME CRITICS, HISTORIANS, and scholars, especially if they were trained in literature, speak of "narrative" in film. Generally, they mean no more than "story." But "story" suggests mere entertainment or even the sort of things one shares with children, while "narrative" connotes substantive stuff, worthy of scholarly explication and analysis.

A narrative, however, is something *told*, and the oldest and truest of observations about films is they are at their best when their makers "show, don't tell."

This problem is revealed when we consider the problem of narration in film. It is axiomatic that a novel is, by definition, a narrative. It is equally axiomatic that a film isn't, or isn't in the same way.

In novels, the narrator is frequently a surrogate for the author. In films, however, a narrator is seldom a surrogate for the filmmaker. Instead, the narrator is usually a character; often, the central figure in the story.

Narration is frequently written after a film is shot, and is often the way the filmmaker rescues a film that was in trouble. *Annie Hall*, for example, was originally titled *Anhedonia*, whose title refers to the inability to experience pleasure, and its central character was Alvy Singer. During the editing of the film, Woody Allen became convinced that the more interesting story was Annie's, so he added material that came directly from one of his old standup comedy routines and a voice-over narration. The narration enabled him to make Annie, not Alvy, the central character. Francis Ford Coppola spent over two years editing the enormous amounts of footage he had shot for *Apocalypse Now*, but it wasn't until he brought in Michael Herr to write a voice-over narration for Willard that the story coalesced into its present form.

In less skillful hands, narration and voice over can become an excuse for lazy or confused filmmaking. When it is well integrated — which is to say when it becomes part of the story rather than an appendage — a narration can be seductive and powerful.

(See also: FLASHBACKS; FOURTH WALL; INNER CONFLICTS)

NEW

WE LIVE IN a time in which most of us demand that nearly everything we consume or embrace must be "new," and in our hubris we reject the line in Ecclesiastes, "There is nothing new under the sun." We want our cars, houses, computers, jobs and even spouses to be new. We want our religions to make us feel new. Even though 90% of what we eat comes from seven grains, a half dozen fruits, and four or five animals, we want our foods to somehow be new.

The film industry is ever ready to adopt new technologies. At certain times in its history, as for example in the 1970s, it has even been prepared to embrace new directors, writers, subject matter, and attitudes. But most often the new elements it accepts deal with style, presentation, and packaging. The *storytelling* continues to derive from an unbroken tradition that goes back to the ancient Greeks. When it comes to stories, the evidence seems clear that what most people want is old wine in new bottles — the *appearance* of the new, but not necessarily the substance.

(See also: ORIGINALITY; CONSERVATIVE)

*Opposites attract but
they do not necessarily bind.*

Obligatory Scenes

Early in a film, a man sends someone on a mission: Find out what a dying man's word meant because it holds the key to that man's life. Throughout the film, the man talks to the people who knew the man best, beginning with his childhood and ending with his death. At the end of the film, the man is asked whether he's discovered the meaning of the dying man's word. He responds by denying the very basis of his mission: "It wouldn't have explained anything. I don't think any word can explain a man's life."

If *Citizen Kane* had ended there, we might today say, "*Citizen* what?" when the film is mentioned and maybe even "Orson who?" when we hear the name of the director. *Citizen Kane* would have been a "shaggy dog story," one without a point or conclusion. But, while none of the characters in the film ever discovers what "Rosebud" means, *the audience* does — in the 30-second epilogue that follows the speech just quoted. The brief shot of the sled burning in the furnace is *Citizen Kane's* Obligatory Scene.

A popular film is constructed upon an unspoken but understood contract with the audience: "If you watch this film, you will see …." It is the obligation of the filmmakers to bring the lovers together at the end of the romantic comedy, to see the hero plug the bad guy at the end of a western, to kill the monster at the end of the horror film, to accomplish the mission in the war story, or to reveal whodunit at the end of a detective story.

The anticipation of the obligatory scene increases the audience's interest in the film and is similar to the experience of watching a magician — we often know in a general way what will happen, but we don't know exactly when or how.

(See also: HOOKS; MISSIONS)

OPPOSITES

OPPOSITES ATTRACT BUT they do not necessarily bind. Therefore, two characters who are opposites provide a fertile premise for either comedy or tragedy. In comedy, this can be a tall skinny guy and a short fat guy, as Laurel and Hardy and Abbott and Costello demonstrate. In war films, cop films, and any other story that revolves around an ensemble, the team, squad, or other unit will often pair a college-educated smart guy with a street-wise high school dropout, or someone from a sophisticated eastern city and someone from the deep south, or white males and members of a minority group. The team may consist of a highly emotional loner and a calm family man, as in *Lethal Weapon*, a hardened and cynical veteran and a young rookie, as in *Dirty Harry*, King Kong and Ann Darrow in the movie named after the hairy one; Joe Buck and Ratso Rizzo in *Midnight Cowboy*, Hannibal Lecter and Clarice Starling in *The Silence of the Lambs*; Snow White and the Seven Dwarfs. At the very least, the team will consist of that most fruitful of opposites that attract but often don't bind — men and women.

The potential combinations are endless, but the structural principle is the same: in some important way, the people who must work together are opposites. (This is in contrast to life, where people in organizations and companies usually look for others who will "fit in"; that is, who are similar to themselves.)

The use of opposites doubles the potential for dramatic conflict as well as for that element that is so important to popular American filmmaking —

humor. During part of the film, the story will deal with the conflict between the team and their common adversary; but during other parts of the film, the story will deal with the conflict within the team. *Butch Cassidy and the Sundance Kid*, *The Wild Bunch*, *Thelma & Louise* and nearly every other film that involves a team could not sustain interest if they did not bring opposites together.

Often, the conflicts between the members of the team are played for laughs, as in *Butch Cassidy and the Sundance Kid* and *Thelma & Louise*, while the conflict between the team and the outside world is deadly serious. This provides the opportunity to modulate the mood, tone, pace, and level. If, on the other hand, the conflict between the members of the team is taken seriously, as it is in *Bonnie and Clyde*, then much of the conflict with the exterior world will be played for laughs.

In real life, marriages or business relationships between two parties that have much in common are more likely to succeed than relationships between those that have little in common. This is because in real life we want harmony. In drama, however, we want conflict. And the best way to produce conflict is to put opposites together.

(See also: BISOCIATION; TEAMS AND COUPLES; DUALITY)

ORIGINALITY

SINCE DRAMA HAS been prolifically produced for more than 2,500 years, there are few elements that haven't already been used. Originality, however, is not the principal requirement of drama — creativity is.

Audiences are motivated to see a film by recognizing elements in it that they have positively responded to in the past. Characters such as James Bond, Superman, Batman, Spider-Man, Rocky and the Terminator follow in the paths set in earlier times by Sherlock Holmes, Tarzan, Frankenstein, and Dracula, and sagas such as *Star Wars*, *The Godfather* and *The Matrix* follow in the paths of epic stories going back to *The Iliad* and *The Odyssey*.

The use of familiar characters or an ongoing narrative is not a phenomenon invented by movies or popular culture. The sacred texts of major religions all deal with familiar central figures who go through a series of episodes.

Consuming film is like consuming food: most of what strikes us as new is really a combination of ingredients we're already familiar with. We look for something that feels new, but we also want the security of elements that feel comfortable. Originality in storytelling most often consists of bringing elements together in a new way, rather than in creating elements that are entirely new.

(See also: BISOCIATION; CHARACTERS, STOCK; NEW)

P.

The greater the character, the more likely it is that he or she is fundamentally paradoxical.

P.O.V.

POINT OF VIEW in literature is usually communicated by the use of first, second, or third person nouns or pronouns. Most novels are told in either the third or first person; if in the third person, characters are referred as "he," or "she," while first person uses "I."

In film, however, point of view, or P.O.V., might more accurately be considered "Point From Which Viewed." What the camera shows the audience is often not what a specific person in the scene actually sees; often, the point where the camera was set up is intended to evoke as much a *feeling* as it is an optical reality.

In *2001*, there is a famous scene in which Dave Bowman and Frank Poole lock themselves in one of the transportation vehicles aboard the spaceship in an attempt to prevent the malevolent computer HAL from hearing what they're saying. Stanley Kubrick frames them so we can see the two men talking in close proximity, with HAL's red "eye" in the distance. Then, Kubrick cuts to a reverse angle, presumably showing us what HAL "sees": a closeup of their lips moving, which tells us that HAL is lip-reading every word they say. Later in the film, as Dave descends towards Jupiter, we see the "Stargate Sequence" that presumably shows us the planet through Dave's eyes. A bit later, Dave is in a strange and sterile room, and someone or something is now watching Dave, and the angle is from their P.O.V. (A point that Arthur Clarke made explicit in his screenplay but Stanley Kubrick obscured.) As these examples demonstrate, P.O.V. shots often shift faster than anyone can consciously keep track of them.. Often, if we ask who's P.O.V. it is, the answer should be, "the director's."

(See also: INTIMACY)

Pain

THE ANCIENT ROMANS' idea of entertainment was to toss Christians to the lions. Although we don't usually do this to real people anymore, our most popular films demonstrate that we, like the Romans, torture people for our pleasure — we just confine it to fiction or sports.

Pain is the basis for both comedy and tragedy. In comedy, the cause of the potential or real pain is presented, but the audience is usually blocked from feeling it because it is converted into laughter. In tragedy, the audience is meant to feel the pain but not enough to make them cry. Being able to control what the audience *does* with the pain is one of the most important jobs of the filmmaker.

(See also: BLOCKING; SACRIFICE; LOSS; DESPAIR)

NIELS BOHR, THE Danish co-founder of quantum physics and one of the most important theoreticians of science in the twentieth century, observed that, "There are trivial truths and great truths. The opposite of a trivial truth is plainly false. The opposite of a great truth is also true." Such a statement could be applied to many of the central characters in memorable popular films. In fact, the greater the character, the more likely it is that he or she is fundamentally paradoxical.

A paradox is not necessarily a contradiction; it merely *appears* that way at first. When presented with a contradiction, we usually try to decide between the elements that appear contradictory. When presented with a paradox, however, we are forced to accept that both elements are true. This is why our reaction when we realize something is a paradox is often the "Ah!" that accompanies discovery or insight.

Contradictions weaken a story but paradoxes strengthen them, and the films that haunt us often contain major paradoxes. In *One Flew Over the Cuckoo's Nest*, the protagonist, R. P. McMurphy, is dead at the end, but he has brought Chief to life. Michael Corleone, in the *Godfather* series, keeps saying that whatever he does is for the family, and yet he is responsible for destroying an important part of it in all three films. At the end of *Casablanca*, Rick Blaine sends away the love of his life, Ilsa Lund, but they'll "always have Paris." Alvy Singer in *Annie Hall* helps Annie stand on her own two feet, but then he can't handle it when, as a result, she leaves him.

In the construction of character and all art, there is power in paradox.

(See also: BUT; DUALITY; BISOCIATION; INCONGRUITY; IRONY)

THE ACTION IN novels usually take place in the past, which is why they are customarily written in the past tense. The first lesson many screenwriters learn is that all films take place in the present and nothing is to be written using past tense — even flashbacks.

The past always evokes an attitude and feeling. In an early scene in *Citizen Kane,* the eight-year-old Charlie Kane has built a snowman and is playing with his sled. That sled, as we learn later, symbolizes all the lost innocence and love that he once had before he was sent away by his mother to be raised by a banker.

The images in *Doctor Zhivago* of Lara in the snow and among the daffodils of spring evoke a sense of beauty but later of loss. In *The Best Years of Our Lives*, Frank Derry is haunted by his wartime past, and his walk among the skeletons of old bombers simultaneously evokes nostalgia and loss. Scottie Ferguson in *Vertigo* is so haunted by his memories of Madeleine that he feels compelled to recreate her through another woman.

One of the most famous evocations of the past in popular films occurs in *Casablanca* when Rick and Ilsa recall their time together in Paris when they were happy and in love. The past can evoke deep and complex feelings, which is why memorable films so often go there. But they're always written in the present — which is also perhaps part of their power.

(See also: FLASHBACKS; BACKSTORIES; LOSS)

PERSONA

A "PERSONA" is not to be confused with a "character." A persona is something an actor has that transcends any particular role. It stems in part from attributes of the actor's personality such as toughness or vulnerability, from his physical attributes, his attitude, the way he or she talks, walks, looks at others, etc. What occurs in many memorable films is a *fusion* of the actor's persona with the character he or she is playing. We think of Charles Foster Kane *as played by* Orson Welles or of Michael Corleone *as played by* Al Pacino, and it is hard to tell where the character leaves off and the actor begins.

Problems occur, however, when an actor's persona is so overwhelming that it makes the characters he or she plays fade into the background, as often happened with the films of Elvis Presley, John Wayne, and Marilyn Monroe.

Casting a star with a clear persona often saves the filmmakers twenty pages of character development. This is one of the reasons actors with clear personas get so much money — they not only bring audiences to the film, they help tell the film's story with economy.

(See also: ATTITUDE)

HEROES DIE FOR their own or other people's sins, get maimed, or at least have to sweat a lot. These are the sacrifices they make so that others may live. In modern memorable popular stories, however, the audience seldom pities the hero.

PITY

For modern audiences, pity is a cheap emotion. It's like being faced with a guy on the street rattling a cup asking for change — our reaction is to get away as fast as we can. In a movie theater, we can't get away, so our reaction to a filmmaker who appeals to our pity may be discomfort at having been manipulated. The skillful filmmaker does not ask us to feel pity; he asks us to feel compassion, which is quite a different thing.

(See also: COMPASSION)

PLAYING IT STRAIGHT

I. A. L. Diamond, Billy Wilder's collaborator who was the co-author of the screenplay for *Some Like It Hot*, once said that a good comedy uses "a sub-structure that's as strong as it would be in drama. I think any comedy, with a slight change of emphasis, should be able to play as a drama" (see: ATTITUDE).

Similarly, many comic actors insist that it's important to "play it straight" — that only badly trained amateurs deliver lines with a wink and a nod to the audience that says, "Look how funny I am."

People who have never learned the essence of telling a joke will often begin by telling you, "This is funny." But effective humor, whether it's in a joke or a feature film, depends on the teller of the story, pretending not to *know* it's funny.

That's why the audience has to "get it" — that is, understand that something is funny without being told.

(See also: COMEDY; JOKES)

Five years after *The Birth of a Nation* convinced everyone from the White House to Wall Street that films were an important new dramatic medium, *Photoplay* magazine published an "encyclopedia" that attempted to codify the basic plots available to motion pictures. As has so often been the case in Hollywood, the writers of this compendium copied a much earlier work; in this case, the Frenchman Georges Polti's *The Thirty-Six Dramatic Situations*. Even earlier than this, the Italian dramatist Carlo Gozzi had said there were twenty-six basic plots (although I agree with Goethe that there probably aren't that many).

Contemporary physicists are largely agreed that there are only four basic forces in the physical universe: the weak atomic force, strong atomic force, gravity, and electro-magnetism. Contemporary biologists are largely agreed that there are only four basic compounds in DNA: adenine, thymine, cytosine, and guanine. From these four forces in the physical world, all the universe is constructed; from the four simple elements in DNA, all life forms are built.

If the entire universe of physical and living phenomena each have only four basic ingredients, perhaps the world of drama is not as chaotic as it seems. Perhaps, like the physical and biological world, there are relatively few basic dramatic structures, but they are capable of being combined in an infinite variety and number of ways.

The essential structural elements of the vast majority of plots that will ever exist already *do* exist. People who claim they have invented a new plot usually know very little of the history of drama and literature, let alone of the countless myths, legends, folktales, and fables that human beings have been telling since language was first invented.

More important than creating an original plot is creating an original character, since it is usually characters — not plots — that most people remember.

(See also: ELEGANCE; COMPLEXITY; CONCEPTS; ORIGINALITY; and the various entries under CHARACTER)

There are two problems with pornography:
1) How can the filmmaker keep people interested
in a film that begins with a climax? and 2) How can
the filmmaker get other jobs?

The solution to the first problem traditionally
has been the structure of "Theme and Variations,"
that is, to begin with one kind of sexual coupling,
go to threesomes, then end up with a finale fea-
turing a room full of people doing everything
conceivable to as many orifices as are evident.

There is no solution to the second problem.

PORNOGRAPHY

POWER

ALL MEMORABLE STORIES are about power.

There are people who approach the subject of power the way the Victorians approached sex: while everyone of a certain age knows it exists, "nice" people aren't supposed to talk about it, let alone admit they desire it. Such prudery about power is unbecoming of people interested in film.

When people say someone is interested in or trying to acquire power, they usually are referring to power *over* someone else. This is the kind of power the villain seeks, but there are other kinds.

Physicists define power as the ability to produce change or to prevent it. This is the kind the hero seeks. While the villain seeks and uses power for his own self-enhancement, the hero seeks and uses power either to help other people or to prevent the villain from harming others.

In the real world, political, social, cultural, and religious heroes are usually people such as Mahatma Gandhi, who gain power in order to produce change. In memorable popular films, however, it is more often the villain who seeks to gain power in order to produce change.

George Bailey opposes Mr. Potter's attempt to take over the town of Bedford Falls. The title character in *Terminator 2* opposes the attempt of the machines to destroy Sarah Conner and her son. In *Chinatown*, J. J. Gittes opposes the attempts of Noah Cross to control both the Los Angeles water supply and his daughter Evelyn. In *One Flew Over the Cuckoo's Nest*, R. P. McMurphy opposes the attempt of Nurse Ratched to impose her will on the patients. In *The Exorcist*, Father Karras opposes the attempt by the demon to control the innocent girl, Regan. In *The Grapes of Wrath*, Tom Joad opposes the attempts of the rich farm owners and corrupt cops to exploit the Okies. In *Mr. Smith Goes to Washington*, the title character opposes the corrupt politicians in the U.S. Senate. In *Star Wars*, Luke Skywalker opposes The Empire's attempt to dominate the universe.

The villain in all these films wants to change things, to remake the world in his image. The hero doesn't want to change the world; he merely wants to stop the villain from doing so. In this sense, he is a true conservative (see: CONSERVATIVE).

Change and power go together. What happens to power during the course of a film defines whether it is structurally a comedy or tragedy:

1) If the central character has power in the beginning and loses it by the end, we call it a tragedy.

2) If the central character has little or no power in the beginning but gains it by the end, we call it a comedy.

3) If the central character has power at the beginning, never loses it, and still has power at the end, or if the central character has no power at the beginning, never acquires it, and still has no power at the end, we call it a flop.

Power is one thing; authority is another. Authority is moral *permission* to use the power one already has. Teachers, doctors, psychiatrists, police officers, judges, ministers, and parents all have power over other people. However, in the morality plays we call movies, they may not use that power inappropriately if they are to retain the audience's respect and identification.

Power must have a purpose the audience approves of, and it must be used for something that transcends the personal interests of the individual who has it. That's why the audience condemns the villain who uses power for his own self-aggrandizement, but praises the hero who uses power on behalf of his friends, family, or community.

(See also: CHARACTER, POWER; GIFTS; BLESSINGS; CURSES; HEROES; CHANGE; SACRIFICE; IMPOTENCE; ACTS, THIRD; PREDICTION)

IN ALL SOCIETIES, throughout all of recorded time, the ability to predict the future has always been recognized as the greatest of powers. This is one of the reasons the entrails of birds, animals, and humans were plucked out in ancient times, and why tea leaves, fortune-tellers, and horoscopes continue to be considered popular fonts of wisdom by some people in our own time.

People are constantly in search of clues regarding the outcome of horse races, athletic events, the stock market, their love affairs, their children's and their own futures, and tomorrow's weather. It ultimately explains why people pray to their gods — they hope that their future will be a good one, in this life or the next. The historical track record of people who have predicted the future is not reassuring, but people keep trying because someone who *could* predict the future would be the most powerful person on earth.

Heroes, not surprisingly, often predict the future. That famous line from *The Godfather*, "I'll make him an offer he can't refuse," is a prediction. And, just before he dies, Vito Corleone predicts that the first person to approach Michael to try to arrange a peace settlement with the other dons will be the traitor, which gives Michael the clue he needs to avoid mortal danger. In *The Searchers*, Ethan Edwards' young protégé, Martin Pawley, excitedly tells him that he's learned that the Indians they have been chasing for several years have told a shopkeeper where they were headed. Martin urges Ethan to mount up and go after them, but Edwards calms the excitable young man down and tells him the tribe of Indians they're after always say they're going one way when they will in fact go "t'other." In *Dirty Harry,* Harry Callahan figures out the route the serial killer will follow with the kidnapped school bus full of terrified children, and in one of the film's most memorable shots, he drops onto the top of the bus like an avenging angel.

Heroes predict the future because the ability to do so is a sign that they *are* heroes.

(See also: KNOWLEDGE; CHARACTER, POWER; INTUITION AND INSIGHT)

THE PRINCIPAL CHARACTER in a memorable film is generally a principled character. This is, however, not always clear for much of the film's running time. In *The Wild Bunch, The Searchers,* and *Unforgiven*, the central characters do many things that make us uncomfortable because they appear ruthless. Sam Spade in *The Maltese Falcon (*and most of the other roles Humphrey Bogart played) is morally ambiguous. Rhett Butler in *Gone with the Wind,* C. C. Baxter in *The Apartment,* Commander Shears in *The Bridge on the River Kwai,* and Terry Malloy in *On the Waterfront* all appear for much of their films to be people who are only concerned with themselves. Eventually, as is true for nearly all American popular films, the character's better nature — which we like to believe is his *true* nature — is revealed.

Star Wars, modern American culture's most popular morality play, places the concern for principles at its core. While Luke, like many another hero, is *tempted* by The Dark Side, he does not succumb to it.

There are many memorable popular films in which the central character appears to have the wrong principles in the beginning but has the right ones at the end. But there are few in which the central character has the right principles in the beginning and abandons them by the end. That would be a tragedy, which would violate one of the most profound principles of the American ethos.

(See also: TRAGEDY; JUSTICE; DUALITY; PARADOX; BISOCIATION)

PRINCIPLES

PROCESS

IN *2001*, WE see the process that enables Dave Bowman to remove HAL's memory bank. In *E.T.*, we see the process the scientists use to examine the little fella. In *Singin' in the Rain*, we see the process used in early sound films for dubbing. In *Tootsie*, we watch the process Michael Dorsey uses to transform himself into Dorothy Michaels.

Film and television, better than any other media, are capable of showing us *how* something is done, which is why many films spend so much time doing exactly that, and why so many television series are what the industry calls "procedurals." The revelation of process can be suspenseful and surprising in itself, causing us to exclaim, "Oh, *that's* how they do it!"

As with everything else, the more people who make films and television help the audience discover something, the more likely the audience is to think their work is good.

(See also: DISCOVERY)

Somebody else's documentary.

PROPAGANDA

PSYCHOPATHS AND SOCIOPATHS

MANY OF THE most memorable villains are either psychopaths or sociopaths. Some writers on human psychology say that the psychopath violates social norms and commits reprehensible acts but doesn't really understand what he's doing, while the sociopath knows very well what he's doing but doesn't *care*. Whatever their state of understanding, dark characters such as Darth Vader in *Star Wars* and Hannibal Lecter are among the most interesting and memorable villains in film.

On the other hand, when we look closely at the behavior of memorable heroes, such as Ethan Edwards in *The Searchers*, Travis Bickle in *Taxi Driver* or William Munny in *Unforgiven*, it is sometimes hard to distinguish what they do from the acts of sociopaths or psychopaths. Why, then, do we identify with them? Because their "heart is in the right place" — they *want* to do right. Villains don't *care*.

(See also: MOTIVATION; VILLAINS; COMMITMENT; MISSIONS; ART VS. CRAFT; SUSPENSION OF DISBELIEF)

IN THE WORK he significantly called *Metamorphoses*, the Roman poet Ovid gives his version of a story that can be seen as a template for countless stories about the relationship of men and women.

Pygmalion was a king of Cyprus who sculpted an ivory statue called Galatea that embodied his vision of an ideal woman. As so often happens, he fell in love with his own creation. But the hunk of marble containing Pygmalion's view of a perfect woman left him even more frustrated than before, so Aphrodite, the goddess of love, took pity on him and gave his creation life.

Myths, religions, and the world's fiction abound with supernatural tales of men giving birth. In the Old Testament, the male God created the female Eve out of Adam's rib. In Greek mythology, Zeus gave birth to Athena out of his brow, perhaps to demonstrate the power of the male intellect.

In *Annie Hall, The Phantom of the Opera,* and *Citizen Kane*, the male literally helps the female character find her "voice" to become a singer. In *A Star Is Born,* Norman helps Esther find her "voice" as an actress. In *Chinatown,* Jake Gittes helps Evelyn Mulwray speak the truth she has hidden for many years. In *Titanic,* Jack Dawson helps Rose speak out and assert her independence from her suffocating family and fiancé. In all these films, a male helps the female fulfill her potential, helps "bring her to life." Ironically, the males do not find fulfillment for having done so.

In *My Fair Lady*, whose film and stage versions were both based on the play *Pygmalion* by George Bernard Shaw that was itself based on Ovid's story, men take a female lump of clay and "bring her to life." Ovid's story and Shaw's play do not end with the union of the two, but *My Fair Lady* on stage and film is more ambiguous. It took *Pretty Woman* to unambiguously unite creator and created at the end, which is perhaps why so many people loved the film.

The ongoing appeal of the Pygmalion/Galatea story is a testament to the ongoing power of male narcissism. It is difficult to think of memorable popular films in which the gender roles are reversed — it is only in real life that women create men.

(See also: NARCISSUS; LOVE; ROMANCE)

King Pyrrhus was a Greek who defeated the Romans in an especially bloody battle in 279 B.C. Afterwards, when informed of his victory and the number of men he had lost, he remarked, "One more such victory and we are lost." A "Pyrrhic Victory" is thus one in which the costs of winning have been so enormous that "victory" becomes an ironic term.

PYRRHIC VICTORIES

In *Apocalypse Now*, Willard fulfills his mission and kills Kurtz but in the end discovers, "The horror." In *Bonnie and Clyde*, *The Dirty Dozen*, *Butch Cassidy and the Sundance Kid*, *The Wild Bunch*, *The Exorcist*, *Frankenstein*, *Dracula* and many more, the title characters are dead by the end of the film. The bridge in *The Bridge on the River Kwai* gets built, but then it and everyone associated with it is destroyed. In *Gone with the Wind*, Scarlett finally tells Rhett she loves him, but by that time he doesn't give a damn. In *High Noon* and *Dirty Harry*, the law enforcement officers who have saved the town toss down their badges in disgust and walk away from it.

People who believe a "Happy Ending" is obligatory if a film is to be popular just haven't paid attention to what actually *happens*. Aside from comedies, *most* memorable popular films end in pyrrhic victories.

This is not to say the endings are "downers." The hero may have lost the world, but he has gained his soul. In so doing, he has transcended what the world calls "victory."

(See also: Endings, Happy; Success; Loss; Transcendence)

R

Realism is the real "ism" of film.

REALISM

REALISM HAS BEEN a goal of drama ever since the Greeks came up with the idea of *mimesis*, which is often translated as "imitation" — although whether mere mimicry is all that mimesis involves has been debated for many centuries.

Edison's early recordings at the end of the nineteenth century were made by speaking into the large end of a big trumpet that used the pressure of sound waves to incise grooves in a spinning wax cylinder. It would surprise anyone today to find that Edison's contemporaries praised these crude records for their astonishing "realism." When the Lumière brothers made some of the first motion pictures by setting a camera in front of an arriving train, it is reported that the footage struck audiences as so realistic that some people jumped out of their chairs to avoid being hit.

Each generation believes that what they are hearing and seeing at the time is "realistic." Each succeeding generation, however, is struck by the artifice and lack of realism of earlier times and wonders how earlier people could have been so naive.

When people say a film is "not realistic" or is "artificial," what they're often saying is that it doesn't conform to their expectations of mimesis. *Everything* in film is based on artifice. Realism is the real "ism" of film — a system of beliefs that may or may not correspond to the real world. Films are not mirrors of that world; they are interpretations of it.

(See also: REALITY FALLACY)

THE REALITY FALLACY is the quaint notion that things work in films the way they do in real life, and therefore the logic of the real world should govern the logic of film.

In *Citizen Kane,* Charlie's mother inherits the world's third largest fortune. What is the first thing she does with it? She sends her only begotten son, an eight-year-old boy on a sled who is the only meaningful thing in her life, to be raised by a banker in New York. Although she lives many more years, she never sees him again. How realistic is that?

Citizen Kane is about a man who is incapable of love, presumably because he was torn away from his mother at an early, formative stage. It is the logic of the story — not the logic of life — that requires his mother to never see him again.

Citizen Kane is also structured around a reporter's search for the meaning of Kane's dying word, "Rosebud." But how does the world within the film know that was his dying word? Raymond, the butler, tells a reporter he was present at Kane's deathbed, but Raymond is a liar — we have seen Kane die and Raymond was nowhere in sight. We saw a nurse tuck Kane into his bed and then close a very thick door. The camera dollied into one of the most famous closeups in film history, and we saw Kane's lips filling up the screen as he *whispers* "Rosebud." There was no one else there. Thus, the entire premise of the film is based on something that could not have happened in the real world the way it is presented in the film.

Casablanca is a film in which an object is central to the plot of the story: two Letters of Transit, which will allow whoever has them to get out of town without question. The film opens with the murder of two German couriers carrying these valuable documents, and then leads to the rounding up of "the usual suspects."

Later, Rick Blaine tells Ugarte, who has the Letters of Transit, that he's impressed the little thief has them. They discuss what makes them so valuable, and Ugarte says that General De Gaulle signed them, and, therefore, no one can question them, not even the Gestapo.

Wait a minute! Casablanca is in northern Morocco, which in 1943 was controlled by the French Vichy government, which was, in turn, controlled by the Nazis — which is why Major Strasser has the power to order police chief Renault to close Rick's Café Americain.

In real life at the time, Charles De Gaulle was part of the defeated French army that had fled France and found sanctuary in England, where he urged the underground forces back home to keep up the good work. Saying De Gaulle's signature is on the Letters of Transit makes as much sense as saying Franklin Roosevelt's signature is on them — no sense at all. Yet, as far as is known, no person watching *Casablanca* when it came out in 1943 ever questioned this blatant contradiction of reality

Films are not about reality, they're about their own inner world, and the logic of life is not necessarily the logic of films.

Realism in art is a style, not a fact.

(See also: REALISM)

As *The Shawshank Redemption*, which regularly places near the top of recent lists of memorable films, demonstrates, it is not enough for the hero to rescue others; he must also redeem himself. Whether you redeem a discount coupon, something you've hocked at the pawn shop, or your soul, the process of redemption is based on a contract between two parties that says if you act a certain way, you are entitled to certain compensations.

Redemption

Rick Blaine says early in *Casablanca* that he sticks his neck out for nobody, and Rhett Butler in *Gone with the Wind*, Terry Malloy in *On the Waterfront*, R.P. McMurphy in *One Flew Over the Cuckoo's Nest* are similar slackers who don't want to get involved. By the end of their stories, though, they have sacrificed themselves on behalf of others and, in so doing, they redeem themselves.

But if redemption is based on a contract between two parties, who is the other party? The hero doesn't redeem himself with the villain, and he seldom has to redeem himself with other characters. He redeems himself with the audience.

(See also: Antiheroes; Transcendence)

REJECTION

YOUNG AND ALIENATED Jim Stark in *Rebel Without a Cause* rejects his parents and runs away to find solace with his new girlfriend, Judy, who also rejects her own family. Young and alienated Benjamin Braddock in *The Graduate* flees the welcome-home party his family has given him and tells his father he wants his life to be "different." George Bailey tells his father, "You're a great guy, pop, but I don't want to be like you." Michael Corleone in *The Godfather* tells his girlfriend a story, but then says, "That's my family, Kay, not me."

Rejection is part of the process the Jungians call "individuation" — becoming your own autonomous being. Like defiance, it is a universal characteristic of heroes.

(See also: DEFIANCE; INDIVIDUATION; COMING-OF-AGE FILMS)

IF A FILMMAKER tries to make something "relevant" to its time, there's a good chance the film will feel dated by the time it is released. Certainly it will lose its "relevance" within a short period of time.

Films are sometimes criticized for not dealing with the issues people think at the time of their release are important. Much of the last half of *The Graduate*, for example, takes place on the Berkeley campus of the University of California, which, when the film was made in the late 1960s, was going through major upheavals because of student demonstrations and strikes associated with the war in Vietnam. Yet none of this appears in the film. *Apocalypse Now* was criticized for not being specific enough about American involvement in the war in Vietnam. As is often true, if either film *had* been more "relevant" to its own time, it might have dated more quickly and ceased to interest later generations.

(See also: TOPICALITY; SOCIAL ISSUES)

RELUCTANCE

WHEN GOD BURNED a bush on Mt. Sinai to get the attention of Moses and then told him He had selected Moses to lead His people out of Egypt, Moses told God He had the wrong guy, that he wasn't a good public speaker — in fact, he stuttered — and surely there were better candidates for the job than he.

Early in *Casablanca, Gone with the Wind,* and *On The Waterfront*, their protagonists declare that they stick their necks out for nobody. Early in *The Godfather* and *It's a Wonderful Life*, their protagonists declare that they don't want to be part of the family business. Early in *The Matrix*, when Neo is told he is "The One" who, it has been prophesied, will save humanity, he insists he is not. At the beginning of nearly all memorable stories about heroes, the hero is reluctant to *be* a hero.

There's a good reason for this: As many a war film demonstrates, the character who steps forward and *volunteers* for a heroic mission often finds himself dead. People who volunteer to be heroes seldom are. It's not a job someone applies for or, if they're in their right mind, *wants*.

The nearly universal reluctance of the hero stems in part from the structural requirements of plotting a dramatic story, and in part from the requirements of building an interesting character. The best way for a hero to develop into a hero is to begin with him *denying* that he is.

(See also: DEFIANCE; HEROES, SINGLE; IRONY)

IN ORDINARY CONVERSATION, we often apologize if we repeat things. In art, there's no need to apologize, since repetition is one of art's most useful tools.

REPETITION

In *Annie Hall*, the title character is heard singing the song, "Seems Like Old Times" twice. The first time she sings it, around an hour into the film, Alvy has helped her gain her confidence, which her rendition of the song demonstrates. The second time we hear the song it is on the soundtrack at the very end of the film, after Annie and Alvy have parted for the last time.

Early in *Dirty Harry,* the title character corners a bank robber he has wounded, and as the man lies on the ground and starts to reach for his gun, Harry asks him, "Do you feel lucky, punk?" The robber backs away and saves his own life. But later, at the end of the film, Harry confronts the serial killer, Scorpio, whom he has been chasing throughout the film. Once again, he wounds a person whose gun lies within easy reach and asks him, "Do you feel lucky, punk?" This time, the punk reaches for his gun and fires off a round, which gives Harry what he — and we — want: moral justification to blow him away.

The most famous line in *The Godfather*, which became a tag line across America for years after, deals with making somebody "an offer he can't refuse." It is spoken only twice, but the repetition is very effective, in part because the first time it is spoken it comes early in the film from Vito Corleone. The second time, it comes from

Michael Corleone, and it signifies that he has learned his lesson well. In the final scene of *Star Wars*, Luke Skywalker hears the line he had heard early in the film from Obi-Wan Kenobi, the most famous line in the series, "The Force, Luke — Trust The Force."

Repetition is a basic building block of comedy. Every standup comedian, comedy series, or late-night television host has lines, gestures, or reactions that become so familiar that any amateur mimic can draw down the house by imitating them. Within comedies, lines that in themselves are not funny can produce a laugh if we hear them repeated, such as someone claiming to have "Type O" blood in *Some Like It Hot*.

When repetition in music becomes identified with a character, it is called a "leitmotif." Films as diverse as *Citizen Kane, High Noon, The Graduate, 2001,* and *The Godfather* all use leitmotifs to great effect and, perhaps not coincidentally, are considered to have some of the most memorable scores in film history.

There is another kind of repetition that bears analysis: why is it that with most films, we see them once and don't care to repeat the experience, but there are certain films we like to see over and over again? The answer may lie in the pleasure we receive watching our favorite comic repeat a routine, or watching a magician perform a trick we have seen before. With most films, our interest is sustained by the question, "What happens next?" and once we know, a repetition of the experience is usually

less interesting. With the films we can stand to see
over again, however, the interest changes from what
happens to *how* it happens, and our interest shifts
from the plot to the artfulness of the filmmaking.
Repetition, to repeat, is one of art's most useful tools.

RESCUE

THE HERO RESCUES other people, but someone who has to be rescued is, by definition, not the hero. The hero rescues people to prove that he *is* a hero.

(See also: REDEMPTION)

WHEN VITO CORLEONE first meets the drug dealer, Sollozzo, he tells him, "I heard that you're a serious man, to be treated with respect." The line is ironic, but nothing is more important than respect to the characters in *The Godfather* and most gangster films.

Permutations on the theme of respect run deep in many memorable films. Terry Malloy in *On the Waterfront,* Rocky Balboa in *Rocky*, Travis Bickle in *Taxi Driver*, Ratso Rizzo in *Midnight Cowboy*, Andy Dufresne and Red Redding in *The Shawshank Redemption*, and many other memorable popular films involve characters looking for respect. The character Atticus Finch in *To Kill a Mockingbird*, which received the most votes in the American Film Institute's poll of all-time favorite characters, is largely defined by his respect for others.

Who does the villain respect? Nobody. That's one reason he *is* a villain.

RESPECT

RESTRAINT

RESTRAINT IS SOMETIMES all that differentiates the hero from the villain. The villain is a fanatic who will stop at nothing to get what he wants; the hero does stop. In the famous scene in *The French Connection* in which Popeye Doyle frantically chases the killer fleeing in the elevated train above, he swerves at the very last second to avoid hitting a woman who pushes a baby carriage. A villain in such a scene would *prove* he was a villain by not swerving.

Villains express their anger all the time, but when a hero does so, it needs to be carefully prepared and is often instrumental behavior, which is to say, it is consciously intended to produce a result, rather than stemming from a loss of control. In *The Godfather,* for example, Vito Corleone, that coolest of men, pretends to become angry with his godson, the singer Frankie Fontaine, when he slaps him. But it is clear Vito is trying to bring Frankie to his senses and that he has not lost control of himself.

The differences in the level of restraint of the three Corleone boys in *The Godfather* demonstrates how important it is to characterization. Like the story of Goldilocks and the Three Bears, in which one bed was too hard, one too soft, and one just right, Sonny is a hothead who is too hard — his lack of restraint is shown in his very first scene, when he stomps on the photographer's camera. We see it again in his final scene when, despite Tom Hagen's warning, he rushes out of the house and drives into a fatal trap at the toll booth. Fredo, on the other hand, is too soft, as he demonstrates when his father is hit with five slugs in the assassination attempt, and all Fredo can do is watch and fumble with his gun. Michael, of course, is just right. He is restrained in the hospital when he saves his father's life, but is also able to overcome his inhibitions as he extracts his vengeance by killing Sollozzo and McCluskey during dinner.

The restraint the hero shows is another one of those things that proves he *is* a hero, because he has the power to control that most difficult of all things: the self.

REVELATION

MANY PEOPLE IN the film industry talk about "the reveal." What they generally mean is the point in the story when the audience learns something important about a character. It is often something filmmakers have withheld from the audience that, as in *The Sixth Sense*, doesn't become clear until the very end of the film. Often, however, the audience feels manipulated by the timing and manner of the revelation.

An even more powerful permutation in film occurs when the audience discovers something *for themselves*. This occurs during that pleasurable moment when you nudge the person next to you and tell them what you've just recognized. But you are discovering what the filmmakers *want* you to discover. It's *all* manipulation. The art of filmmaking lies in not letting it *feel* that way.

(See also: DISCOVERY)

"REVENGE IS A dish best served cold" is a line in Mario Puzo's novel *The Godfather*, where it is attributed to ancient Sicilians. Some attribute the line to *Les Liaisons Dangereuses,* the 1782 book by Pierre Ambroise de Laclos, others to the writer Dorothy Parker; still others to the Klingons. Like many another famous line, it has probably been coined many times.

REVENGE

Revenge underlies a good many Greek and Roman works, such as Euripides' *Electra* and almost any play by Seneca. The Elizabethan playwrights frequently wrote revenge dramas, including Thomas Kyd's *A Spanish Tragedy*, Marlowe's *The Jew of Malta*, and Shakespeare's *The Merchant of Venice, Hamlet, Othello,* and others. In film, all three of *The Godfather* films are filled with revenge, and it plays a major role in *All About Eve, Amadeus, The Deer Hunter, Jaws, The Searchers, The Wild Bunch, Taxi Driver, Unforgiven,* and *Pulp Fiction* — not to mention the numerous comedies that play the revenge impulse for laughs.

In comedy, a character seeking revenge can be hilarious, in part because of the fun he and we have when the person who did the original bad deed gets his comeuppance. But in tragedy, revenge is nearly always associated with dire results.

Revenge is always something done *in return* for some injury another has caused. This creates a problem, because there are no rules that govern when revenge-seeking *stops*. In the meeting with the heads of all the families in *The Godfather*, Vito says, "I forego the vengeance of my son," but it's only a strategic move so he can wait to serve it cold, and we take delight when his son Michael is able to say he's "settled all the family business" by rubbing out the heads of the other families.

Revenge has no end because it is impossible to truly settle old scores as long as anyone is left alive on either side. In *Lawrence of Arabia*, when Gasim, whom Lawrence had rescued from the desert, kills a member of Auda Abu Tayi's tribe, Sherif Ali Ibn el Kharish's tribe demands revenge. But this will only continue the long-standing blood feud between Gasim and Auda's tribes. So, Lawrence offers to execute the man he had saved because his doing so will not be for personal revenge but for a legal principle.

Revenge is a primitive form, a *predecessor* of justice. The person who seeks revenge is merely "evening the score" for something that directly affects him. Justice, however, involves a third party who will not personally benefit from the action.

Revenge contains qualities drama seeks: simplicity and clarity. Justice that *transcends* revenge, however, can be even more interesting.

(See also: BETRAYAL; JUSTICE; MOTIVATION)

Romance

The GENRES IN which romance appears most often are romantic comedies and musicals, and they are the two — and the only two — genres that are obliged to have happy endings.

Few genres are as predictable as romance. Everyone knows when he buys a ticket how the romance will end; yet he pretends that he doesn't (see: Suspension of Disbelief).

Boy meets girl, boy wins girl, boy loses girl, boy regains girl. There is not much creative potential in this plot. Perhaps that is why what we remember best about movie romances are often the humor, singing, and dancing.

There is no question that romance is popular — most compilations of the top ten films at the box office each year contain one or more romances. Yet romances do not fare well when it comes time to getting awards, nor are they often on lists of the most memorable films. Like comedy, as much as people love them, they get no respect.

While all romances deal with love, not all love stories are romances.

(See also: Love; Endings, Happy; Comedy)

S

Success, as Americans define it in real life,
is not something the hero aspires to, and
happiness is something the hero no longer is
concerned with — or perhaps even capable of.

SACRIFICE

HEROES ARE BETTER than we are, not necessarily because they possess greater powers than we do, but because they are willing to sacrifice more than we are.

"Sacrifice" comes from the same root as "sacred," and throughout history there has been a reciprocal relationship between the two. What people hold sacred often demands sacrifice; conversely, when someone makes a sacrifice, he and his actions tend to take on an aura of the sacred.

There is a big difference between sacrificing others and sacrificing yourself. When we watch people sacrifice others, we may accept it, but they do not generally rise in our esteem. When people sacrifice themselves, however, and voluntarily accept pain, loss, deprivation, and suffering on behalf of a cause or other people, their sacrifice often raises them to a higher, more sacred, plane.

Ideologies and religions always demand sacrifices — often of others. The stories that remain in our memories, however, usually deal with the sacrifice of the self. In *Lawrence of Arabia* the title character returns to the Nefud desert to rescue Gasim, and the possibility that he may be sacrificing his own life for someone else raises him to a higher ethical sphere, which is why, when Lawrence returns, the Arabs anoint him with new clothes and a new name (see: NAMING). Later, however, when Lawrence orders, "No prisoners!" and massacres the retreating Turkish soldiers, his butchery is a tragic turning point, and he is never the same in the eyes of his men, the audience — or himself.

The hero generally gains little or no reward for his sacrifice — it is the community that gains. To the extent the hero does personally gain from his sacrifice, he ceases to be a hero and becomes simply a smart operator.

Sacrifice becomes sacred when it is truly selfless.

(See also: TRANSCENDENCE; LOSS; TESTS; PAIN)

SCENES

WHEN WE WERE young, our mothers taught us not to make a scene. But that is exactly what the hero *does*. Making scenes is the essence of being a hero and it is also the essence of making memorable films.

Great films consist of great characters in great scenes. What makes a great character? Someone who appears in great scenes.

In memorable films, *every* scene helps define character. From a structural standpoint, no scene in most of the memorable films can be removed without substantively altering what the film is about.

Scenes may be filled with action, but if they are merely exciting or merely advance the plot, rather than simultaneously advancing the audience's understanding of the character, they miss an opportunity for greatness.

Memorable scenes invariably contain one or more of the following elements:

1) They often contain considerable incongruity, bringing together elements that have not generally been thought of as belonging together (see: BISOCIATION). These elements can be characters, places, genres, moods, or plot. By themselves, the individual elements may be quite familiar; often, what makes the scene memorable is the juxtaposition of elements.

2) They surprise us.

3) They contain some element of deception. Things are never quite what they seem, which forces the audience to look beneath the surface, to engage in an active attempt to figure out what's really going on (see: DECEPTION).

4) They create a trap for their characters. (see: TRAPS).

5) They involve some kind of sacrifice (see: SACRIFICE).

6) They deal with separation or loss (see: Loss).

7) The scene involves an important decision (see: DECISION).

8) On some level, there is a physical or psychological chase (see: CHASE).

9) They follow the Principle of Parsimony, using only as many elements as are necessary (see: ELEGANCE).

Memorable scenes are frequently a microcosm of the macrocosm; that is, what the scene is about is what the film itself is about.

SCIENCE FICTION

SCIENCE FICTION FILMS are almost invariably set in the future and spring from one of the oldest and most compelling forms of storytelling: prophecy. As is true for any prophecy, one must understand not only the specifics of what is predicted but also the yearnings and fears they express.

Although the future time frame of science fiction is unique among film genres, its location is not. In war films, the action takes place on a "front"; in westerns and science fiction, it takes place on a frontier. Dramatically they are equivalent places. At the front/frontier, the organized forces of society are weak, get in the way, or trap the hero. In *Alien,* for example, the corporation back on earth that has sent the spaceship on its mission is treacherous, as is the government agency that has sent Dave Bowman and his crew on their mission in *2001.*

Not only can one lose one's life on the front/frontier, one can also lose one's soul. This is why most memorable war films, westerns, and science fiction films deal not only with physical conflicts but also with ethical and moral battles.

Space is a barren place, a desert. As any reader of the Hebrew, Christian, and Islamic bibles knows, deserts are traditionally the places where moral and spiritual battles take place. The question is not merely, "Who will survive?" it is also, "Who *deserves* to survive?"

While the definitions and boundaries of any film genre are difficult to maintain, some critics distinguish between science fiction and science fantasy. *2001, Blade Runner*, and *Soylent Green*, they say, are science fiction because they respect what is known about the natural world, i.e., science. *The Time Machine*, *Star Wars*, *Back to the Future*, and *The Terminator*, on the other hand, often ignore or contradict what science teaches.

2001, one of the pillars upon which modern science fiction films are built, was scrupulous in adhering to what science knew about space travel. Appearing before anyone had actually gone to the moon, everything in the film was substantiated by real life the following year, when men landed there.

Star Wars, the greatest example of science fantasy, simply ignores science. The only Academy Award the film received was for sound, and as any person who has taken ninth grade science knows, there *is* no sound in space because it's a vacuum. That vacuum also means there's no air, so the aerodynamics of the dogfight sequences with the Millennium Falcon would also be impossible. Nor does the film bother with trivial things like gravity, the lack of oxygen, or the speed of light, which the Millennium Falcon routinely exceeds. Similarly, science fantasies such as *The Time Machine*, *Back to the Future* and *The Terminator* totally ignore the scientific fact that time moves in only one direction, and it is impossible for the future to affect the past.

In science fantasy films, the power of technology is invariably awesome, but ultimately it's not what is most important. Rather, what counts is the power of "the force" (*Star Wars*), the power of love (*E. T.*), or will power (*The Terminator*).

Most of what we label "science fiction" is actually science fantasy. As is true for so much else in film, it seems clear that people *want* to ignore what they know to be true in favor of what they *wish* were true. But then, this has always been a characteristic of prophecy.

(See also: FANTASY; TECHNOLOGY; SUSPENSION OF DISBELIEF; REALITY; POWER)

IMAGINE THAT YOU were in a public forum with
Bernard Herrmann, the composer of the musical
score for *Citizen Kane*, and you told him how much
you admired the violin crescendo at the end of the
film when Rosebud is being consumed in the furnace. Or that you told Elmo Williams, the editor of
High Noon, that his montage of twenty-two four-
second cuts as the clock approaches noon was the
greatest part of the film. Or that you told Robert
Surtees, the cinematographer of *The Graduate*, how
awestruck you were at his focus pull on a 500mm
zoom lens in the scene where Benjamin Braddock is
racing to the church to stop Elaine's marriage.

As much as each master of his craft might
inwardly be pleased by your perceptive compli-
ment, the chances are good that in this public
forum, each would respond by saying that the techniques of filmmaking should not call attention to
themselves, but rather should be an integral part of
the overall film. This is the Hollywood party line.
Often called "the seamless web," this theory of
filmmaking has dominated American filmmaking
since its earliest days.

It is not the only possible theory of filmmaking. Josef von Sternberg, who was one of the most
lauded and popular directors of the 1930s, made
films with Marlene Dietrich in which his composition and lighting made it impossible to take your
eyes off her; but he had little interest in story and
character. *Pulp Fiction* and other works directed by
Quentin Tarantino make no attempt to construct

SEAMLESS WEB

seamless webs. But these are exceptions. Most films continue to aspire to an integrated whole in which the individual elements do not call attention to themselves.

(See also: Elegance)

"MRS. ROBINSON, YOU'RE trying to seduce me
… aren't you?" Benjamin Braddock's line in *The
Graduate* invariably produces a laugh because he
dares to verbalize what the audience knows is
going on.

In *The Maltese Falcon, Casablanca, Gone with
the Wind*, nearly all of the James Bond films, and
countless others, the male protagonists *appear*
to be seduced by attractive, powerful women.
None of these males are that naïve, however; all
of them know the game and are merely playing
along. They never really lose control, and they are
never seduced.

In other films, such as *Double Indemnity, Sunset
Boulevard*, and *Chinatown*, however, the protagonist
is seduced, and the results are not pretty. All heroes
are tempted, and the temptation is always a test, but
it is difficult for someone to be truly seduced and
still be called a hero.

(See also: TEMPTATION; WILL POWER)

SEDUCTION

Self-Denial

A CHARACTER WHO *needs* the accoutrements of worldly success will never be seen by the audience as heroic. Heroes are invariably ascetic, denying themselves pleasures and comforts that ordinary people take for granted.

In the production of *Apocalypse Now*, Francis Coppola shot an expensive scene in which Willard has sex with a beautiful woman on a former French plantation. In the production of *The Godfather*, Coppola shot a scene early in the film in which Michael Corleone and Kay Adams have sex in a fancy hotel room. In both cases, Coppola removed the scenes before the film's initial release, not because of censorship or prudery but because the hero's pleasure does not enhance him; it may, in fact, diminish him.

In war films, the hero often declines invitations to partake of food or sex, although he usually encourages his men to relax and have some fun. The hero *can't* relax, *can't* have fun.

In westerns, the hero rides in from the right side of the screen at the beginning and rides out from the left side of the screen at the end, and all he owns in this world is in that tiny bundle behind the saddle we see when he first appears. We don't know if he ever changes his shirt or if he even *has* a shirt to change into, so minimal are his earthly possessions.

In detective, police, mystery, and spy films, the central character usually lives in a one-room apartment or, as is the case with *Lethal Weapon*, a trailer, but it's hard to say the hero *lives* there — it's where he flops when he's overcome with exhaustion. If he drinks, it's beer, not wine; if he has a car, it's a beat-up old clunker.

Does he wish he could get a new car, new apartment, or new shirt? If he does, he never lets on. Like religious and mythical heroes of earlier years, the hero is in this world, but not *of* it. He denies himself the pleasures ordinary mortals yearn for precisely because he *isn't* an ordinary mortal.

(See also: HEROES; DESIRE; MOTIVATION)

SELFISHNESS

FOR WHOM DOES the villain do what he does? For himself. For whom does the hero do what he does? For others.

What does the villain gain by what he does? Power. What does the hero gain by what he does? If he's lucky, as *Shane* demonstrates, maybe a "thank you" from a little boy.

If the hero did what he did for *himself*, he would cease to be a hero.

(See also: SACRIFICE)

CRITICS HATE SENTIMENTALITY, which they usually define as an excess of feeling or feelings expended on someone or something that doesn't deserve it. Films intended for women have frequently been derided as "soap operas," "women's weepies," and "chick flicks." Too much *feeling*.

What is an *excess* of feeling? Obviously, it depends on attitude, culture, audience, the times, and other factors that are not inherent in the specific work but in the person or group making the judgment. What people often condemn is too much of the "wrong" kind of feeling.

There really is no such thing as a film with too much feeling; there are only films that fail to control how its feelings are received by the audience.

(See also: PITY)

SEX

WHILE IT IS almost universally assumed that popular American films are filled with sex and violence, any careful analysis of the films that have been both popular and memorable will reveal that, while there is a very high level of violence, there is comparatively little sex.

Memorable scenes and memorable movies in American history usually find people in pain or people in danger; only rarely do they find people in bed. This is because, while sex is an integral part of life, its *depiction* has never been an integral part of drama.

It is usually enough to be sexy; that is, evocative. Few scenes in memorable popular films depict actual sex.

(See also: LOVE; ROMANCE; REALITY FALLACY)

P. T. BARNUM, who called his circus "The Greatest Show on Earth," at first staged his performances like everyone else — putting up a big tent with a ring in the center into which he brought a succession of elephant acts, sword swallowers, trapeze artists, clowns, monkeys, and anything else that might entertain people. But in 1870 he came up with an idea that has since been emulated in every other entertainment media: simultaneous, rather than sequential, action.

SIMULTANEITY

Instead of a succession of acts, Barnum put three large rings in front of the audience. If some people became bored watching the elephants lumber around in one, they could laugh at the clowns in the second or gasp at the sword swallower exhaling fire in the third.

Film, like the circus, is not limited to presenting sequential action. More than any other art form, film excels at representing *simultaneous* actions, as D.W. Griffith demonstrated when he laid the foundation for parallel editing or "crosscutting" — the presentation of different characters in different locations acting simultaneously.

There are several kinds of simultaneity in film. When Griffith in *The Birth of a Nation* and John Ford in *Stagecoach* staged last-minute rescues of characters who are in dire straits, they conveyed actions that were going on at the same time but in different locations. The audience watching the film pretends that the action freezes in the first locale while we watch the second.

Close to the end of *The Godfather*, Michael Corleone stands in church as godfather to his nephew, renouncing Satan while the action crosscuts among quick shots of his hit men simultaneously assassinating the heads of the other gangster families. The crosscutting is a *tour de force* of cinematic editing and direction, and in quick succession we feel shock, horror, admiration, and amusement at the juxtaposition of these events.

At the very end of *The Godfather*, Coppola demonstrates another way in which film can present different elements simultaneously: through the use of split focus. We see Kay, in the foreground, pouring a drink for her husband, while in the background, we simultaneously see Michael's minions kiss his ring and, for the first time in the film, call him "Godfather." While both of these actions are going on, the door separating Kay from Michael starts to close, throwing her face into shadows, and visually commenting on the now-unbreachable gulf between the two of them.

The ability of film to present simultaneous actions is one of its greatest powers.

WHY DO WE have situation comedies but not situation tragedies? Are not both comedy and tragedy the result of the *situation* that characters find themselves in?

Tom Joad returns home and finds his family and neighbors destitute as a result of the dust bowls in *The Grapes of Wrath*. Rose Sayer and Charlie Allnut find themselves drifting down the Zambezi River in Africa during World War I in *The African Queen*. Steve, Curt, Terri, and Laurie find themselves facing life after high school in Stockton, California, in *American Graffiti*. C. C. Baxter finds himself caught between his bosses' demand for his apartment and his own desires in *The Apartment*. Joe and Jerry find themselves in a garage during the St. Valentine's Day Massacre in *Some Like It Hot*. Travis Bickle finds himself on the streets of decaying New York City in *Taxi Driver*. Atticus Finch finds himself called upon to defend a black man accused of rape in a Southern town in *To Kill a Mockingbird*.

All comedies are situation comedies and all tragedies are situation tragedies. Sometimes, we don't so much identify with the characters as we identify with the situation they're in.

(See also: TRAPS; ATTITUDE)

SOCIAL ISSUES

THE GRAPES OF WRATH is a film about The Depression, *The Best Years of Our Lives* is about America's readjustment after World War II, and *On the Waterfront* is about corruption in the longshoreman's union in the Fifties. That's how these films have sometimes been described, especially when they first came out.

While all of these films dealt with current issues, the fact that these films have *continued* to interest people long after they were released indicates that they are "*about*" much more than the social issues of a specific time and place. All of these films deal with the corruption of society and its destruction of a sense of community — a subject that is always timely. Each also deals with love and loyalty, whether within the family, as in *The Grapes of Wrath*, or between men and women, as in *The Best Years of Our Lives* and *On the Waterfront*.

A film that is *only* about a social issue relevant to a specific time and place will date very quickly. A film that is also about issues that transcend time has a better chance of lasting.

(See also: RELEVANCE; HISTORICAL FILMS; JUSTICE; LOYALTY)

THE IDEA OF community is quite different from the idea of society. Society is usually an amorphous "they" — government agencies such as the CIA, the Presidency, the military, or large corporations. "They" can be the medical, legal, law enforcement, or some other powerful establishment. "They" can be the rich, well-born, well-placed, or powerful.

While "society" in popular films is usually a negative force, "community" is usually depicted positively.

(See also: COMMUNITIES)

SOCIETY

SPECTACLE

ARISTOTLE DIVIDED DRAMA into six parts: plot, character, diction, thought, spectacle, and song. Spectacle, he said, was the least worthy element, and this has tended to be the attitude in the theater ever since. Spectacle doesn't necessarily imply the spectacular; it simply refers to all that is seen, as opposed to what is heard. In the large outdoor amphitheaters in which Greek drama was performed or in the dark, gas-lit Elizabethan theaters, there wasn't much that *could* be seen. As for the spectacular, it often consisted of nothing more than rattling sheets of metal backstage to simulate thunder. By the late nineteenth century, electricity made it possible to simulate a chariot race by having horses run around a revolving carousel. But the spatial, physical, and financial limitations of theatrical performance usually left spectacle less than spectacular.

It is often said that film is a visual medium, which is only part of the story. But it is certainly true that spectacle — what we *see* — is far more important and potentially powerful in film than in theater. In addition, films have the potential to generate a great deal more money than live theatrical performances, and, therefore, filmmakers can afford real chariots, special effects, or computer-generated imagery. Equally important, while the spectacle must be produced in real time in the theater, months can be devoted to producing the spectacle in film.

However, nothing dates more quickly than spectacle, in part because the technology used to produce it constantly improves. Thus, what seemed to be spectacular in one film quickly becomes standard fare.

(See also: HABITUATION; CHARACTERIZATION)

STRUCTURE

STRUCTURE IS THE relationship of the parts to the whole and to each other. Many of the world's most important ideas, theories, and discoveries have dealt primarily with structural relationships. Newton, Darwin, Einstein, and others who made significant contributions to human understanding each discovered in his own field "the relationship of the parts to the whole and to one another."

If an element is genuinely important to the structure of something, changing or eliminating it will usually change its overall effect. If eliminating it does *not* change the work significantly, it isn't structurally important.

The structural elements of film include but are not limited to plot, characters, settings, time, place, actions, objects, sounds, color, light, and movement. Anything we see, hear, or feel in a film can potentially be an important structural element.

Films move through real time but consist of imaginary events that are not bound by reality. Therefore, nothing is more important to a film than finding the appropriate relationship between real and imaginary time, between the running time of the film and the time that elapses within the story.

When a film doesn't work, it is often because one or more important events were placed too early, before the audience was ready for them, or too late, after they had ceased to need them. The sequence of events, their pacing, and their relationship with one another are all important structural concerns.

While watching a film, the audience is generally not aware of structure because its members can't *know* the relationship of the parts to the whole and to each other until the film is over. A film's creators, however, must be acutely aware of its structure.

(See also: ELEGANCE)

STRUCTURE, DRAMATIC

THE POWER OF dramatic structure is so great that it influences all other forms of storytelling, even news and documentaries. Dramatic structure resembles that of a joke: there is rising development that reaches a climax and releases the tension it has set up. Drama that does *not* create tension had better be short; otherwise, it will be dull.

In dramatic structure, everything is regarded as meaningful and everything is intentional, because dramatic structure operates like Newtonian physics — everything has a cause, and for every cause there is an effect. Accidents and coincidences occur all the time in real life, and the history of individuals and entire societies often turns on them. But dramatic structure is based on the fundamental assumption that what individuals do *determines* what happens — not fate, God, history, accidents, or coincidences (see: DESTINY; INDIVIDUALISM).

The logic of life, as we all learn through experience, is that all too often there *isn't* any logic. Ironically, a drama that tries to simulate this lack of logic stands a good chance of being called unrealistic.

What audiences seek in drama is a structure they seldom find in real life.

(See also: STRUCTURE; STRUCTURE, EPISODIC; STRUCTURE, JOURNALISTIC; ACCIDENTS; DESTINY; REALITY FALLACY)

Structure, Episodic

CHILDREN AND OTHER inexperienced storytellers tend to tell episodic stories. The dead giveaway to episodic structure is that actions are linked by the word "and." Any story that follows the form, "This happened, and then that happened, and then the next thing happened," is episodic. Dramatic structure, on the other hand, links its events with the word "but." It uses the familiar form, "The good news is ... *but* the bad news is ...." The danger in using episodic structure is that the story becomes less compelling or even boring as it develops because we do not see the *relationship* between events.

Road pictures, whether they literally take to the road as in *Easy Rider* and *Thelma & Louise*, follow the yellow brick road, as in *The Wizard of Oz,* or flow down a river, as in *The African Queen* and *Apocalypse Now,* face the challenge of episodic structure. While the events that occur on the road are not bound by a cause-and-effect structure and could often have been arranged in a different order, the *internal* development of the central characters and their reactions to events does, in memorable films, follow a dramatic structure.

The structure of dramatic stories can be represented by drawing a triangle that resembles a mountain. Episodic stories, on the other hand, can be represented by a straight line with bumps in it. Stories with a dramatic structure end in a climax; stories with an episodic structure often just end.

(See also: BUT; STRUCTURE; BIOGRAPHIES)

STRUCTURE, JOURNALISTIC

EVERY JOURNALISM COURSE begins by instructing students on the "Five W's of Journalism": Who, What, Where, When, and sometimes Why. The structure of a journalistic report is often represented as an upside-down triangle, as opposed to drama, which is often shown as a pyramid. The difference in the two structures stems largely from *where* the most important elements of the story are placed.

Journalists learn to "get to the point" in the very first paragraph, partly because newspaper readers search for the gist of a piece, and once they find it, they often skip to the next article. Equally important, newspapers are supported by advertising, which usually takes up the bulk of the space in the newspaper. If the editor decides that another article or ad must be squeezed into a space, he must have the ability to cut the later parts or move them elsewhere.

Journalistic stories usually get less interesting the further you get into them. With drama, it is just the opposite —if the later parts of a dramatically structured work were cut out, the consumer would feel cheated.

Journalistic structure has remained quite consistent in print media for the past three hundred years. In television and movies, though, journalistic structure is difficult to sustain, because if you're going to tell people who, what, where, when, and why early in the piece, why continue to watch? The element of real time in television and movies forces its creators to move away from journalistic structure and into dramatic structure. This is why often in documentaries and even newscasts, the "best" is saved for last.

(See also: STRUCTURE, DRAMATIC)

Subplots have been defined in various ways: sometimes as a storyline that is entirely separate from the primary storyline, sometimes as one that is separate but related to the primary storyline. As with everything about effective storytelling, what's important is the concentration of energy and focus. If the subplot deals with something that doesn't affect the central characters, it may not belong in the film.

SUBPLOTS

It is possible to create an interesting character in interesting scenes that don't really contribute to the main story of the film. When this happens, the filmmaker may find too late that instead of adding to the total impact of the film , he has diffused it. For example, many people found that the most interesting part of *The Godfather: Part III* was the story of Vincent Mancini, who succeeds Michael Corleone as don in a story that parallels the original *Godfather*. But *The Godfather: Part III* is also Michael Corleone's story — as the audience expected. Vincent's story competes with Michael's. The result is the audience is never sure what or who the film is about — which is always dangerous.

(See also: Conflict, Single; Backstories; Elegance)

SUCCESS

EVERYONE KNOWS THAT Americans aspire to success, which they hope will bring them happiness. Everyone also knows that "success" in America is manifested in expensive homes containing lavish furnishings and appliances, complete with an ideal spouse and a coveted car in the driveway.

But no memorable popular film is *about* such success. If the character aspires to it early in the film, as do George Bailey in *It's a Wonderful Life*, Esther Blodgett in *A Star is Born* and Bud Fox in *Wall Street*, you can be sure the character will realize before the film is over that there are more important things in life.

Success, as Americans define it in real life, is not something the hero aspires to, and happiness is something the hero no longer is concerned with or perhaps even capable of.

The hero's life is filled with pain, sacrifice, loss, and death. What person aspiring to "success" would choose such a path?

In the tough-minded world Americans live in, what do we call someone who works really hard, puts up with excruciatingly difficult and painful situations, makes immense sacrifices, and then gets no reward commensurate with his time and effort? In other cultures at other times, such people might have been called "saints"; in contemporary culture, they are often called "losers."

This helps explain why, as much as we seem to admire them, we seldom seek to emulate the heroes we see in films.

(See also: ENDINGS, HAPPY; SELF-DENIAL)

EARLY IN *Lethal Weapon*, Martin Riggs sits alone in his tiny trailer, drinking as he fondles a picture of his dead wife. Grief overcomes him and he opens his mouth and puts a gun into it and starts to squeeze the trigger. *It's a Wonderful Life* begins with George Bailey on a bridge about to commit suicide. In *M★A★S★H*, the dentist discovers he is impotent and plans to kill himself and instead of trying to talk him out of it, his buddies make elaborate plans for the ceremony. As he does, "Suicide is Painless," the theme song for the film and the popular long-running television series, plays merrily on the soundtrack.

None of these suicides is completed. If they were, *Lethal Weapon* and *It's a Wonderful Life* would have nowhere to go. *M★A★S★H* could continue on because the dentist is not one of the central characters, but the emotional effect would be so great that the film would have difficulty continuing to provoke laughs because, despite what the song says, suicide is not painless.

In *The Wild Bunch, Butch Cassidy and the Sundance Kid*, and *Thelma & Louise*, the endings depict the thinly disguised suicides of the title characters. But the recognition of their self-destruction is blocked by the fact that the acting, music, and direction are upbeat and even gleeful.

"It is better to die on your feet than live on your knees" is a line attributed to heroes of both the Mexican and Spanish civil wars; a similar expression is captured in the American description of people who, like those at the Alamo, "died with their boots on." Such suicidal gestures are inherently paradoxical, which is why *The Wild Bunch, Butch Cassidy and the Sundance Kid,* and *Thelma & Louise* all end in freeze frames. If they gave their audiences a chance to *think* about their endings and see the consequences, the audience might realize that what they thought was a blaze of glory was also the extinguishing of a flame.

(See also: ENDINGS, HAPPY; WILL POWER; PARADOX)

ALFRED HITCHCOCK WAS famously known as "The Master of Suspense." The fact that nobody of comparable stature was known as "The Master of Surprise" tells us that there is an important distinction between the two.

Hitchcock differentiated between surprise and suspense by saying that if two people sit down at a table and a bomb goes off, we are surprised; but if we first see someone plant a bomb under the table and then two people sit down at it, we have suspense. This is demonstrated in the famous scene in an Italian restaurant in *The Godfather*. Michael plans to kill the drug dealer, Sollozzo, and the crooked cop, McCluskey, who acts as his bodyguard. The suspense builds as the driver of the car carrying Michael to the restaurant reverses direction on a bridge: where are they taking him? Once inside the restaurant, Michael speaks to Sollozzo in Sicilian; as the conversation is untranslated, we wonder what's going on. He goes into the bathroom where a gun is supposed to be hidden but has trouble finding it. When he finally does, Michael resumes his seat at the table and waits for the subway to clatter by before he makes his move. Finally, when the tension has reached its peak, Michael plugs the two bad guys at point-blank range. We knew what was going to happen; we just didn't know when and how.

The difference between surprise and suspense lies in the state of the audience's knowledge. As is so often true, when filmmakers *share* something with their audience, as happens with suspense, the audience becomes more deeply invested in the story than if they passively witness events that the filmmaker totally controls, as happens with surprise.

(See: MYSTERY)

THE POET SAMUEL Taylor Coleridge wrote of the "willing suspension of disbelief," a term that has become a fundamental concept in our understanding of the relationship between the audience and the screen.

On the one hand, we all know that romantic comedies will end with the lovers' embrace, that the monster will be dead by the end of the horror film, that the gunfight at the end of the western will leave the villain dead and the hero still standing. We could stop the projector ten minutes into almost any popular film, and if we asked the audience how it will end, we would find that they guess correctly nearly all the time.

On the one hand, we know that what we're watching is "only a movie," yet we suspend that knowledge and act as if we were experiencing something real. That is why our palms sweat, our breath is bated, and adrenaline flows.

To accomplish this, everything that happens in a popular movie is centripetal, that is, draws us into its center. Anything that might draw us *away* from that center — to consider the real world, for example — is avoided.

(See also: MANIPULATION; SEAMLESS WEB; FLOW; DOCUMENTARIES)

SUSPENSION OF DISBELIEF

T.

Nearly all memorable popular movies could appropriately be titled "Trapped."

TALKING HEADS

WRITERS NEW TO filmmaking often give characters speeches that fill a page or more — creating what the industry refers to as "talking heads" — and are then chagrined to discover that this is considered amateurish.

Most speeches in films last no longer than a single shot, which, in contemporary films, is measured in seconds. But there have been intensely dramatic scenes that far exceed this generalization. In the opening scene of *Patton*, for example, the title character tells his men: "No bastard ever won a war by dying for his country. He won it by making the other poor dumb bastard die for his country." The line comes in the middle of a *very* long monologue. In *Apocalypse Now,* Kurtz advises Willard: "You must make a friend of horror. Horror and mortal terror are your friend." This, too, comes in the middle of a very long monologue.

Casablanca is a very talky film, as is the more recent *Pulp Fiction*, and many memorable popular films are full of talk. There is ultimately nothing wrong with talking heads — if what they are talking about is interesting. If it's just talk, it's too long no matter how short it is.

(See also: DIALOGUE)

Team**WHILE ALL TEAMS** are not couples, all couples are a
team. What holds a team together is loyalty; what
destroys it is betrayal. At the center of both loyalty
and betrayal lies the issue of respect (see: RESPECT).

Members of a team act in ways that will
enhance one another's power. When this is not so,
when the actions of one diminish the power of the
other, the members are antagonists, whether they
are aware of it or not.

The antagonist and the hero often *could* be
on the same team, and a cliché of team-oriented
genres such as the western and the gangster film is
that the protagonist used to be on the same side as
the antagonist.

Team members, though, are not defined by
their similarities; they are defined by their similar *goals*. In fact, one of the basic principles of the
formation of teams is, "Opposites attract" (see:
OPPOSITES).

"Buddy films" such as *Butch Cassidy and the
Sundance Kid* are those in which the members of the
team behave in many ways as if they were a couple.
Whether there is an erotic component or not, such
stories often take on many of the attributes of a love
story (see: LOVE).

As we see most clearly in sports or business, a
team comes together for a specific occasion or task,
and when it is over, members of the team can, if
they wish, go their separate ways. Couples, however, have no specific occasion or task; they remain
together for a wide variety of events over a relatively long time.

TEAMS AND COUPLES

Many of the most memorable teams in film history are so intertwined that it is common for people to get their specific identities confused. Which one, for example, was Laurel and which Hardy? Butch Cassidy and the Sundance Kid? Thelma and Louise?

When two individual characters fuse so that audiences have trouble remembering who is who, it can be a mark, not of a creative failure, but of its success. When this happens, the answer to the question, "Who is the protagonist?" is, "*They* are."

(See also: Heroes; Heroes, Single; Antagonists; Love; Loyalty; Betrayal)

IN EARLIER STORIES, nature was often associated with the wilderness or jungle — dangerous and chaotic places that needed to be brought within human control.

In modern times, however, nature has often come to stand for that which is peaceful and harmonious. The dangerous and chaotic forces in popular storytelling now are often machines, as HAL the computer in *2001*, the Replicants in *Blade Runner* and the robots in the *Terminator* series all demonstrate.

As always, what lies at the center of powerful storytelling is the issue of power. When we say that nature or machines are "out of control," what we really mean is "out of *our* control." When *anything* is beyond human control, there is fertile ground for storytelling. Technology fails to save young Regan in *The Exorcist,* and it threatens to destroy the human race in *The Terminator* and *The Matrix.* The solution to out-of-control technology only occasionally lies in better technology; more often, it lies in some uniquely human quality that lies within, as *Star Wars* demonstrates.

(See also: CHIMERAS; MONSTERS; POWER; CHAOS; TOOLS)

TELEVISION VS. FILM

THE STRONGEST STORIES in film and drama deal with a single individual and a single problem. Television, however, is devoted to series rather than to individual stories, and usually deals with multiple individuals and an endless sequence of problems.

Half of television consists of situation comedies; the other half consists of situation tragedies (see: SITUATIONS). For both forms, there is none of that "Call to Adventure" stuff that comes up in myths and movies (see: CALL TO ADVENTURE). In television, which is rigidly governed by the clock, there is no time to sit around waiting for a "call." Characters must be presented with one crisis after another — preferably more than any normal mortal or group of mortals could ever handle in a single day.

In the most memorable films and dramas, all the action and all the other characters generally revolve around a single central character. This structure has been supplanted in contemporary television by the drama of the group, in which action moves back and forth between several different characters and there is no single narrative thread. (Not coincidentally, this makes the suturing of commercials into the story feel less disruptive.)

The need to sustain a series over dozens and sometimes hundreds of episodes and to get into its stories quickly explains why television characters so often work in the medical, police, detective, and law fields. In these fields, you don't have to go looking for adventure, you just show up for work.

(See also: HEROES, SINGLE; CONFLICT; STRUCTURE, EPISODIC)

AT A CRITICAL point in *The Sound of Music*, Captain von Trapp says of the Nazis who have taken over his beloved country, "To refuse them would be fatal for all of us; to join them would be unthinkable." In *The Maltese Falcon*, Sam Spade tells Brigid O'Shaughnessy he loves her but says, "I won't play the sap for you ... I won't because all of me wants to, regardless of consequences." In *Star Wars*, Darth Vader urges Luke to "Join me and I will complete your training." Temptations are tests, some of the many inevitable crises that confront the hero. They occur for the reasons all tests do: to see whether the hero's got the right stuff.

(See also: SEDUCTION; TESTS; WILL POWER; DEFIANCE)

TEMPTATION

Tests

You become a hero the way you become a doctor or lawyer — by passing tests. Unlike these professions, however, the tests heroes are given are not based on education and knowledge, nor are they taken in front of a computer terminal; they're taken in front of a tribunal called the audience.

Arthur C. Clarke, the co-writer with Stanley Kubrick of *2001*, originally intended that it be clear to the audience that the black obelisks on the earth, moon, and in Jupiter's orbit were placed there as a test to determine whether humans deserved to evolve beyond their current state. (Kubrick decided to obscure the point of this test, which left many in the audience puzzled.) In *Star Wars,* the tests are much clearer — the training, battles, and tortures inflicted on Luke Skywalker are all there to determine whether he is worthy of becoming a Jedi Knight. In *North by Northwest* Roger Thornhill faces one test after another, as do all of Hitchcock's protagonists. In *Lethal Weapon*, Martin Riggs is tested and tortured throughout the film, as is the custom in detective films, thrillers, and virtually all action/ adventure films.

In all film genres — perhaps in all *stories* — heroes are trapped, tortured, and wounded because we recognize the profound truth that lies behind clichés such as, "No pain, no gain."

Without a test there is no way to keep score, no way to know whether someone *deserves* the recognition and status we have the power to give them when we label them "heroes."

(See also: Wounds; Sacrifice; Heroes)

HERMAN MELVILLE ONCE declared, "To produce a
mighty course, you must choose a mighty theme."
We might say of memorable characters that you
produce a mighty character by linking him to a
mighty theme. The word "theme," however, is like
"character" — we all toss around the word, but few
of us bother to examine it very closely.

What is a theme? Often, it is simply an idea
repeated often enough that people begin to see that
it has been used over and over again. For Jesus, it
was compassion, for Marx it was oppression, for
Freud it was the unconscious.

Is theme important to popular film? Of course.
But not if you think of it in the way so many people teach it — as some statement about "the human
condition," filled with pompous gravitas. "Man's
inhumanity to man," for example, is the most-cited
theme in fiction and drama, yet it's also what underlies most articles on the front pages of newspapers
and the evening news on television. There's nothing
especially interesting in the theme of man's inhumanity to man, the power of love, the dangers of
lust, the self-destructiveness of greed, the crippling
legacy of jealousy. We've heard 'em all many times.

In order to be compelling, themes must be
expressed, not as platitudes but as actions. Themes
must not be just talked about. The truest of
clichés about film commands, "Show, don't tell,"
and that is how memorable popular films handle
their themes.

THEME

Time

WHAT TIME IS it when a film begins? While novelists
habitually write in the past tense, films always take
place in the present, so the time is *now*.

Partly because it moves through real time, film
has only rudimentary tools for indicating something
that is *not* "now." The filmmaker can superimpose
a title card that says "1890" at the beginning of the
film, or the audience can be allowed to take its cues
from the lack of automobiles and the funny clothes
and hairstyles. But 1890 is the *present* time of the
film, and unless and until the filmmaker tells us otherwise, it remains so.

Films have a limited repertoire for indicating
otherwise — a title card that says, "1910," perhaps,
or the leaves falling off the trees, the seasons changing, or the pages of a paper calendar being torn off.
There are not a lot of devices to indicate a time
change in film that are *not* clichés, and they frequently are heavy-handed.

It takes only a small amount of manipulation of
time for a film to feel experimental. *Citizen Kane*,
for example, basically follows chronological order
once it gets past the introductory newsreel. But,
because one character tells his part of the story in
flashback, and the film then returns to the present
and introduces another character, and a couple of
times Orson Welles has that person's story over-
lap the preceding story, the film *seems* to have
experimented with time in significant ways, even
though its experimentation is quite modest.

Whenever a film moves out of a straight-
forward chronological progression, filmmakers

have to carefully devise their strategies. Playing with time can be very interesting, but it can also be confusing. Conversely, when the passage of time is clear and compelling, as in *High Noon,* the effect can be riveting.

(See also: FLOW; CRISIS POINT, ONE-HOUR; DEADLINES; FLASHBACKS; BACKSTORIES; MYSTERY)

TOOLS

HEROES USUALLY DON'T have superior tools; they have a superior morality.

If the hero does possess superior tools, these will very frequently be lost or broken before the story is over. The reason for this is simple: the person who *relies* on superior tools is, by definition, not a hero. Losing them or losing the power they possess exposes the protagonist to mortal danger ... and gives him the opportunity to *become* a hero.

(See also: TECHNOLOGY; ARMOR; WEAPONS)

WHEN THE MOVIE *Casablanca* came out in 1943, it happened to coincide with a meeting the Allied leaders were holding in the actual city in North Africa. While neither the politicians nor the film-makers had anything to do with this coincidence, the fact that the city was suddenly in the news gave the film a recognition value it would not otherwise have had.

When *The China Syndrome*, which dealt with the meltdown of a nuclear reactor at an American power plant, came out in 1979, it was the good fortune of the film but the bad fortune of the nuclear power industry that an accident occurred at the Three Mile Island nuclear plant in the eastern United States, which seemed to validate the plot of the film.

When someone says, "I think that would make a good film," it usually takes two years — and frequently as long as nine or ten — to develop a suitable screenplay, receive sufficient funding, attract appropriate stars, attach the right director, and get onto a distribution schedule. No one is capable of accurately predicting that their film will be in synch with current events when it is released. The depiction in the original *The Manchurian Candidate* of a plot to assassinate a presidential candidate became *too* topical when John F. Kennedy was killed, and the film was pulled from release.

Topicality is not something filmmakers are good at injecting into a film; rather, it is something audiences perceive in it — or don't — when the film is released.

(See also: RELEVANCE; SOCIAL ISSUES)

TRAGEDY

WE HAVE BRITISH comedy, American comedy, German comedy, etc., but while we have ancient Greek tragedy, in modern times there isn't anything we can point to that is uniquely British tragedy, American tragedy, or German tragedy. While comedy is bound in with specific cultures, places, and times, tragedy tends to be universal. Early in the development of television, laugh tracks were added to comedies, but nobody has ever suggested adding a *crying* track to tragedy. We may need to be told something is funny, but we do not need to be told it's tragic.

However, if we look at the way American films are marketed to the public, we would never know there *is* such a thing as tragedy. In the United States, the word "tragedy" is banned as sternly as other cultures ban certain terms for sex and bodily functions. In American culture, which prizes above else the power of the individual to determine his destiny, the fatalism of tragedy is heresy (see: DESTINY).

This does not mean that the tragic *sensibility* is banned; in fact, it is alive and well in a good proportion of America's most memorable films, most of which are, in fact, closer to tragedy than they are to comedy. It is a sensibility, though, that dare not speak its name.

Tragedy usually ends with its central character dead, on his way to prison, or cut off from other human beings. Comedy usually ends with a wedding, a party, or some other celebration of human community. If, however, a film *begins* with such a celebration, there is the danger it will move towards tragedy.

Whether a story is ultimately a comedy or a tragedy depends largely on the way it structures the relationship between the protagonist's desires and duty. If a film spends a lot of time focusing on the central character's desire, it will probably move toward comedy. If it spends a lot of its time focusing on the central character's duty, it will probably move toward tragedy.

The most memorable actions of the protagonist in comedy often take place near the end. In tragedy, however, they more often take place near the beginning. Lear gives his kingdom to his daughters; Macbeth kills the king; Charles Foster Kane and Michael Corleone seize power. Once they do, they spend the rest of the story dealing with the *consequences* of their actions.

Tragedy tends to affirm law, order, and the supremacy of reason. Charles Foster Kane, Michael Corleone, Lawrence of Arabia, and the majority of our most memorable characters are seldom carried away by emotion. They *think* about what they are going to do and then they do it coolly and with as much forethought as they can muster. When they don't, when they are swept away by their passions, it is likely to end badly. Thus, when Kane impetuously decides to stay with Susan, his story goes downhill. When Michael marries the Sicilian girl, Apollonia, she quickly dies. When Lawrence suddenly declares "No prisoners!" his story enters its darkest moments. Oedipus impulsively kills the man who turns out to be his father; Romeo impulsively drinks poison; and Stanley Kowalski in *A Streetcar Named Desire* impulsively commits rape. Impulsivity, we see over and over again, leads to tragedy.

The common belief that Hollywood films need a "happy ending," which is synonymous with the acquisition of power, stems from comedies (see: ENDINGS, HAPPY). The course of tragedy is, inevitably a *descent* from power.

Many tragedies resemble the myth of Icarus, who at first soared above the ground, but then, ignoring the warnings, flew too near the sun and plummeted to his death. Tragedy constantly takes the position that the power that enables someone to rise above other people is flimsy and fleeting, leading to what the Greeks called *hubris*, or overweening pride, and that it all too easily leads to a fall.

Tragedies invariably end in a way that confirms the audience's sense of justice. However, modern audiences don't have much use for the "fatal flaw" that was so common a feature of earlier tragedy — in part because justice has nothing to do with a flaw. Modern tragedies more often stem from decisions and actions the central character is responsible for, rather than from things over which he has no control (see: DESTINY).

Comedies such as *Some Like It Hot* often get away with arbitrary endings where there is a miraculous personality transformation. Tragedies such as *Citizen Kane*, however, end the way they do because they *must* — because of the inexorable logic of the character's actions.

If we knew how things were going to turn out, we would never begin many of them. It is the denial of consequences that so often allows us to laugh. The recognition and *acceptance* of the consequences of our decisions and actions, however, lies at the heart of tragedy.

(See also: COMEDY; DECISIONS)

TRAN-SCENDENCE

THE HERO SEEKS power, but it is never for his own self-aggrandizement; rather, it is for something *beyond* the self, something that is higher and more valuable than one's own pleasure or even one's own life.

The transcendent cause the hero struggles for can be an idea, a discovery, or saving other human beings. Whatever it is, the benefit is not just to himself. Without transcendence, one cannot become a hero.

(See also: TRANSFORMATION; PYRRHIC VICTORIES; SACRIFICE; HEROES; CAUSES; MISSIONS; MOTIVATION)

MANY OF THE most memorable stories involve the birth of consciousness, where a sense of the self and the possibility for action in the world is born. Tom Joad in *The Grapes of Wrath*, Willard in *Apocalypse Now*, the three returning soldiers in *The Best Years of Our Lives*, and the narrators in both *To Kill a Mockingbird* and *Forrest Gump* all awaken to powers they did not know they had. Sometimes, as in *Lawrence of Arabia* or *Gandhi,* an entire culture awakens to its potential.

When either an individual or a society awakens to its own potential, the most powerful of all possible transformations occurs. The fact that it happens so often in American films helps explain why the world has been so receptive to them.

(See also: INDIVIDUATION; GIFTS; POWER; IMPOTENCE)

TRAPS

NEARLY ALL OF the most memorable popular movies could appropriately be titled "Trapped."

James Bond in *Goldfinger* is strapped to a table with a laser beam inching upward between his legs. Dave Bowman is locked outside the spaceship in *2001*. Bonnie and Clyde and Butch Cassidy and the Sundance Kid are surrounded by a posse. R. P. McMurphy is bound in a straitjacket in *One Flew Over the Cuckoo's Nest*. Roger Thornhill, in *North by Northwest*, is trapped by a crop-dusting plane and later on the face of Mount Rushmore. Thelma and Louise are trapped between the police on one side and the Grand Canyon on the other.

Heroes are people who, when caught in a trap, use all their strength, intelligence, ingenuity and will to escape *through their own efforts*. That is why they are trapped in the first place — to give them a chance to prove that they *are* heroes.

(See also: ACTION; WILL POWER; HEROES; RESCUE; TEMPTATION; TESTS; TRIALS)

TRIALS

As EVERY LAWYER knows, many trials adhere to dramatic principles. Conversely, many films are structured like trials, whether or not they are actually situated in a courtroom.

In each, there is an audience watching, weighing both what is said but also what is not. Each questions motives and intentions, watching for clues in behavior and body language. As the audience/jury acquires information and observes, it leans one way, then, it leans the other. If this back-and-forth movement is missing, the audience/jury is likely to become increasingly bored.

It has been customary since the Romans to invoke the image of the scale when discussing trials. The image is equally useful for drama, sports, and other contests that appeal to large numbers of people. The most interesting stories and contests, like the most interesting trials, are those in which the scales tilt first one way and then another, and the outcome isn't clear until the very end.

(See also: TESTS; DUALITY)

TRUE STORIES

FILMS ARE OFTEN advertised and begin with the claim that they are "based on a true story," which often invites critics, historians, and people who have nothing better to do with their time than to point out how many things in the film are *not* true.

If we wanted the truth, we would go sit on a street corner and watch life pass us by. What we search for is some *pattern* to the many potential truths, some *story* that makes sense out of the cacophony of voices, images, and experiences we encounter in real life — some *structure* that gives it meaning.

Is *Citizen Kane* a true story? A great many of the events and details parallel in substance and even in chronology the life of William Randolph Hearst, the powerful newspaperman who nearly destroyed the film. If Hamlet, Macbeth, Julius Caesar, and others had not been long dead when William Shakespeare told their stories, these mighty figures might also have sought to destroy this upstart hack who dared put words in their mouths.

Nearly all "true stories" have been reshaped, with major events deleted and major scenes, events, and dialogue invented to suit the needs, not of truth, but of effective storytelling.

(See also: REALISM; REALITY FALLACY; ADAPTATIONS; BIOGRAPHIES)

TRUTHTELLERS

THE CHILD WHO exclaims "the emperor has no clothes" may cause shock or panic in other characters, but the audience laughs. The old person who blurts out the truth, especially if it's to some pompous authority figure, will also get laughs. The child speaks the truth because it doesn't know any better and is not aware of the consequences; the old person because he or she doesn't care.

Because telling the truth has consequences, scenes in which the truth is told are often highlights of drama. The hero is a special kind of truthteller: he knows the consequences, and he does care, but he *dares* to tell the truth — which is one of the things that makes him a hero.

(See also: UNMASKING; DECEPTION; DETECTIVE FILMS; MISDIRECTION; REALISM)

U

*Deep down inside many of us
lies the fear that there
is* no deep down inside.

UNMASKING

DEEP DOWN INSIDE many of us lies the fear that there *is* no deep down inside — that all we are is what our genes, our society, our schooling, and other forces outside ourselves have made us. This leads to the fear that, if other people saw what we were *really* like, they would cease to love us, cease to respect us, and cease to have anything to do with us. And so, we pretend to be what we are not.

Memorable comedic and dramatic scenes often involve an unmasking, where the pretenses of character are stripped away. *Singin' in the Rain, Tootsie, The Graduate,* and *Some Like It Hot* all have them, and so do *Citizen Kane, Sunset Boulevard, The Godfather*, and *Chinatown*. So much energy goes into masking; it follows, therefore, that scenes of unmasking are inherently powerful.

(See also: DISCOVERY; REVELATION; REDEMPTION)

V

One of the great themes in religion and popular storytelling is that those who have power often lack virtue, while those who lack power possess virtue in abundance. If this were an accurate reflection of our values, there would be more striving in life and in film for virtue, and less for power.

Values

Next time you're at home watching a film on DVD with others, try stopping the film halfway through and asking the people in the room to rate the power of each of the characters at that point in the film relative to the others. You will nearly always find substantial agreement.

But if you then ask them how they *value* those same characters, there will frequently be significant disagreement. People often value characters differently at different points in the story, and their valuation often correlates with their opinion of the film as a whole. If you see Michael Corleone as nothing more than a ruthless gangster determined to wipe out all opposition, you will value *The Godfather* one way. If you see him as a man forced to take desperate measures to save his family, you will see the film in another way.

Nothing is more complicated nor more personal than someone's values. And nothing is as likely to manifest the contradictions and paradoxes in us, as well as in the characters on the screen, as the values we and they hold. For example, one of the great themes in religion and popular storytelling is that those who have power often lack virtue, while those who lack power possess virtue in abundance. If this were an accurate reflection of our values, there would be more striving in life and in film for virtue, and less for power.

(See also: Ethics; Power; Justice; Sacrifice; Wounds)

THE HERO IS a victim who refuses to be victimized, who instead of passively taking the mistreatment he receives, defies what is happening to him. He suffers and sacrifices, but it would be wrong to feel sorry for him, because ultimately he will transcend victimhood and transform himself into the opposite of a victim: a hero.

(See also: SACRIFICE; DEFIANCE; PITY; TRANSCENDENCE)

VICTIMS

VILLAINS

WHAT DO *Star Wars, Silence of the Lambs, Apocalypse Now, Alien,* and *The Terminator* have in common? Their villains are more interesting and memorable than their heroes. Children dress up as Darth Vader far more than Luke Skywalker. We remember Kurtz's final line "the horror, the horror" in *Apocalypse Now*, but probably not Willard's. And while we may remember that Hannibal Lecter ate the liver of a census-taker with fava beans and a nice glass of Chianti, who knows — or cares — what Clarice Starling dined on?

Heroes can easily become boring. This is because they have to *act* like heroes — and what a limitation that is! Villains, however, can do all kinds of interesting and even horrifying things. This is why horror films are usually about the villain, who is also generally the title character. It may also be why horror has become such an important part of so many recent films — such villains can be *fun*.

There are, however, few, if any, memorable popular films in which villains prevail over the hero at the end of the film. We know well in advance how the battle between heroes and villains will end, but we pretend we don't so that the story can continue (see: SUSPENSION OF DISBELIEF).

The power of the villain is usually established early in a film, and he is usually more powerful than the hero throughout most of the film — otherwise the story has no place to go. But the villain does not necessarily gain strength as the story progresses, while the hero always does.

The hero need not stand out from the crowd; if Luke Skywalker, Captain Willard, or Clarice Starling walked into a room, nobody would notice. But if Darth Vader, Kurtz, or Hannibal Lecter did, all eyes would turn to them.

Villains often want to change society, but it is invariably for their personal benefit. Heroes either want to keep society the way it is or restore it to what it once was. In this sense, villains are inherently radical and heroes inherently conservative.

Ethical decisions play an important part in the battle between villains and heroes. As Darth Vader demonstrates, it is as important for the villain to *choose* to be bad as it is for the hero to choose to be good.

Like the hero, the villain is usually surrounded by a community. But the villain's community consists of underlings whom he dominates, whereas the hero is at the forefront of a community whose members seldom need to be commanded and certainly cannot be coerced.

Villains often represent corruption or perversion. They often lack restraint and are out of control, engaging in acts of random cruelty and violence. Kurtz in *Apocalypse Now* demonstrates this in his admiration of the Viet Cong, who chopped off the arms of babies, in his dumping the head of Chief onto Willard, and in his writing "Drop the bomb — kill them all!" in his book. The hero also engages in violence, but it is never random and is always under control (see: SELF-DENIAL; WILL POWER).

Memorable villains are not simple. The title character in *All About Eve*, Mrs. Robinson in *The Graduate*, Nurse Ratched in *One Flew Over the Cuckoo's Nest*, the various British officers and diplomats in *Lawrence of Arabia,* and the demon in *The Exorcist* all are complex characters.

Filmmakers too often think they have to dehumanize their villains because they fear the audience may care less about the hero if they care at all about the villain. But one of the achievements of *2001* is that HAL, the computer that attempts to kill everyone onboard, comes off as the most humanized character in the film. Caring *about* the villain is a crucial element of characterization.

Heroes are never perfect, but villains often are. The title character in *The Terminator* can't be stopped, and no matter how badly it is injured, it heals itself and keeps on going. The title character in *Alien* is "a perfect organism" and so too is the title character in *Jaws*, who is described as a "perfect eating machine." Their perfection is often what makes villains fascinating.

It is in their reactions that the true character of the villain is revealed — the villain's heart beats more gladly watching the suffering and tears of others. Mr. Potter in *It's a Wonderful Life* cannot restrain his delight when he talks to George Bailey about the impending demise of George's Savings and Loan. Lt. Col. Kilgore in *Apocalypse Now* loves "the smell of napalm in the morning." All of the characters in *Dr. Strangelove* are having a great time as they bring about the destruction of the human race.

The best villains are not totally different from the hero; they, in fact, are often quite like him. What ultimately differentiates the villain from the hero is that villains act totally on behalf of their own self-interest, whereas heroes act on behalf of other people or a cause.

(See also: HEROES; HEROINES; DUALITY; PARADOX)

VIOLATION

WHEN MCCLUSKEY, THE corrupt cop in *The Godfather*, breaks Michael Corleone's jaw, or the man with a knife in *Chinatown* slits Jake Gittes' nose open, the physical violence they perpetrate on the protagonist eventually heals. But when the title character in *Gandhi* is thrown off the train because he dared to sit in the first-class compartment reserved for white men, his psyche (the Greek word for soul) has been violated, and such injuries never heal. That is why scenes of violation are so powerful and often so much more memorable than mere violence.

(See also: VIOLENCE; REVENGE)

Films, like drama since the Greeks, have been filled with violence. In fact, if people were killed or wounded as often in real life as they are in films, our planet might now be nearly devoid of *homo sapiens*. We see so much violence that we scarcely notice it, and it has little effect (see: Habituation). If you look at the list of memorable popular films near the beginning of this book and count the acts of violence in them, you may be astonished at how many of them there are.

Violence

Women are often repelled by what they see as "excessive violence." Men, on the other hand, are repelled by what they see as excessive feelings — "that sentimental stuff" (see: Sentimentality). The films that seem to attract men and women equally combine violence and sentiment in ways that overcome the resistance of each gender. *Gone with the Wind, Casablanca, From Here to Eternity,* and *The Godfather* are all love stories. But they are also war stories, and it is the *combination* of love and war that often brings success.

Both love and violence involve a "letting go," a loss of inhibitions. "I couldn't control myself" is often used to justify both violence and love. All societies have sought to control how and under what conditions people are allowed to "let go" because both love and violence affect a society's survival, one helping to create it and the other having the potential to destroy it.

There are those who think that love will produce a just world, and those who think that violence will. Any examination of human history shows that both methods have repeatedly been tried, and neither, by itself, has produced the intended result. That's bad for humanity, but good for drama.

(See also: VIOLATION; LOVE; SEX; CHAOS; JUSTICE)

It is often said that it helps if the hero is vulnerable, but why is this so? Vulnerable to what? What's the difference between vulnerability and weakness?

Vulnerability humanizes characters and helps us to identify with them. But so, too, does strength. We understand someone's vulnerability; but we admire their strength.

There are fairly strict boundaries for the ways in which a hero can be vulnerable. They cannot be vulnerable to corruption, cruelty, greed, or self-seeking power. They can, however, be vulnerable to the demands of love, family, and people who need them.

Will Kane in *High Noon* is vulnerable when he talks to his mentor, the former sheriff who refuses to help him, or to his ex-mistress, his new wife, his deputy, or his best friend. We understand why Kane seems to be vulnerable to their advice that he leave town, but we admire the fact that he refuses to take it.

In *The Exorcist*, Father Karras expresses his vulnerability in his very first speech, when he tells Tom, a fellow priest, that he fears he has lost his faith. His vulnerability is increased when he goes to see his elderly mother, who will soon die alone and leave Karras filled with even more remorse and guilt. The demon that has possessed the young girl, Regan, knows how vulnerable Father Karras is, and attempts to exploit this when Karras performs the exorcism.

Characters are made vulnerable not simply to enhance audience identification; their vulnerability sets up one more test that the hero must pass in order to prove that he *is* a hero.

(See also: Power; Tests; Weapons; Tools; Goofy)

W

It is will, more than any other single quality,
that determines heroic behavior.

WAR FILMS

THE DARK SECRET about war films is not that war is hell; it is that war is a hell of a lot of *fun*. If it were not, war films and other genres that use the basic elements of war — cops, detectives, gangsters, science fiction, horror, and westerns — would not be the staples of popular filmmaking that they are.

The first half of many wars films deals not with war but with the preparation for it. This is because the social unit is central to war films, and it takes time to socialize people into a coherent fighting force, as *The Dirty Dozen*, *Platoon* and *The Deer Hunter* demonstrate. But this creates a major structural dilemma in war films: the formation of the community may take too long and become boring and audiences may want the filmmaker to "Get on with it!"

But if the film plunges into the action scenes too early, before we have had time to care about the unit and the individuals in it, the battle scenes risk becoming repetitive and numbing. *Saving Private Ryan*, for example, placed its most gripping and memorable scenes at the very beginning of the film, and never reached the same level of emotional intensity.

The art of war is the art of strategy; similarly, the art of making a war film depends heavily on making the right strategic decisions about how the story will be structured.

(See also: CONFLICT; DUALITY; PYRRHIC VICTORIES; DISASTER FILMS)

A CROWD IS gathered in the village square around a large stone into which a glistening sword has mysteriously been embedded. It has been prophesied that the person who pulls the sword out of this stone will be "The One" who will free the people from their oppression.

The local blacksmith huffs and puffs, but all his strength fails to budge the glistening sword. The scion of the local noble puffs and huffs but fails to budge the weapon. Finally, an inconspicuous lad nobody paid any attention to effortlessly pulls the sword out of the stone, proving he is the prophesied leader.

From this point until very late in the story, the powerful sword will protect the hero from harm and bring instant death to all his enemies, all of whom will, of course, try to seize it because they think it is why he is so powerful. But in many stories the weapon is lost, broken, or abandoned.

At the end of *Star Wars*, the fate of the universe depends on dropping a bomb precisely into the center of the Death Star's reactor. Luke's men aim their computer-controlled weapons but are easily destroyed by Darth Vader. Eventually, Luke is all alone, with Vader hot on his tail. As he looks at his computer and his fingers clench the trigger, Luke hears Obi-Wan Kenobi's disembodied voice reminding him, "Trust the Force." Luke responds by pushing the computer aside and relies on his *feelings* to find the right moment to drop the bomb.

WEAPONS

No one ever tells the hero, "Trust the sword." While it is fun to watch the hero twirl his weapons and use them expertly throughout most of the film, ultimately what is important is not the weapon the hero holds, but what he holds inside.

(See also: ARMOR; TECHNOLOGY; TOOLS; GOOFY)

ONE DAY, A bright and inventive group of filmmakers will make a western in which, at the very end of the film, the hero and the villain walk toward one another in the blazing sun, and as they eye each other, the hero will say, "Why don't we submit this to binding arbitration?" That film will be one of the great flops in film history.

However much in real life people resort to lawyers, courts, and judges, they are never the means to resolving the conflicts in westerns. The conflicts in westerns, horror, gangster, and science fiction films must end in a man-to-man, man-to-monster, or man-to-machine climax.

Throughout most of human history, towns were situated next to dependable rivers. Western towns in films such as *High Noon*, *The Searchers, The Wild Bunch,* and *Unforgiven*, however, are situated in the middle of some of the driest places on earth. Perhaps that's because deserts, in the Hebrew, Christian, and Islamic Bibles, are places of *spiritual* conflict.

Westerns are set in frontiers and war films are set at the front. Both are places where colliding forces clash against one another. At the front in war films, large numbers of people follow rigid rules that come from military organizations. At the frontier of the western, there are usually few people, and because they are far away from any organization's power, the rules are weak or nonexistent. The emphasis in war films is thus on courage and tests of strength, while in westerns it is on morality and tests of will.

THE POWER OF FILM ⌒ HOWARD SUBER   407

Most people recognize that the line that begins, "A man's gotta do…" ends with "…what a man's gotta do." While the line has its origins in John Steinbeck's novel, *The Grapes of Wrath*, most people think it must come from a western. What *is* it that a man's gotta do?

War is about violence, so there is no question whether it will be used — only how and to what effect. The central problem of the western, however, is the *legitimization* of violence, rather than the violence itself, as *High Noon*, *Shane* and *The Searchers* attest.

What a man's gotta do in the western is kill another man — not, as is true of the villain, because he wants to but because he *has* to. As is true of so many other mythic stories, the central concern of the western is justice.

(See also: GENRES; HEROES; JUSTICE; FRONTIERS)

DAVE BOWMAN IS outside the spaceship in *2001* in a small pod, having unsuccessfully tried to rescue his partner whom HAL has murdered. He issues the command, "Open the pod bay door, HAL," but the computer tells him that he "can't do that." Dave suddenly realizes that he has forgotten to put on his space helmet and is trapped inside the pod. As happens so often in memorable popular films, the hero faces what appear to be insurmountable odds. And then, he surmounts them.

What enables Dave to overcome HAL's superior power? Will power. Dave, like the heroes in *Mr. Smith Goes to Washington, The Bridge on the River Kwai, The African Queen, Ben-Hur, Gandhi, Lawrence of Arabia, Butch Cassidy and the Sundance Kid, Apocalypse Now, The Terminator, Thelma & Louise, The Matrix*, and most other memorable films, simply will not stop and will never give up. It is will, more than any other single quality, that determines heroic behavior.

(See also: CHARACTER, POWER)

WISDOM

IN MOVIES, AND occasionally in real life, the most powerful of all forms of knowing is what we call "wisdom."

In *The Godfather,* Michael Corleone comes up with a plan to kill the corrupt cop who protects the drug dealer, Sollozzo. Everyone else protests that if you kill a cop, terrible consequences will ensue. It is not Michael's Ivy League college education that leads him to propose his plan; it is Michael's wisdom. In *Fargo,* Marge Gunderson is the pregnant, slow-moving sheriff of a small town who appears not to be too bright, but she turns out to have an innate wisdom that solves the crime. The heroes of all of Frank Capra's films are generally goofy and apparently quite ordinary people — until they reveal themselves to be the wisest people in the film.

Wisdom in popular films is not something you inherit or get in school; it comes from what lies within.

(See also: CHARACTER, POWER; GOOFY; INTUITION AND INSIGHT; POWER; INDIVIDUALISM)

SIGMUND FREUD BELIEVED that the two most important qualities of adulthood were the ability to work
and the ability to love. In films, as in life, people are
often successful at one or the other, but it is often
difficult to be simultaneously successful at both.

Work consists of a transformation of the world;
love consists of a transformation of the self. Charles
Foster Kane in *Citizen Kane* and Michael Corleone
in *The Godfather* both succeed in the first, but not
the second. In *High Noon*, Sheriff Will Kane nearly
fails in both but succeeds when his bride, Amy, joins
him to defeat the gang at the last minute. In *It's a
Wonderful Life*, George Bailey nearly fails in his work
life, which, in turn, affects his ability to love.

There are many examples in film of men who are
successful in the world of work but unsuccessful in
the world of love: *Gone with the Wind, The Maltese
Falcon, Casablanca,* and *The Godfather.* It is difficult to
think of memorable popular films, however, that end
with a person who is successful in the world of love
but unsuccessful in the world of work.

When a character's work life and his love life are
treated as separate entities, what is often called "the
love interest" is likely to feel like a tacked-on appendage. But films as diverse as *Citizen Kane, Casablanca,
Gone with the Wind, The Best Years of Our Lives, The
Apartment,* and *Bonnie and Clyde,* manage to weave
together the characters' work lives and love lives.
When this happens — when love and work become
part of the *same* story — the film is likely to be much
more powerful than if they are unrelated elements.

(See also: DECISIONS; LOVE)

WORK AND LOVE

WOUNDS

ABOUT HALFWAY THROUGH *The Godfather*, Michael Corleone goes to a hospital and saves his father's life through the use of sheer will power and ingenuity. However, immediately afterwards, the corrupt police captain, McCluskey, pulls up and confronts him. Instead of recognizing that "discretion is the better part of valor," instead of deferring to the greater power of McCluskey, Michael defiantly asks McCluskey how much he was paid to remove the protection surrounding his father. McCluskey breaks Michael's jaw.

In *The Grapes of Wrath*, Tom Joad tries to save his friend Casey from an attack of local police thugs, and for his trouble, he gets whacked with a board that leaves a gash across his face that makes him a marked man.

Toward the end of *On the Waterfront*, Terry Malloy goes to the headquarters of mob boss Johnny Friendly and taunts him with the truth. Terry is beaten so badly he can barely stand up.

In *Lawrence of Arabia*, the title character celebrates his destruction of a Turkish train by strutting majestically atop it, provoking a wounded Turkish soldier to fire his pistol at him. Lawrence looks at the wound in his shoulder and says, "Good — good!"

In *Chinatown*, Jake Gittes sticks his nose where it doesn't belong and it is sliced open.

As these scenes demonstrate, heroes are inevitably wounded in body or soul — often in both. Whatever the cause, the function of wounds is the same in all of the world's stories, myths, and religions: they are a *stigmata* that prove their bearer *is* a hero.

(See also: ARMOR; PAIN; SACRIFICE; TESTS; WEAPONS)

THERE IS NO writer alive who has not been advised,
"Write what you know." And there are few writers who have not, in the course of following this
advice, spent weeks, months, or years producing a
personally cathartic but predictable work.

Too often, people who train writers and writers themselves act as if "write what you know"
means "write what you've lived." Yet, few writers
lead dramatic lives; if they did, they wouldn't have
much time or energy for writing. Writing what you
know therefore can constrict a writer to a very narrow perspective.

But what you "know" is not just what you
have experienced. What did Paul Schrader know of
pimps and prostitutes when he wrote the screenplay
for *Taxi Driver*? What did Mario Puzo know about
gangsters when he wrote the novel *The Godfather?*
What did Shakespeare know of Danes and Italians
and Jews and Romans? How many writers of
America's myriad westerns have known much of
anything about the period they were depicting? Of
the supernatural experiences in horror films? And
what *could* writers of works such as *Star Wars, E.T.,
The Terminator,* and other science fiction films know
about the future?

What a writer "knows" is his own personal
experience, which is never that broad and is never
enough to sustain him throughout a productive
career. This is not to denigrate the value of experience; it is to suggest that, all by itself, personal
experience can lock creative people into a limited
sphere of understanding that they quickly use up.

WRITING
WHAT YOU
KNOW

What is of primary importance in the creation of memorable films is not personal experience and not research, but feeling joined with understanding that yields compassion. Someone who has sufficient compassion can make a film about *anything*.

ABOUT THE AUTHOR

Howard Suber has taught generations of screenwriters, directors, producers, and film scholars at UCLA's celebrated film school, and his former students are today creating films and television programs and teaching film studies throughout the world.

During his forty years at UCLA, Suber has taught over sixty-five different courses in film and television, including screenwriting, directing, producing, film history, theory, and criticism. He founded and chaired UCLA's Critical Studies and Ph.D. program in the history, theory, and criticism of film and television. He was a founding director of the UCLA Film Archive, dedicated to the preservation of American film history, where he built the largest collection west of the Library of Congress. He created and chaired UCLA's current Film and Television Producers Program, which is focused on the realities of the modern motion picture and television industries. He has team-taught with, or brought into the program, many of the most important movie studio heads, agents, producers, lawyers, and executives in the industry.

In his foreword to *The Power of Film,* Geoffrey Gilmore, Director of the Sundance Film Festival, states that "Howard Suber is one of the foremost teachers of film in the world" and "is clearly a man with an incredibly restless intellect and creative energy." These characteristics and his achievements have been recognized by the award of the Distinguished Teaching Award from the UCLA faculty and students, and of a Life Achievement Award from the Temecula Film and Music Festival.

Howard Suber is also well-known and widely respected outside the academy. He has done more work as a consultant and expert witness on issues involving authorship, creative control, creative process, and copyright than probably anyone else in the country. He has also been retained by corporations to advise them on strategic business plans and to explain to their own employees the nature and structure of the film business.

This book is a distillation of over eight thousand pages of notes, handouts, and articles that Suber has produced during his prolific and fertile career in film.

Owners of this book may subscribe to a free newsletter from the author. See www.ThePowerOfFilm. Com.

INDEX

MICHAEL WIESE PRODUCTIONS

Since 1981, Michael Wiese Productions has been dedicated to providing both novice and seasoned filmmakers with vital information on all aspects of filmmaking. We have published nearly 100 books, used in over 600 film schools and countless universities, and by hundreds of thousands of filmmakers worldwide.

Our authors are successful industry professionals who spend innumerable hours writing about the hard stuff: budgeting, financing, directing, marketing, and distribution. They believe that if they share their knowledge and experience with others, more high quality films will be produced.

And that has been our mission, now complemented through our new web-based resources. We invite all readers to visit www.mwp.com to receive free tipsheets and sample chapters, participate in forum discussions, obtain product discounts — and even get the opportunity to receive free books, project consulting, and other services offered by our company.

Our goal is, quite simply, to help you reach your goals. That's why we give our readers the most complete portal for filmmaking knowledge available — in the most convenient manner.

We truly hope that our books and web-based resources will empower you to create enduring films that will last for generations to come.

Let us hear from you at anytime.

Sincerely,
Michael Wiese
Publisher, Filmmaker

www.mwp.com

Archetypes for Writers: *Using the Power of Your Subconscious*
Jennifer Van Bergen / $22.95

Art of Film Funding, The: *Alternate Financing Concepts*
Carole lee Dean / $26.95

Cinematic Storytelling: *The 100 Most Powerful Film Conventions Every Filmmaker Must Know* / Jennifer Van Sijll / $24.95

Complete Independent Movie Marketing Handbook, The: *Promote, Distribute & Sell Your Film or Video* / Mark Steven Bosko / $39.95

Creating Characters: *Let Them Whisper Their Secrets*
Marisa D'Vari / $26.95

Crime Writer's Reference Guide, The: *1001 Tips for Writing the Perfect Crime*
Martin Roth / $20.95

Cut by Cut: *Editing Your Film or Video*
Gael Chandler / $35.95

Digital Filmmaking 101, 2nd Edition: *An Essential Guide to Producing Low-Budget Movies* / Dale Newton and John Gaspard / $26.95

Directing Actors: *Creating Memorable Performances for Film and Television*
Judith Weston / $26.95

Directing Feature Films: *The Creative Collaboration Between Directors, Writers, and Actors* / Mark Travis / $26.95

Elephant Bucks: *An Insider's Guide to Writing for TV Sitcoms*
Sheldon Bull / $24.95

Eye is Quicker, The: *Film Editing; Making a Good Film Better*
Richard D. Pepperman / $27.95

Fast, Cheap & Under Control: *Lessons Learned from the Greatest Low-Budget Movies of All Time* / John Gaspard / $26.95

Fast, Cheap & Written That Way: *Top Screenwriters on Writing for Low-Budget Movies* / John Gaspard / $26.95

Film & Video Budgets, 4th Updated Edition
Deke Simon and Michael Wiese / $26.95

Film Directing: Cinematic Motion, 2nd Edition
Steven D. Katz / $27.95

Film Directing: Shot by Shot, *Visualizing from Concept to Screen*
Steven D. Katz / $27.95

Film Director's Intuition, The: *Script Analysis and Rehearsal Techniques*
Judith Weston / $26.95

Film Production Management 101: *The Ultimate Guide for Film and Television Production Management and Coordination* / Deborah S. Patz / $39.95

Filmmaking for Teens: *Pulling Off Your Shorts*
Troy Lanier and Clay Nichols / $18.95

First Time Director: *How to Make Your Breakthrough Movie*
Gil Bettman / $27.95

From Word to Image: *Storyboarding and the Filmmaking Process*
Marcie Begleiter / $26.95

Hollywood Standard, The: *The Complete and Authoritative Guide to Script Format and Style* / Christopher Riley / $18.95

Independent Film Distribution: *How to Make a Successful End Run Around the Big Guys* / Phil Hall / $26.95

Independent Film and Videomakers Guide – 2nd Edition, The: *Expanded and Updated* / Michael Wiese / $29.95

Inner Drives: *How to Write and Create Characters Using the Eight Classic Centers of Motivation* / Pamela Jaye Smith / $26.95

I'll Be in My Trailer!: *The Creative Wars Between Directors & Actors*
John Badham and Craig Modderno / $26.95

Moral Premise, The: *Harnessing Virtue & Vice for Box Office Success*
Stanley D. Williams, Ph.D. / $24.95

Myth and the Movies: *Discovering the Mythic Structure of 50 Unforgettable Films* / Stuart Voytilla / $26.95

On the Edge of a Dream: *Magic and Madness in Bali*
Michael Wiese / $16.95

Perfect Pitch, The: *How to Sell Yourself and Your Movie Idea to Hollywood*
Ken Rotcop / $16.95

Power of Film, The
Howard Suber / $27.95

Psychology for Screenwriters: *Building Conflict in your Script*
William Indick, Ph.D. / $26.95

Save the Cat!: *The Last Book on Screenwriting You'll Ever Need*
Blake Snyder / $19.95

Save the Cat! Goes to the Movies: *The Screenwriter's Guide to Every Story Ever Told* / Blake Snyder / $24.95

Screenwriting 101: *The Essential Craft of Feature Film Writing*
Neill D. Hicks / $16.95

Screenwriting for Teens: *The 100 Principles of Screenwriting Every Budding Writer Must Know* / Christina Hamlett / $18.95

Script-Selling Game, The: *A Hollywood Insider's Look at Getting Your Script Sold and Produced* / Kathie Fong Yoneda / $16.95

Selling Your Story in 60 Seconds: *The Guaranteed Way to get Your Screenplay or Novel Read* / Michael Hauge / $12.95

Setting Up Your Scenes: *The Inner Workings of Great Films*
Richard D. Pepperman / $24.95

Setting Up Your Shots: *Great Camera Moves Every Filmmaker Should Know*
Jeremy Vineyard / $19.95

Shaking the Money Tree, 2nd Edition: *The Art of Getting Grants and Donations for Film and Video Projects* / Morrie Warshawski / $26.95

Sound Design: *The Expressive Power of Music, Voice, and Sound Effects in Cinema* / David Sonnenschein / $19.95

Special Effects: *How to Create a Hollywood Film Look on a Home Studio Budget* / Michael Slone / $31.95

Stealing Fire From the Gods, 2nd Edition: *The Complete Guide to Story for Writers & Filmmakers* / James Bonnet / $26.95

Ultimate Filmmaker's Guide to Short Films, The: *Making It Big in Shorts*
Kim Adelman / $16.95

Way of Story, The: *The Craft & Soul of Writing*
Catherine Anne Jones / $22.95

Working Director, The: *How to Arrive, Thrive & Survive in the Director's Chair*
Charles Wilkinson / $22.95

Writer's Journey, – 3rd Edition, The: *Mythic Structure for Writers*
Christopher Vogler / $26.95

Writing the Action Adventure: *The Moment of Truth*
Neill D. Hicks / $14.95

Writing the Comedy Film: *Make 'Em Laugh*
Stuart Voytilla and Scott Petri / $14.95

Writing the Killer Treatment: *Selling Your Story Without a Script*
Michael Halperin / $14.95

Writing the Second Act: *Building Conflict and Tension in Your Film Script*
Michael Halperin / $19.95

Writing the Thriller Film: *The Terror Within*
Neill D. Hicks / $14.95

Writing the TV Drama Series – 2nd Edition: *How to Succeed as a Professional Writer in TV* / Pamela Douglas / $26.95

DVD & VIDEOS

Field of Fish: *VHS Video*
Directed by Steve Tanner and Michael Wiese, Written by Annamaria Murphy / $9.95

Hardware Wars: *DVD* / Written and Directed by Ernie Fosselius / $14.95

Sacred Sites of the Dalai Lamas – DVD, The: *A Pilgrimage to Oracle Lake*
A Documentary by Michael Wiese / $24.95

CPSIA information can be obtained
at www.ICGtesting.com
Printed in the USA
BVOW11s1454020817
490953BV00026B/787/P